ETERNITY'S GENERALS:
THE WISDOM OF APOSTLESHIP

An Essential Guide & Comprehensive Tool for
Contemporary Apostles

Dr. Paula A. Price
D.Min., Ph.D.

Flaming Vision Publications
Tulsa, Oklahoma

Unless otherwise indicated, all scriptural quotations are from the *King James Version* of the Bible.

Cover photo is courtesy of US Air Force.

Design by A. Peterson.

Eternity's Generals: The Wisdom of Apostleship

Flaming Vision Publications

Tulsa, Oklahoma 74136

ISBN 1-886288-12-7

*This book is dedicated to God and Christ's
next generation apostles, of which I have had the privilege of
birthing and molding a few.*

Table of Contents

Preface

As I undertook writing this book, I was motivated by three repeating words that ultimately became its backdrop: embassy, ambassadorship, and diplomacy. Having sat through many "Apostolic Summits" where discussions on apostleship led to more questions and confusion than answers, I had no problem discerning why the Lord thought these words were important to this work. With them came the phrase "Next Generation Apostleship." As I thought on what they collectively meant and how they related to what I was writing, the Lord impressed upon me the urgency of collaborating with Him in His shift to next generation apostolism[1]. He reminded me of the truth that "Every new move begins in the womb of the old." In regard to apostleship, I understood Him to mean that the first generation of apostles was born in the womb of the evangelical church. For that reason it differed at face value, little from what people had come to know as the New Testament church. The shift the Lord had in mind was His apostles' move from under the umbrella of evangelical theology and doctrine to the reestablishment of the mantle that brought us the New Testament. Upon this mantle is Christ's New Creation ecclesia founded.

The Lord is ready to relieve His apostles' mantle of its initiating strands of charismatic and word of faith influences that shaped and regulated it up to now. For this reason, little of what people detect about apostleship; or what they are taught that it is, strikes them as very unlike traditional Protestantism. Most see very little variation in conventional church protocols,

---

[1] As it stands today, present apostleship is evangelical. From doctrine to applied ministry, apostles as observed to date operate their mantles and execute the office pretty much the way church has been done. They practice the office on an evangelical platform as high ranking evangelists, mostly answering to and governed by the pastorate, conforming their regulations and guidelines to the Charismatic Pentecostal ecclesiastical model. The reason is the New Move-Old Womb Syndrome. Jesus' parable of the old wine and old wine skins expresses it best.

doctrine, dogma, or theology they learned under the fundamental evangelicalism. Consequently, most Christians cannot see what makes apostles different or entitled to church headship.

Eternity's Generals takes up its part in the apostle's reinstatement journey to present apostleship as the Lord Jesus ordained and practiced on earth. It responds to the Savior's call for His next generation apostles to shift from the old move that birthed it to peel it away from the new. *Eternity's Generals* refines the somewhat blurred lines that presently distinguish apostles from the remaining officers of Ephesians 4:11. Its wisdom facilitates next dimension apostleship, as the early church comprehended the ministry. As you read the book, you will learn what the Lord did to give apostles their unique standing in His kingdom and also how He authorized them alone to accredit the other ministries of His body. Because of apostleship's unequivocal standing as the last office of the Old Testament and the first office of the New Testament, traditional answers to their invalidity are utterly discredited. *Eternity's Generals* tells you why and how Christ's apostles concluded Moses' Law, and predating the Church, established the government and order into which it was born. Government as used here defines the laws, codes, statutes, judgments, penalties, legislation and the officials empowered by a state or sovereign to protect its interests, prosper its citizens, restrain criminality, uphold and dispense its laws and overall see to its security, serenity, and perpetuity. These reasons alone settle why Jesus set His apostles as first ranking officers of His kingdom and His Church. After reading this book, their perpetual status as God's first officers in creation and in the ecclesia will remain forever uncontestable.

2

Chapter One

Next Generation Apostleship

Chapter Discussions

New Move, Old Womb • The Second Motivating Thought •
Distinguishing Apostles' Acts from Title • Praxis &
Apostleship • Metonymies of Apostleship • Substance of this
Material • Basic Fundaments of Apostleship

T his is the second of my books on apostleship.
Entitled ***Eternity's Generals***, it expands on the first
book, *God's Apostle Revived*, released in 1994. A three
book series, this work covers the subject of
apostleship extensively from many vantage points. It
opens with a basic understanding of apostleship, its purposes
and work, commission, and missions.

New Move, Old Womb

Two primary thoughts motivate this work. The first is that every new move begins in the womb of the old. Second, defining the apostle must be separated from describing the function. Here is a statement replete with suggestiveness. It means that when someone says God is doing a new thing and begins to act on it, he or she, although inspired by the spirit of the change the Lord wants to ignite, is hindered by the old culture. New moves initially are bogged down with mindsets that must be loosened; new ways of doing things embraced; and established guards of the spiritual and natural that must be either transformed or displaced. The wisdom for achieving all of this often comes much later in the process because it takes time for change agents to be taken seriously, and to earn the credibility that attracts a reliable following. For David, it took nearly two decades.

The necessary events that provoke the new move's changes can span years. Until it happens though, what change agents say and do appears to vary little from what the masses are accustomed to over the last several decades. Other than a few dissenting remarks, and controversial comments, working and walking out the change tends to be a ways off. Those affected find that aside from a different message (usually well blended with the old) and a fluctuating disparity with the norm, sounds from the pulpit or in private discussions surface little to deviate the status quo. Only the Lord's persistence causes that to happen.

All this is to say that new moves take time to move away from their old lineages. Language and vernacular have yet to be devised and disseminated as forms and functions take their time. For a while, the new words may be just that, new words that have no corresponding action. Herein lays the church's conflict with those announcing God is doing a new thing. In

4

reality, all it sees is its beloved devotions and institutions criticized. If no radical power and wisdom accompany the new word, the new move stays locked in its old grip. Thus, the baby is born, but is never cleaned from its birth grease, the covering that enables its survival in the womb. Often it is called the birth anointing.

Jesus' parable of the old wineskin, old wine, old garment, and old cloth take hold at this stage, because new words and often, new ways of saying the same old things are all people hear until the Lord forces His change on the church. Claims of fresh new revelations from God initially receive lukewarm receptions because they lack the accompanying power to alter what people come to know and recognize as God in action. The Lord must impose His changes on His body, but how does He do it? By removing or reducing His favor from its old messages and messengers and their words to sound hollow and repetitive, or non-appealing. The hearts of supporters disenchanted with the same messages they have served closes as its now unsatisfactory fruit loses its glitter. Frustration, disillusionment, and outright boredom take hold as God challenges those sitting in the pews to reach beyond the norm and familiar for something more, something deeper.

Though the old guard sermonizers may not want to go to the next level in God, indeed many of them have no choice. It is the only sift they can make now that their move is ended. Those assigned to the next move crave it. Funds dry up, attendance drops, and maintenance of the old move's systems and orders deteriorate. Often the present guard in defense of its hold on the body argue that God is still moving with them and begin to castigate the new message; vilifying it as heresy. However, over time, the Lord's will is done and He simply shifts His body to their successors.

5

The Second Motivating Thought

The second thought that motivated this work is a clear-cut meaning of the word *apostle*. Regularly it is touted that no one can really define an apostle; a belief that rests on the confusion between the noun (what the apostle is) and its verb (what the noun, the apostle does). If the two are not distinguished, any hope of conceptualizing the officer and succinctly defining what makes an apostle an apostle may never be resolved. A noun asks for what names apostles, while a verb states the action that substantiates the noun. Naming apostles distinguishes and classifies the titles that best identify their calling, see Luke 6:13. In the way of explanation, a noun is an appellation that declares the meaning over the actions of apostleship, its praxis[2].

A most interesting word in the list of nouns for the apostle is the word *action*. In the Bible, a Greek word that corresponds to it is praxis. Though the two, the apostle's title and action, are close for ease of definition, they must be distinguished for those not familiar with the mantle and its prevailing culture. A sound definition of apostleship then, should describe its name according to what may be understood from its title. The word serving as the name, its nomenclature should include its calling and clarify its appellation (designation and title) as part of the definition. That is what the following meaning does for the word apostle. An apostle is *"a deity's specially commissioned[3] messenger who is delegated miraculous power and sent as its ambassador to*

---

[2] The Original Roget's Thesaurus of English Words & Phrases, Revised & Modernized by Robert A. Dutch, O.B.E., St. Martin's Press, 1965 #561n.

[3] Apostles unending training mandate from "The Diplomat's Dictionary," Chas. W. Freeman, Jr., pp 292-293:

"As the most senior member of his profession present in an embassy, an ambassador has a duty to tutor his juniors in the essentials of diplomatic tradecraft, to evaluate their potential successfully to pursue a diplomatic career, and to ensure that the most promising among them are assigned to places and positions where they can begin to develop into what they have the capacity to be."

6

overturn strongholds, establish its kingdom, and deliver or return a nation *to its god*" (The Author). Understanding apostleship always hinges upon two immutable things: gods and nations. Nations belonging to gods and apostles as their dispatched representatives or ambassadors are sent to deliver or return a nation to the god that birthed or won it in combat. Consider the following extracts from scripture that certify this truth:

Seven References Clarify the Gods Theme in Scripture

1.	Your god	182
2.	Your gods	34
3.	Their god	81
4.	Their gods	34
5.	Our god	208
6.	Our gods	2
7.	Gods of the nations	7

Deuteronomy 32:18 says expressly that Israel was begotten by Yahweh while Jesus calls Satan the father of the unregenerate, from whose line Cain came, as said in Matthew 13:38.[4]

Suggested Activity

Review the above definition given for the apostle for a moment; turn it over in your mind to start to visualize what type of person this describes. Take it apart if you will and explore each word's meaning to the end. What you would get from such an activity is a practical profile of what God had in mind when He declared, first apostles in 1 Corinthians 12:28. Develop your profile based on the following ten points taken from the above definition:

---

[4] John 8:44 and 1 John 3:12.

1. Deity

2. Specially Commissioned

3. Messenger

4. Delegated

5. Miraculous Power

6. Sent Ambassador

7. Overturn Strongholds

8. Establishing Kingdoms

9. Deliver or Return to a Deity

10. A Nation's God

Distinguishing Apostles' Acts from Title

A good way to simplify the essential character of apostleship is by looking at the word and separating its syllabus. As simplistic as this may sound, those just becoming familiar with the term may find it a fast way to fix the officer's distinctives in their mind. Consider this, how the word **APOSTLE** contains a messenger term at its core. Look at it below:

A POST LE

At the risk of appearing too elementary, the center of the word *apostle* is the word *post* suggesting in this little illustration that apostleship is strongly connected to a post in several of its aspects. The core of the word hints at its essential character. The word post includes the following:

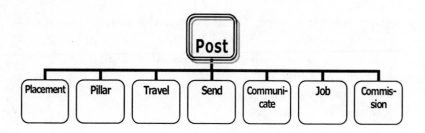

Just think about it, seven features of apostleship emerge from merely concentrating on this core word. They epitomize the officer's functions with a simple understanding of the word *post*. Definitively, its varied uses go from station (placement as a pillar), to action (sending and communication), to commission and status, a job. That simple exercise in no way encapsulates the scope of apostleship as the Lord views it, but it does give a quick way to focalize a person's introduction to the founding office of what the New Creation church looks like in action.

What takes longer to explain about apostles are the features and functions of the acts commissioned to those designated as apostles. Title definitions are given at length elsewhere in this series, but for now, here is a list of the apostle's actions that often cloud who the minister is with what he or she does. The word *praxis*, as one of the several nouns or nomenclature for apostleship is used in scripture. It means "practices, acts, work, functions, deeds, an office and or its work, or one's official work." When Luke's Gospel was dubbed the "Acts of the Apostles," the gospel's title aptly fit because it showed Luke truly sought to present an orderly account of the events, activities, and elements of the apostles' ministry, past, present and future. Its first sentence however, states that he set out to narrate for Theophilus the "acts/praxis" of Jesus Christ; what He began to do and to teach. It indicates Luke's aim is to perpetually recall what the Lord Jesus began and continues to do (praxis or practice) in and through His apostles, the primary

9

subjects of his account. When compared with those synonyms given in our stated reference for a noun, the word *praxis* says what qualifies its inclusion. When traced, its synonyms surface an extensive string of words illuminating apostleship. Given below, these further prepare you for the largely atypical treatment of this subject.

Praxis & Apostleship

From religious and secular sources, the "Acts of the Apostles," their *praxis* if you will, outlines for us the apostle's fundamental:

Actions	Perpetuity	Operations	Campaign
Deeds	Performance	Interaction	Force
Works	Execution	Commission	Administration
Doings	Agency	Influence	
Militancy	Routine	Labor	Achievements
Move/ Movements	Procedures	Business	Exploits
	Practices	Feats	
Policy	Behavior	Employment	
Dispatch	Conduct	Occupation	

In all, thirty-one actions functionalize apostleship. Taking them one by one and exploring the actions normally associated with each one, expands your comprehension of the works of an apostle even further.

The two phrases, "new move" and "old womb," along with a succinct definition of the apostle, comprise the essential thoughts behind the whole of this series and its teachings on apostleship. While on the subject of synonyms, it might be a good at this stage of our discussions to present its metonymies for you as well. A more in depth treatment of these words comes later; the words below are to open your mind to the reality that apostles are more than just missionaries or lateral church leaders.

Metonymies of Apostleship

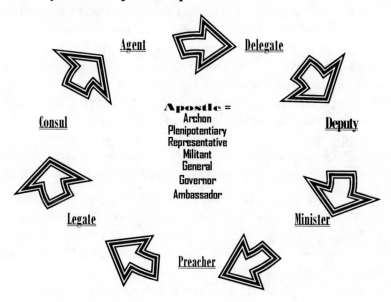

Apostle =
Archon
Plenipotentiary
Representative
Militant
General
Governor
Ambassador

Agent
Delegate
Consul
Deputy
Legate
Minister
Preacher

Substance of This Material

This material aims to facilitate God's full-scale reinstatement of the apostle's office by giving the founding officer of the New Testament a cursory overview of the ecclesiastical side of ministry. The three books' in this series, *Eternity's Generals* Volumes 1 and 2 effectively profile Christ's apostleship; His first, early, and succeeding apostles; their spheres of authority and the grounds for the office's strength in official and occupational terms and contexts. These may be easily understood and related to by apostles emerging or serving today. Discussions proceed to examine and explain God's objectives for His apostles in the Body of Christ and in the world using extensive definitions and etymology with thoroughly probed scripture to ground the teaching with sound wisdom and eternal practicality.

All efforts endeavor to contrast accurately for the reader the distinctives of Bible apostles from the apostles in the world, as well as from the other ministers serving Christ's church. The phrase *"Bible Apostle,"* used frequently in these writings speaks to the ministry and mantle of apostleship the Lord Jesus, the Great Apostle, brought to earth, deposited in His church, and unleashed on the world. Discussion emphases revolve around how apostles educate, organize, legislate, and strategize their jurisdictional spheres under Christ's leadership to steer current and future apostles' commissions toward God's ordained paths.

The texts' teachings reveal the Lord's mind on the subject, its value to Him now and forever, and the apostle's obligations while equipping His body for its eternal inheritance. Beyond these, discussions encircle the apostolate's labors and exhaustive apostolic profiles, executions, and activities covered in later volumes. All subject matter is thoroughly scrutinized in order to treat comprehensively apostleship from its broadest perspectives. Addressing God's heart on the apostle's ministry enlightens the Church and accelerates the mantle's reinstatement in God's leadership. Overall, the goal is the adequate education of any serious learner on the subject.

The core premise of this book is "Eternity in the Now." That is, how the apostle expresses and executes the Creator's eternal word, will, wisdom, and works in our now. The phrase explains the value He places on educating instated apostles to occupy the head of the New Creation church. Such a premise enlarges present beliefs and attitudes on apostleship to shift the reader's traditional mindset to apostleship as Christ practiced it.

12

Frequently the point is made that the Bible is written and founded upon apostles and prophets, a truth confirmed by Jesus Christ in Luke 24:44. Unquestionably, the New Testament is written by His apostles, despite the scribes, they used to pen it. For this reason the apostle's duties and responsibilities are delegated on His behalf and for the good of His people. This is best understood and communicated by apostles, the mantle that received and disseminated the order in the first place.

Classifications of the minister, the apostle's office and mantle and apostolic work express how early apostles instituted government, enacted legislation, and wrote directives for the church as a model to guide their successors. All its doctrine and dogma being substantiated by scripture began with apostleship, from Moses the Old Testament type of the apostle to Jesus, the first recognized apostle in the church. God's government remains in the hands of this extraordinary officer as foretold in Isaiah 9:6 regarding the Great Apostle, who declares apostles co-govern with Him throughout eternity. In comparison, none of the other offices, namely evangelist, pastor, and teacher, contributed anything to the construction or compilation of the New Testament or its sacred text. Their non-involvement in these two vital processes suggests God ordained a minimal role to them in initiating or establishing the church's order and government at the first. This glaring historical fact indicates all the more how unsuited they are to define or regulate His church and completely disqualifies them to legislate or define the apostle's office.

Thoughts such as these, along with many other very provocative overtones related to biblical apostleship permeate discussions to encourage apostles laboring today and those on the horizon for the future. You will find this series exciting, challenging, explosive, and yet profoundly conformational. Many of your attitudes will shift as old mindsets are radically altered to transform your present ideas on the Bible believing church, its trends, leadership, government, and culture. Your knowledge and wisdom levels soar as this book dynamically fortifies your comprehension of apostleship. Consistently, you will find yourself, as an apostle, more accurately exemplifying your divinely delegated commission. Over time, you will unmask the apostle's ordained range and the purpose of authority as you undertake the task of converting your ministry world to God's eternal government. Ultimately, you will come to formulate the unique apostles' message and doctrine God dispensed to you so that your mantle explodes with the accompanying signs and wonders that critically confirm your apostleship.

While there is much important material to be known on this subject by all serious apostles to do the job, what is essential to its quality understanding and fair treatment by the New Testament church is what is addressed here. That includes the following basic fundaments.

Basic Fundaments of Apostleship

- The Heavenly and Earthly Origin and History of the Apostle

- The Bible Apostle's Commission, Message, and Mandates

- God's Basis for Divinely Authorizing and Perpetually Backing His Apostles

- Discussions on the Pre-Christ Apostle

- The New Creation Church and the Apostle

- The Apostle in the World

14

- Insights and Disparities Between Secular and Kingdom Apostleship

- Understanding The Apostle's Nature

- Exploring the Depth, Range, and Scope of the Apostle's Service

- Delving into The Work of the Apostle

- Probing the Apostle's Make Up

- Comparing the Apostle with the other Five-fold Officers

- Unlocking What Constitutes the Apostle's Personality

- What Gives the Apostle Authority and Power

- The Ongoing Dynamics of Apostleship and the Resurrected Christ

The preceding thoughts though not addressed in the above order sum up the apostle's meditations. They are covered at length throughout the series under various headings. Below is a diagram to show how apostle's teachings (the Bible calls it doctrines) differ from the others. Apostolic concentrations generally revolve around the following:

The Apostles Message is for Christ's New Creation Children of Creator God. They are distinguished by an unusual thought process and otherworldly contemplations that characterize their ministry emphases. Their emphases constitute what scripture call The Apostles Doctrine that is discussed later. Below is a snapshot of what that looks like in action.

Snapshot of Apostles'

Thought Line & Doctrinal Emphases

The Apostles Message: For Creator God's Eternal Nation
Diagram of Apostles Thoughts & Concentrations
These Contribute to the Apostles Doctrine

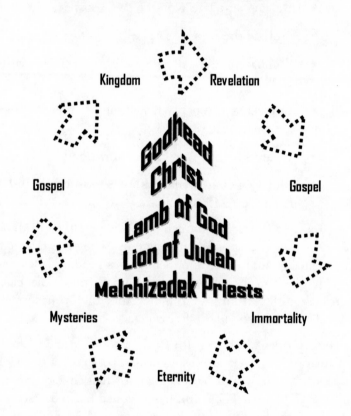

Eternity's Generals, as a textbook and handbook, intricately details the apostle's office, and repeatedly serves as a functional instruction guide for those appointed by God to stand in the office. In addition, as a handbook, it is indispensable in building and leading modern apostolic orders and organizations today. From their wisdom, apostles can confidently and competently exercise God's authority in the earth; make quality and relevant apostolic decisions on His behalf, and effectively execute the divine operations of the Godhead. What any apostle of today gains from this information will promote a viable understanding of who and what the messenger is and what the Church of the Lord Jesus is to become because of the office's revival, reinstatement, officiations, and regard for its apostles.

Chapter Summary

1. Two primary thoughts motivated this work.

2. Every new move begins in and is pushed from the womb of the old; defined by its traditional predecessor.

3. Apostles can and should, be defined by who they are before describing what apostles do.

4. Apostleship hinges on two immutable things: gods and nations.

5. Apostles' acts and titles must be separated to identify and qualify the office.

6. The word *post* is the central core of apostleship

7. Part of the apostle's name includes praxis, a Greek term used to designate the Acts of the Apostles.

8. There are fourteen metonymies for apostleship.

9. All apostles should be well versed in and have an understanding of the fifteen basic fundaments regarding apostleship

Chapter Two

A Quick Summary of the Who, What, & Why of Apostleship

Chapter Discussions

How Apostleship is Generally Received Today • Christ's Type
of Apostleship • Why Apostleship is Vital to the Lord • Why
God Summons Apostles • How Apostles are Inducted • Not
All Apostles Are Directly Commissioned by Jesus • Apostles &
Incumbent Leadership • Recognizing an Apostle How the
New Testament is Wholly Apostolic • Apostleship Serves Jesus
Christ Forever • The Original Apostles Not Guaranteed

T his chapter introduces the subject of apostleship
as it has probably not been viewed previously,
because if it was, much of the debate on the
subject would most likely have been settled by
now. That is what *Eternity's Generals* accomplishes. Many

practical thoughts and functions proffered here open your mind on the subject of apostleship as it may not have been opened before. The information to come provides a quick overview of apostleship summarizing apostleship in general covering its, who, what and why covered, giving important insights into apostles' ministries and mantle.

In preparation for what is to come, this chapter gives a flash look at the apostle as God intends and uses the messenger. To acquaint readers with its extensive material, this book opens with a panoramic view of apostleship. The goal is to begin to shift or fortify readers' existing thoughts, explanations, and beliefs on apostleship so that they accommodate what the Lord is doing in His body in these last days.

Since the Lord is summoning and installing apostles en masse in this era, it is responsible for all those being summoned or affected by them to grasp the Godhead's descriptions and plans for the mantle. These discussions propose to do just that by capturing apostles' ministry: how it serves Christ and His body. Meant to serve as a quick review, the chapter begins the reader's initiation and orientation to what may be learned about the extraordinary offices of 1 Corinthians 12:28, 29 and Ephesians 4:11.

How Apostleship is Generally Received Today

By now, it is accepted by the wider body of Christ that apostles are retaking their places as head leaders in Christ's church, a reality met with decidedly mixed responses. Those called to be part of the Lord's shift of His church from its traditional pastoral, teacher, and evangelical dominance to apostleship welcome His changes with glee. They rejoice at God's long overdue overhaul of His kingdom as it has operated over the last several centuries. On the other hand, those who fear the brunt of the shift and its costs are not quite as enthusiastic and

20

see the effects of the change in entirely different ways. These servants fear what it will do to them personally, to their works economically, and their visions and religious persuasions overall. Their concerns are all very understandable.

The responses to God's establishment of His Son's apostleship as the New Testament church's most dominant office fluctuates from indifference to dread, because so few people really know what apostleship is. They are concerned with how it looks and acts in today's world. These people are withholding judgment until they get satisfactory answers their curiosity. They sound something like this: "Quite frankly, I don't know what it (apostleship) is. So until I better understand it, I don't know what to say about it." Others, because they have so little information to go on, cannot quite fathom what all the commotion is about and simply resolve to ignore it or study the subject deeper on their own to arrive at the right conclusion. The majority of the people tackling the matter today however possess only hearsay knowledge of the office. Many would be simply glad to know what apostles are and what makes them so important. Generally, this group is more open minded and willing to listen and learn about them before deciding for or against apostles' as valid and credible heads of the New Testament church. The material to follow greatly expedites their objective.

Christ's Type of Apostleship

To start to unravel the heretofore, unwieldy question of apostles today, let us explore Christ's type of apostleship: what it is and why it is needed? The God-ordained offices to head the staff of New Testament ministers begins with apostleship. They are appointed by the Lord to identify for the New Creation body of Christ, in scripture and action, the staff of ranking ministers chosen and ordained by God to perpetually lead and empower His church. Paul establishes in 1 Corinthians

21

12:28, 29 and Ephesians 4:11 that God's staff begins with apostles.

Since apostleship is eternal, it makes sense that it must also be perpetual. Apostleship, if one took scripture at face value, are the one office in the New Testament church that validates the remaining ministers and ministries of Christ's ecclesia on earth. This bold statement is indisputably substantiated by scripture when the New Testament is viewed and practiced as intended by its writers and the Holy Spirit. The following statement may be stunning at first, but after consideration, its truth becomes obvious.

Here we discuss the Lord's continued endorsement of apostles as the ground for their credibility. The New Testament used to structure and govern the church, administrate its dispensations, was written by apostles and only apostles for very good reasons; that is, except where they used scribes, something prominent personalities did back then to record their activities., Scribes for the ancient world served the exact purposes that cameras and tape recorders do today. As a staff, scribes accompanied rulers and influential leaders and teachers, such as kings, prophets, priests, and warriors and wrote down every detail of their public activities.

Presumably, before filing their chronicles with the others in the celebrity's official annals, new records were reviewed and approved in advance by their authors. Unless, of course, the recorder was an antagonist or historian, in which case everything scribed suited his or her point of view and became history. That means Jesus would have been diligent enough to prescreen His narratives before permitting them to become part of His final record. His integrity as God's Son, Messiah, and God incarnate would have seen to it. In addition, He would have been scrupulous in His selection of scribes. His would have been eternally chosen and intimately screened.

Scribes were not considered authors, only witnesses that inscribed what they observed as followers of a certain leader. For these reasons, when it comes to the New Testament no other officer of Ephesians 4:11 and 1 Corinthians 12:28, 29 could have contributed to its development, since they did not yet exist. Scribal recorders are in keeping with the spiritual authority of a religious founder in Christ's day. His ministry demonstrates specifically an apostle's purpose that is to found, organize, and to legislate God's government. They are also to establish their religious order's official canon and catechize their deity's populace. In Christ's church based on this truth, the only mantle that can accurately legislate and regulate His New Creation ecclesia is the apostle for reasons that become clear as you continue reading. As a consequence this truth makes it clear why none of the other ministers of the church's positions listed in the New Testament is qualified to define, regulate, or legitimize the apostle's office because the apostle's is the sole mantle that launched the church. Therefore, it takes an apostle to comprehensively describe the duties, authorize, and authenticate the ministry of apostleship and those of the other mantles as well. Only when they do so can the church claim compliance with the Bible's divine order.

Why Apostleship is Vital to the Lord

Why apostleship is vital is answered in two thoughts. The first one requires reclaiming and restoring the state of the world, in particular the Most High's people in the world. The second answer comes from what has happened to the purchased possession over time or more specifically, what happens to its descendents throughout the church's eras on earth. Apostles understand their place among the myriad of deities that proliferated and dominated the world before Christ. The Creator's true faith is always rivaled as the fallen spirits of Satan's regime wrestle to retain control of the souls of

23

humanity. For this reason, the apostle's mantle is repeatedly revived to counter what causes Christ's holdings in this world to be at risk since His ascension. In every generation, they are sent at critical periods in history to retrieve the souls and strongholds of the ecclesia from secularism, humanism, and demonics when these overtake its doctrine, practices, and authority in the church and the world. The implications of both sentiments defend why God always needs apostleship. In their eras, apostles recover God's possessions and return the Lord's people to His dominion.

Why God Summons Apostles

As suggested earlier, God summons apostles and mobilizes them especially when the church becomes overrun with humanist, secular or pagan ideologies and rhetoric. They begin with those inhabited by His Holy Spirit those who have no idea of what true Christianity as Christ birthed it means. Usually, these are the post Joshua generation so to speak, that know not the Lord or His works in the church. Another fundamental aim of apostleship is to help the world to know and appreciate the value and presence of the church within it. Under these circumstances, apostles are commissioned to return the heart of God's people to Him and His holdings to His household. Customarily, apostles are forerun by prophets. The next logical question then is why apostles? What makes them more qualified for the job than the other ministers?

The answer to these questions rests in the very essence of the office. Apostleship from Christ is typically not a "from within the ranks" position. The very reason the apostle is called upon establishes this royal or divine motivation. If the problem for which the apostles are activated is within the entity to which they are sent, it makes little sense to resort to its present leadership or government to resolve it. Apparently, that the difficulties continue despite the ruler's wishes indicates the existing power is either incapable of or disinterested in its reparation for any number of reasons.

The Lord like any good leader in the same situation sends an outsider with no personal interests, no at risk ties with the existing order to handle it for Him. These people have nothing to loose except their relationship with the sender and easily resolve to restore His control and preeminence in the eyes of those He redeemed because of it.

In heaven's case, that sender is the Father of our Lord Jesus Christ and His sending of the apostles according to Luke 11:49. Jesus' apostolic awareness and attitude is seen in nine other passages of scripture that commence the process of unveiling the apostle's ministry for us. They show how the Lord Jesus as God's Sent One had no identity crises. He was incognizant to the purposes, impact, and class of His official calling. He was sent by a God His audience did not or barely knew, to achieve something on His Father's behalf that was no longer happening: to act, declare, and otherwise witness His Father God as the Creator of all things simultaneously witnessing Himself as Yahweh's Sent One. Likewise, Jesus understood His duty to send others like Himself to a world that does not know Him or His Father, to do the same thing, not just for Israel but also for the whole world. They are to make the world know that their Creator is God and that their Maker rules all. This is no vague preaching assignment. It is a definite commission to accomplish something those without a special encounter with the Risen Jesus cannot achieve.

- *(Luke 4:18)* *"The Spirit of the Lord is upon me, because he hath anointed me to preach the gospel to the poor; he hath <u>sent me to</u> heal the brokenhearted, to preach deliverance to the captives, and recovering of sight to the blind, to set at liberty them that are bruised."*

- *(John 5:30)* *"I can of mine own self do nothing: as I hear, I judge: and my judgment is just; because I seek not mine own will, but the will of the Father which hath sent me."*

- *(John 5:36)* *"However, I have greater witness than that of John: for the works, which the Father hath given me to finish, the same works that I do, bear witness of me, that the Father hath sent me."*

- *(John 5:37)* *"And the Father himself, which hath sent me, hath borne witness of me. Ye have neither heard his voice at any time, nor seen his shape."*

- *(John 6:39)* *"And this is the Father's will which hath sent me, that of all which he hath given me I should lose nothing, but should raise it up again at the last day."*

- *(John 6:44)* *"No man can come to me, except the Father, which hath sent, me draw him: and I will raise him up at the last day."*

- *(John 6:57)* *"As the living Father hath sent me, and I live by the Father: so he that eateth me, even he shall live by me."*

- *(John 7:29)* *"But I know him: for I am from him, and he hath sent me."*

- *(John 20:21)* *"Then said Jesus to them again, Peace be unto you: as my Father hath sent me, even so send I you."*

Matthew chapter ten answers how and why apostles are normally not readily welcomed in the ranks of those to whom they are sent. As a rule, only two types of people invite Christ's apostles into their ranks. The first group is those that have been begging God to intervene and change things because of institutional abuse or neglect by their present leadership. The second group is those called to work with apostles to ignite the changes the worn out and disillusioned implore Him to launch; and launching change is what apostles do.

So what is an apostle's greatest call in a word? In brief from many sources, it may be simply stated that, *"An apostle, as a specially commissioned officer[5] of the Lord Jesus Christ, is sent to recover His contemporaneous church and to enlarge His earthly possessions by harvesting a given generation."* This somewhat broad explanation, when examined closely, gives an intriguing idea of what apostleship is, and it indicates the circumstances that resolve its perpetuity throughout humanity's generations. For more insight see the apostolic indicators to be extracted from Judges 2:10-12: *"And also all that <u>generation</u> were gathered unto their fathers: and there arose another <u>generation</u> <u>after them</u>, which knew not the LORD, <u>nor yet the works</u> which he had done for Israel. And the children of Israel <u>did evil</u> in the sight of the LORD, and <u>served Baalim:</u> And they <u>forsook the LORD God</u> of their fathers, which brought them out of the land of Egypt, and <u>followed other gods, of the gods of the people that were round about them,</u> and bowed themselves unto them, and provoked the LORD to anger. And they forsook the LORD, and served Baal and Ashtaroth."*

Apostasy, idolatry, and paganism always precede and indeed ignite apostolic moves. See also another significant indicator of apostolism from Judges 17:6 and 21:25 respectively. *"In those days there <u>was no king in Israel,</u> but every man did that which was right in his own eyes."* a practice that Moses, scripture tells us, condemned in Deuteronomy 12:8, *"Ye shall not do after all the things that we do here this day, every man whatsoever is right in his own eyes."* In relation to kingship, see Exodus 22:28 and Numbers 22:12. Collectively, these passages depict the world and kingdom conditions that necessitate the Lord's activation of the apostle's mantle in a given generation. They signify not only the basis of their calling, but hint at some of the work the apostolic type is to do.

---

[5] "...An officer is a member of the service who holds a position of responsibility. Commissioned officers derive authority directly from a sovereign power and, as such, hold a commission charging them with the duties and responsibilities of a specific office or position. ...Commissioned officers generally receive training as leadership and management generalists, in addition to training relating to their specific trade or ...functionality...." *Wikipedia.com*

27

Taken as one, the passages give good reason for the corresponding authority apostles needs to succeed.

How Apostles are Inducted

The reason that apostles alone are qualified to articulate their functions and mantles is because they are sent expressly by Jesus. Remember the church did not exist when they were being trained or installed by the Savior. This statement is important to understanding the apostle's primacy in Christian ministry. Apostles' method of investiture into Christ's ministry itself empowers their comprehension of the office in ways the others cannot. Much of the original apostles training was received over the three and a half years the Lord walked the earth to establish the characteristic way the Lord inaugurates them to His service. Apostles' appointments come about by way of a face-to-face encounter and extensive interactions with the risen Lord, a major criterion for filling their post. Jesus, in directly commissioning apostles as His specially empowered messengers, literally by His visitations, brings them onto His staff and sets them in His eternal divine office of apostleship. As the Father bestowed it upon the Son, so the Son dispenses it to those He sends to His service by the Holy Spirit.

When apostles are sent to their assignments, it is never to a vague non-descript field of endeavor. Instead, they are pointedly endowed, authorized, and commissioned by the risen Christ to recover, enlarge, and sustain His world possessions; and overall, protect and perpetuate the church as long as it remains on earth. Central to those possessions is the body of people that Jesus purchased with His blood and inhabits by His Spirit. Apostles' eternal mandates presuppose their everlasting service in God's creation.

Not All Apostles Are Directly Commissioned by Jesus

Apostles may be inducted into Christ's service in several ways. The main one is, as we have been discussing, by direct divine encounter with the Resurrected Jesus. The others are by the church and by other apostles. Apostles may be installed into their posts by elder apostles such as how Matthias was chosen to replace Judas Iscariot. They may also be installed and dispatched by the church. (Philippians 2:25) Paul's sending of Timothy and Titus fits this category.

Apostles inducted apart from the Lord's direct dispatch must rely on their elder apostles for affirmation of their calls, corroboration of their legitimacy in the office, and development to succeed in it. That is not to say that the Lord is not involved in their procedures, nor is it to say that they are inferior to the other apostles. It does suggest however, that a reduced level of the persuasion essential to overcome the trials and tribulations associated with the office may exist. In addition, much of their duties are determined by elder apostles with minimal divine input from the Lord. Consequently, these apostles must depend on the apostle that discovered and announced them for certainty and need much human interaction to feel secure and excel in their call. They are likely to be less apocalyptic and not exhibit the scope of wisdom and apostolic insight in their words. Customarily, those apostles called to found their movements, not just buildings and enterprises, are summoned by direct confrontation with the Risen Lord.

Apostles & Incumbent Leadership

One thing the Lord would remind today's apostles of is that the problems they are sent by Him to redress developed under, and with, the previous or incumbent leadership. The apostle is activated because those in command refuse to be corrected from the inside. They have hardened their hearts and obstinately stiffened their necks to resist the word of the Lord to prevent His intervention in their affairs. As a result, He must go outside the status quo to get normally detached or unaffiliated servants to go in and reverse the situation for Him. Those delegated the assignment, often called a commission, ordinarily come from anonymity as part of the Lord's readiness program marked by their deliberate isolation from the mainstream church; a pattern seen in Moses being driven into the wilderness of Midian and later moving the Lord's tabernacle away from the remainder of Israel's camp. See also Joshua, who stayed in the temple when Israel disobeyed the Lord's direct command (see Exodus 33:7, 11). These examples are in addition to the Savior's thirty-year isolation and anonymity, along with Paul's Damascus wilderness experience.

The prophet Jeremiah, to elaborate further, also provides a good example for the Lord's decision to initiate or enhance His apostolic presence among His people. *"But this thing commanded I them, saying, Obey my voice, and I will be your God, and ye shall be my people: and walk ye in all the ways that I have commanded you, that it may be well unto you. But they hearkened not, nor inclined their ear, but walked in the counsels and in the imagination of their evil heart, and went backward, and not forward."* Lastly and for many people, most important, to understanding apostleship is how one can recognize the mantle of an apostle resting or descending on someone?

Recognizing an Apostle

With eighty-five precise mentions of the apostle in the New Testament, including the outright apostolic statements of 1 Corinthians 9:7; 2 Corinthians 10:4; 1 Timothy 1:18; and 2 Timothy 2:3,4 there is more than enough biblical content to deduce and describe an apostle according to the New Testament. Besides the New Testament epistles being penned by named apostles; beginning with Romans and ending with John's Revelation, it is hard to ignore the weight of importance the Lord places on this office. From Paul's writings, Romans, first and second Corinthians, to Galatians, Philemon and maybe the book of Hebrews, apostolic scores run throughout the Bible, including James, Peter, and Jude. The apostle John's Gospel is joined by his three epistles and the Apocalypse to close out the New Testament and the entire Bible. Thus, it is proved how the church's New Testament doctrine was received and recorded by apostles. Their revelations developed the church's doctrines, canon, and government. With the Gospels being the scribal record of the Lord Jesus' ministry, and Luke's book of Acts being dedicated solely to the ministry of the apostles, there is more than ample information to substantiate this apparently significant minister of the body of Christ. What follows was taken from that collection.

How the New Testament is Wholly Apostolic

A most amazing revelation to the one seeking to validate apostleship in every age is the discovery that the New Testament is purely apostolic, as has been stressed repeatedly. Every time one reads about Paul the apostle, one is encountering an apostle. Paul is referred to in scripture more than one hundred and fifty times. Adding all Paul's references with Peter's and the others finds apostleship addressed in the New Testament more than five hundred times. That is about 300 times more than even prophets are mentioned. With such copious information to go on, it is hard to fathom why people cannot identify apostolic behavior, conduct, talents, and aptitudes; and what it takes to accredit the minister's value to the church. Here are but a few of the aspects of apostleship that shed further light on the minister, although the following list is by no means complete.

31

Beyond the characteristics of divine order and governmental roles of the mantle that, by now, are etched in many ecclesiastical minds, along with its parenting aspects, here are other vital features of apostleship to consider.

Feature, Criteria, or Quality Scripture Reference

- Apostles are separated to God's gospel.　　　　　　　　　Rom. 1

- Apostles are called according to promise (to Christ)　　　　Rom. 1

- Apostles are stewards of God's mysteries　　　　　　　　1 Cor. 4:1,2

- The apostle's ministry is confined to Jesus Christ.　　　　Rom. 1

- Apostleship is an office.　　　　Rom. 11:13

- Apostles are of Jesus Christ through God's will. (5 times)　　1 Cor. & 2 Cor. 1:1

- Apostles are free to exercise God's authority over His people.　2 Cor. 10:8

- Apostles have particular service rights.　　　　　　　1 Cor. 9:1

- Apostled people are the apostle's seal of approval and success.　1 Cor. 9:12

- Apostles have specials signs beyond the rest of the body or its ministers.　Lk. 10:17 Mk. 16:17-18

- The Apostle signs include wonders, mighty deeds, and special or unusual miracles.　2 Cor. 12:12; Acts 19:11

- Apostles are not made so by the will of men or the acts of men.

  Gal. 1:1

- Special manifestations or apparitions of the resurrected Christ, the essence of their calling and mantle's authority, induct apostles.

  Acts 26:16; 1 Jn. 1:1

- Apostles of Jesus Christ are specifically by God the Father's commandments.

  1 Tim. 1:1

- Apostles of the church are summoned, empowered, and employed by Jesus Christ.

  2 Cor. 2:1

- Apostles are preachers and teachers of God's truth.

  1 Tim. 1:7; 2 Cor. 4:2

- Apostleship exists for God's purpose of life in Jesus Christ.

  2 Tim. 1:2

- Apostles are Jesus' servants.

  1 Pt 1:1

- Apostles have distinct powers and authority to cure, heal, resurrect dead, and proclaim the Lord's kingdom.

  Mat. 10

- Apostles legitimately exercise supernatural authority on God's behalf.

  Acts 13:7-11

- Apostles are witnesses of Christ's special manifestations and kingdom

  1 Cor. 9:1; Acts

revelations.	18:9,10
• Apostles are privy to much interaction between God and man's worlds.	Jn. 1:51; Acts 12:7-11
• Apostles are generally called to forsake all for Christ, ministry and His kingdom.	Mk. 10:28-31; Mat. 19: 27-30
• Apostles carry the revelations of eternity and its life as given to believers.	Jn. 6:68
• Apostles link prior prophecy with unfolding revelations fulfillment.	Rom. 16:25,26
• Apostles are uniquely informed by God's Spirit.	Eph. 3:5
• Apostles are authorized to execute Divine judgment in defense of God's righteousness.	Acts 5:13; 1 Tim. 1:20
• Apostles are ambassadors for Christ	Eph. 6:20
• Apostles have distinct doctrine, fellowship, and communion.	Acts 2:42, 43; 5:25; 15:35.
• Apostles reiterate God's warnings.	Jude 1:17
• Apostles establish centers for their ministries.	Gal. 2:8; Acts 8:14

35

- Apostles are noted for their extensive non-earthly wisdom. — 1 Cor. 1:21; 1 Cor. 2:5-7; Col. 1:28

- Apostles are ordained by Divine decree. — Acts 16:4

- Apostles are joint foundations of the church. — Eph. 3:5

- Apostles make known the eternal mysteries, blessings, powers, authority of Christ to His church. — Eph. 3:3-5; Mat. 13:11

- Apostles are transfixed by the mysteries of God and His kingdom. — Lk 810; 1 Cor. 4:1; Rom. 16:5.

- Along with mysteries, apostles are equally preoccupied with the Lord's kingdom revelation. — Gal. 2:2; 1 1 Pet. 1:13.

Thirty-six distinct features substantiate apostleship for the church, giving more than enough to establish its guidelines, standards, and criterion. They exclude the ten, sent one references essential to apostleship given above. Taken together however, they all present sufficient information on the ministry in the New Testament. Furthermore, the term *criterion* used above is important. Derived from Greek terms, it defines judgment, determination, and the legal resolution of a controversy as handed down by a tribunal or court of justice. How insightful is that to understanding the office and its operations? Anyone seriously envisioning the apostle's profile could logically apply these principles today for enhanced wisdom on this office and its work.

To connect the meanings of criterion elaborate on Acts 26:16-18, a key apostolic passage of scripture further rounds out the subject. Paul used them to corroborate his apostolic agenda and its ongoing activities. As a little self-test, assign a duty, task, or functional description to the thirty-five (plus the ten) areas above to the range of work and responsibility the Lord placed upon this office.

Apostleship Serves Jesus Christ Forever

Based on Christ's words in two separate gospels, apostles' are the only ecclesiastical mantles to serve Christ's eternal cabinet. See Matthew 19:28 KJV, *"And Jesus said unto them, Verily I say unto you, that ye which have followed me, in the regeneration when the Son of man shall sit in the throne of his glory, ye also shall sit upon twelve thrones, judging the twelve tribes of Israel."* See also, Luke 22:29, 30, *"And I appoint unto you a kingdom, as my Father hath appointed unto me; That ye may eat and drink at my table in my kingdom, and sit on thrones judging the twelve tribes of Israel."* While the word *throne* in these passages is self explanatory, the words *appoint* and *judge* are worth exploring.

The word *appoint* as used in the two passages refers to an assignment to dispose of what has been bequeathed by a testator. What is according to a will and conferred by a designated authority. Add to this meaning the intentional applications of the word *judge* and what the Lord Jesus decrees His everlasting apostles will do forever becomes known. In relation to their eternal tasks, apostles convene without end as His perpetual apostolic council to render His solemn judgments as regnant agents beneath His reign. They comprise heaven's human-divine tribunal to whom creation's continuous questions and litigation are brought. The apostles that end up sitting on those twelve thrones render decisions and kingdom determinations for the masses of redeemed lives entrusted to Christ forever. They answer and enforce eternity's judicial laws of life, righteousness, and holiness, and carry out all their duties perpetually as under-regents of the King of kings.

With that being the case, it is clear why apostleship is the mantle authorized to legitimize and govern the rest. What also vivifies with this explanation is how and why the Lord so heavily endows the apostle's mantle in the first place. The truth of this deduction derives from the apostle's charge and authorization by Jesus, directly or indirectly, to inscribe His post ascension creation with His will, laws, and government. The Lord ordained and endowed His apostles to be exceptionally privy to His new will and testament with the world, upon which the New Creation church of the Lord Jesus Christ is built.

The remaining officers appear or are alluded to as serving the Lord Jesus throughout eternity, but none is promised a throne or mentioned as composing the twelve foundations of the walls of the great city of New Jerusalem. See Revelation 21:10-14.

> *"And he carried me away in the spirit to a great and high mountain, and showed me that great city, the holy Jerusalem, descending out of heaven from God, Having the glory of God: and her light was like unto a stone most precious, even like a jasper stone, clear as crystal; And had a wall great and high, and had twelve gates, and at the gates twelve angels, and names written thereon, which are the names of the twelve tribes of the children of Israel: On the east three gates; on the north three gates; on the south three gates; and on the west three gates. And the wall of the city had twelve foundations, and in them the names of the twelve apostles of the Lamb."*

For these reasons, every generation of apostles is groomed, trained, and screened for success on His staff. Those of you that consider the decision made should think about it, because that may not be so.

The Original Apostles Not Guaranteed

Just because the twelve started out with Jesus does not mean they are assured of their seat on that eternal tribunal. For instance, Judas fell before the Lord was crucified. Furthermore, on this subject, Jesus made a point of declaring that those that begin with Him must endure to the end. So vehement is He about this that in Luke 9:2 He says no one that puts his (or her) hand to His plow and looks back is fit for God's kingdom. As you read the following, you just may learn something interesting about those twelve men that lived, ate, drank, and labored with Jesus for nearly four years. Let us trace their careers after His ascension and the birth of the church.

The Lord Jesus started out with twelve apostles representing the twelve tribes of Israel. By the time, they are in the midst of His ministry, He has settled on three that He trusts with His most secret thoughts and experiences. These three end up on the Mount of Transfiguration witnessing His eternal glory and Moses and Elijah preparing Him for His death. Afterward, the four of them, Jesus and His chosen three, come down from the mount and continue ministering until He is crucified, and rises from the dead. Once the church is born, the recognized apostles' names and numbers shift greatly as James John's brother is martyred and Paul enters the picture. From this time forward, Peter and John are the only apostles of the original twelve the New Testament tracks. Aside from them, Paul and an entire new staff of apostles are recognized.

One wonders then, whatever became of the other apostles: Andrew, Philip, Bartholomew, Thomas, Matthew, James

Alphaeus, Simon Canaanite, and Matthias who replaced Judas Iscariot. These men were a team for more than three years. They did everything together with the Lord Jesus. Yet after Acts 1:13 their names are conspicuously absent, replaced by new converts. For sure, they would have undergone the Sanhedrin's lashing for Christ's name, and been together in the place shaken by the second apostolic outpouring, but their specific ministries and exploits appear to trail off not long after Acts 8:1.

True, there are apocryphal writings recording their apostleship, but in what has become canonized scripture by the Lord's Spirit, largely written by Paul, they are never mentioned again. The bickering competitive souls that Jesus frequently chastened for their self-interest and aggrandizement are omitted from the remainder of scripture. Even Paul omits them in any of his writings as if their paths never significantly crossed again. Neither Peter nor John refers to any of the remaining apostles at all, as if all contact with their once close compadres ceased. It is as if they fell off the planet.

You would think that their paths would have crossed now and again during that time, or that the others would have labored with Peter, Paul, or John in some apostolic endeavor. However, it appears from Acts chapter sixteen to the end of John's Apocalypse, that the other apostles that started the church left no indelible or eternal mark on it. Except for some spurious writings that are brought into question by the three main New Testament writers ignoring them in their letters, they are not mentioned or alluded to by the Holy Spirit. One can adduce that Paul's repeated mentions of the chiefest and most eminent apostles and such includes them, but by name, they are not discussed outside of assuming they remained perpetual members of the Jerusalem council. What this all says to our discussion is that the apostles to reign with Christ on twelve thrones were not settled even at the time of the writing of Revelation.

Chapter Summary

1. Today people greatly fear and avoid or discredit apostleship for many reasons.

2. Christ's type of apostleship is the only trustworthy model for today's ministry.

3. Apostles only authored the New Testament.

4. Two conditions make apostleship vital to the Lord, they are why He keeps the office active and occupied.

5. Humanism, polytheism, paganism, and apostasy are the main reasons for new apostolic moves.

6. Apostles are sent from outside the ranks of incumbent leadership.

7. Apostles are brought into God's service three ways.

8. Apostleship is the entire nature and character of the New Testament.

9. Two scriptures say why and how apostleship will serve Christ forever.

10. Original apostles splintered and all but two of them are remembered in scripture.

Chapter Three

A Historical Backdrop

Chapter Discussions

Prolific Apostleship Scriptures in the New Testament • How the Bible World Saw Apostleship • True Apostleship Separates Redemption from Religion • Spiritual Initiations Begin with Priests • God's Eternal Cosmogony & Apostleship • Apostleship Is a Franchise • Preparing to Face Off with Other Gods • The Eternal Truth about Religious Freedom • The Sent One Consciousness of Jesus' Day

H istorical knowledge of apostles forms the strongest ground of comprehension. Much of what is experienced or disseminated as apostleship is presented as if it merely developed out of nowhere. For people to appreciate the place and importance of apostles and their ministries, they must see how they fit in what people consciously or unconsciously know of God. Believers have to know where the apostle was and is in

God before they can respect the officer in the New Testament church. This chapter provides the beginnings of that trace. Going back to the world where apostleship was common, discussions track the apostle's ministry (or secular service) and study the mantle from eternity to eternity.

While it is the most important of the Church's offices presented in 1 Corinthians 12:28, 29, and Ephesians 4:11, historically the subject of apostleship has been the one ministry given the least amount of concrete attention; lagging behind the scant treatment of the ministry of the prophet. Despite the church's neglect of the subject, the New Testament treats apostleship more than the rest of the remaining ministries, exceeding over three thousand references in all. Yet, the office of the apostle remains an ignored and rejected subject in the church. Look at the following revelations extracted from the twenty-seven books of the New Testament. See how it shows up:

Prolific Apostleship Scriptures in the New Testament

The express mentions of the word apostle	85
Apostleship as the sent one	149
Apostello, specifically used for official sent ones	72
Jesus' name Himself, as the Great Apostle	983
Christ as the anointed apostle	555
Lord, Jesus' the Great Apostle title	711
Paul, apostle to the Gentiles, author of 14 NT Books.	156

Peter as the rock of apostleship	158
The twelve designated apostolized disciples	132
The eleven mentioned after Jesus' death	6
James, John's twin and member of Christ's first apostles	29
Barnabas as Jesus' companion apostle	29
John as the apostle responsible for four books of the New Testament	96
Junia, Andronicus all mentioned by Jesus (1 each)	2
Epaphroditus, Jesus companion	2
Jesus (Jesus' Companion)	7
Silvanus (Jesus Companion Apostle)	4
Apollos	10
James the Lord's brother who seems to head the Jerusalem Council	9
Matthias, Judas' replacement	2
Jude the brother of James, the Lord's brother	1
Writer of book of Hebrews	5
Jesus' young companion, apostolic delegate	7

Titus, Jesus' other apostolic delegate	13
Other mentions	2

Approximate times the New Testament Treats the Subject of **3228** *Apostleship*

Omitting direct references to Jesus the Founder of the institution, still leaves nearly a thousand mentions of the apostles, even when overlooking the "sent one" designations that characterize them. However, it would be errant to omit Jesus, so the minimum number of apostolic references stands at a little over 3,200 times.

The many times apostles are recognized in New Testament definitely verifies their sole apostolic authorship of the sacred texts, and emphatically establishes the importance of the institution to the Godhead and the ecclesia. The Bible, the church's constitution then is strictly comprised of, and founded upon, the apostles' anointing, a reality that will stun many modern religionists. Amazingly, this degree of concentrated attention is found in the twenty-seven little books of the New Testament where a book of the Bible can amount to a single page with as few as two to three paragraphs. Still that does little to alter the truth. Without question, apostles categorically authenticate and vindicate their office's perpetuity on earth, in heaven, and in the church. Confining their existence as the church's founders and leaders in twenty-seven little books indisputably accredits apostleship and to do without them is to entirely throw out or renounce the New Testament as spurious. Of course, that strips the Christian church of its constitutional basis for existing and eliminates its authority to represent the Godhead in this world. Comparatively speaking, how often have we heard of Jesus scholars or church traditionalists seeking to eliminate the office of the pastor?

No one would think of shifting pastoral work to, whosoever wills; nor would it be done with the evangelist or teacher. Yet it seems the ministries of the apostle and prophet, the church's essential leaders and legislators are presented as dispensable and worse, heretical beyond Jesus eras. Additionally, their lack of uniform qualifications and functional service criteria appears to advocate that those occupying these two offices need no specific gifts or talents, or dedicated training, to fill the office. The positions are rather implied as conformable to whoever happens to show interest, desire, or sympathy toward them, when it is not conferred upon anyone that goes on the missions field.

For all these reason and in spite of its prolific concentration in scripture, the office of apostleship remains greatly misunderstood and only vaguely explained. Being without clear-cut, well-defined explanations of its official contributions to the body of Christ to date, its well-deserved reverence and repute have yet to be built. Much of what is available to studious seekers on the ministry tends to revolve around little more than casual learning and far too often a knee jerk reaction to the church's criticism of the ministry's resurgence. In comparison, no other officer listed in scripture has such meager information to go on in ministry even though this one begins all that goes into bringing a church into existence and sustaining it with God's supernatural power and revelations. *"And they continued stedfastly in the _apostles' doctrine_ and fellowship, and in breaking of bread, and in prayers. And fear came upon every soul: and _many wonders and signs were done by the apostles_. And all that believed were together, and had all things common"* (Acts 2:42-44). See also Acts 4:33: *"And _with great power_ gave the apostles witness of the resurrection of the Lord Jesus: and great grace was upon them all."* These two passages alone would suffice to make the point but there are two more worth adding to them. First, 2 Peter 3:2: *"That ye may be mindful of the words which were spoken before by the holy prophets, and of the commandment of us the apostles of the Lord and Saviour"*; and Jude 17: *"But, beloved, remember ye the words which were spoken before of the apostles of our Lord Jesus Christ."* Four resonant passages testify incessantly for us how God designed and ordained this mantle to serve Him in the church.

How the Bible World Saw Apostleship

The apostles, as society knew them in Christ's day, were not the dominating force in the religious, political, and military world they eventually became in the church: although theirs was certainly not an inferior position. Apostleship then, it seems, found its greatest prominence in periods of war and territorial upheaval. Perhaps that is why militaristic and ambassadorial connotations permeate its definitions. While many religions had their undeclared share of them, the apostle started out as a largely secular (as if the word could apply back then) ministry. See note below:

> **Note**: *The reason the word secular is dubious, as discussed later, is that everything in Christ's day and before was tied to a god. All the world was under the sway of the wicked one as the apostle John writes.*

Therefore, even though apostles may have governed ships, and seized and magistrated military strongholds, the era in which they did so was thoroughly polytheistic and pantheistic, keeping all humanity preoccupied with the gods. Whether they traveled land or sea to carry out their diplomatic negotiations with other countries or launched and led wars on foreign soil, it was understood by the cultures of the day that apostles acted on behalf of or at the behest of their gods, or the gods of their sending monarchs. See the following:

47

"Jesus saith unto her, touch me not; for I am not yet ascended to my Father: but go to my brethren, and say unto them, I ascend unto my Father, and your Father; and to my God, and your God" (John 20:17); and Revelation 3:12: "Him that overcometh will I make a pillar in the temple of my God, and he shall go no more out: and I will write upon him the name of my God, and the name of the city of my God, which is new Jerusalem, which cometh down out of heaven from my God: and I will write upon him my new name."

Moses' dispatch on what may be seen as the equivalent of an apostolic assignment shows the practice of theocratic rulers sending significant officials to act on their behalf goes back in history. The word for sending or being sent by one's deity with such a commission before Christ in scripture is *shalach*, from which comes the Hebrew counterpart of the apostle, *shaliach*, discussed later. Exodus chapter three makes the point: *"And Moses said unto God, Behold, when I come unto the children of Israel, and shall say unto them, The God of your fathers hath* **sent (shalach)** *me unto you; and they shall say to me, what is his name? What shall I say unto them? And God said unto Moses, I AM THAT I AM: and he n said, Thus shalt thou say unto the children of Israel, I AM hath sent* **(shalach)** *me unto you. And God said moreover unto Moses, Thus shalt thou say unto the children of Israel, The LORD God of your fathers, the God of Abraham, the God of Isaac, and the God of Jacob, hath* **sent (shalach)** *me unto you: this is my name for ever, and this is my memorial unto all generations"* (Exodus 3:13-15). This is a classic example of an apostle's dispatch. *Shalach* essentially means:

♦ To send away

♦ Appointed to bring

♦ Sent to conduct

- Forsake as a consequence of being sent

- Set forth to sow, spread, stretch out

See how much it mirrors the Greek word *apostello* for the sending forth of Christ's apostles? From John 7:29: *"But I know him: for I am from him, and he hath sent (apostello—apostolized) me."* Jesus was acutely aware of His status and commission as a sent one. Thirty-eight times, He used the phrase "sent me" in relation to His Father's assigned task that brought Him to earth. Of the thirty-eight times He uses the phrase, at least fifteen of them refer to His being apostolically sent. Paul the apostle uses the phrase once in 1 Corinthians 1:17. The remaining times the Savior called Himself a sent one, referred to His being sent as one dispatched on a journey. As opposed to the apostolic inference found in the word *apostello* for *to send*, the primarily dispatch implications appear more in the term *pempo*. While both apply to sending, the particular nuance of the assignment is different. Pempo is essentially to be sent on a journey from a distant point of origin. The *sendee* is remarkably interposed in the distant location for a specified purpose, with a clear understanding that his or her departure from the original point and presence in the land are strictly temporary.

The sent one will, is expected, to return upon completion of the assigned task. The same is not necessarily, so of apostleship. A commission can mean a long-standing occupancy of a distant and foreign land, bringing to fore, the two high features of ambassadorship upon which a proper commission is founded. To see the distinctives of the two words, *pempo* and *apostello*, turn first to John 20:21. Peculiarly, among all the Lord's uses of this term as recorded by His scribes in the gospels, only John records His sending as pempo and apostello.

Apostolic insight suggests that he did so as the one writer to underscore Christ's eternality. John emphasizes Jesus as the eternal Son of God, an eternal being altogether and the incarnate member of the Godhead separated from the other two and dispatched—synonym for pempo—to earth on a journey. To distinguish when Jesus referred to His visit as an errand over His understanding of that errand to be generated by an apostolic commission, twenty-three times John chooses the word *pempo*. When Jesus applies it to His apostles, He subtly invokes the term to convey to them that, once they enter His service, His apostles cease to be citizens of their world and are thus dispatched to it for His express purposes. Upon completion of their assignment, they like Him will return to their home base, which as it was with Him, is not of this world. With the word, *apostello* it is a bit different in the same way an errand differs from a mission, in particular a commission. Apostello then transmits the following:

♦ To set apart

♦ To send out on a mission

♦ To send forth

♦ To set at liberty for departure

Reaching back to Isaiah 48:16 the idea of the sent one, popular in Bible eras, shows up prophetically to predict the Holy Spirit's apostolism. *"Come ye near unto me, hear ye this; I have not spoken in secret from the beginning; from the time that it was, there am I: and now the Lord GOD, and his Spirit, hath sent me."* This resurfaces in Acts chapter thirteen. In all scripture examples, the Lord Jesus' sending principal was the Almighty. The Savior reiterates many times how He was sent by God the Father, Israel's covenant God.

Later, His apostles show their grasp of the same truth as they declare they are sent by Him. From Matthew chapter ten, where the Lord Jesus inducts them into apostolic service (see

50

10:40) up to the end, the apostles understood theirs to be a dispatch on a mission with authority to invoke, perform, or impose some heavenly charge, legislation, demand or business on the inhabitants of this world. That makes it more of a commission as they were to overall, carry out the tasks and duties the Lord delegated to them.

True Apostleship Separates Redemption from Religion

With the climate of the pre Christ world being saturated with deities and the supernatural, apostles today should understand that religion is merely the helpful tool of syncretism—the blending of many or all religions into one. However, during the Jesus years that was not the prime focus. The contest was ever between the gods and their people were not fixed on their religions back then; they were obsessed with the celestial personas that fueled their spiritual climates. They sought not to blend religion but to fuse the world's gods into one common pantheon, to determine what nation's god would rule the world, as they knew it. The ancients concentrated on gods, coming and going, wooing, winning and warring in their world. Civilizations were birthed by them, ruled by them, conquered, and in many ways overrun with the latest, strongest most fortuitous deity entering a land. To best, understand this truth, replace the word religion with god or deity and the spiritual ambiance of the ancient world becomes clear.

The Bible was never written to religious zealots. It was inscribed to the children of the Most High God. To children ordained to become world rulers with their Sovereign Ruling God. True, they were labeled Christians by the secular world, but no one ever downplayed their status as the offspring of the most difficult, unapproachable constantly interfering and overruling God that declared and proved Himself Creator and Lord. What has become the church eras of isolated dogma and doctrine began as express personifications of the conduct, behavior, and adoptive citizenship guidelines for offspring of the deities that populated the ancient world. The religious piece entered when decreed rules of approach, appeasement, petition, blessings, and provisions were stipulated by a deity, or an imperial ruler claiming him or herself to be one. Religious requirements, rituals, keep worshippers in contact and favor with paternal deity. Sacrifices symbolizing a death like surrender to its will and lifestyle begin the process.

Spiritual Initiations Begin with Priests

All spiritual initiation, that is once a deity has overtaken a land and its people, begins with a priest that quickly installs an order of spiritual ministers to stand and serve the deity's altar. The name for this order is priesthood. God follows this pattern up to Revelation 7:15 where the international multitude caught up from the earth in the first rapture are permanently installed in God's temple. This event culminates the ancient appointment of priestly orders that began in scripture with Melchizedek and ends with its eternal institution under Jesus Christ the Lamb.

After a proper priesthood is established, demands for offerings of food and drink (oblations) are followed with burning incense to symbolize prayers and words that amount to praise, thanks, and requests. These serve as the tasks the god will assign the priests and through them the inhabitants of his or her land. See Revelation 5:8, 8:3, 4 for its eternal precedence. Once all these are rendered as prescribed, the atmosphere is thus ready for the worshipper's petitions or audience with the deity. Never, in ancient times, were these seen as mere religious forms acted out of commemorations of dramatic, ethereal, or spiritual moments in a single individual's life. Worship and rituals, for them, were always ascribed to some supernatural or preternatural being credited with personality, sentiment, intelligence, volition, and desire.

Superior heavenly beings were pursued and venerated for their ownership of the land, powers over nature, or an aspect of it, and superior eminence over human life and its affairs. Reading the Bible from this vantage point answers a host of questions regarding what is or is not characteristic of the Most High God, what is or is not acceptable to Him. These explanations say how and why the Lord reacts to certain human behaviors, attitudes, and pursuits the way He does. Elevating popular religious ideals to what they should be, that is the literal sentiments and acceptance demands of the personified god to whom the worshipper belongs, brings arguments over what religion is what and what deity one should worship into a different light. Many people choosing a religion under these circumstances would be more careful about doing so if they knew their choice was not over what rituals or regulations they valued or could live with, but rather over the god to whom they surrendered their lives and souls and how their proposed deities demand they behave to court their favors. The decision then would be seen as having everlasting more than temporal or trendy effects.

God's Eternal Cosmogony & Apostleship

The word *cosmogony* speaks to the origin of a world. Typically, it is applied to the origin of the universe in view of its respective worlds. Prefixing the term with the word eternal focuses attention on its application to the Creator's never-ending world and its perpetual governments and agents. The ensuing discussion links the apostle's concentrations to what is beyond and above the world in which he or she lives and works.

Apostles know their entire campaign in the world pits them against Satan on God's behalf: 1 Thessalonians 2:18 and 1 Corinthians 4:9 makes it clear. Apostles know the conflict between God and Satan targets humanity as the everlasting prize. The Risen Christ indoctrinates His apostles on the reality of their clash with the world's defeated deities and admonishes them not to become mired in the world's religions to triumph. They are further admonished by the resurrected King to avoid viewing theirs as a commission dispatched to the world to confront its dry ideologies; His will is that they not approach anything spiritual or religious as if it is detached from a personal being. Religions are the will, ways, worship, and customs of deities, not the beings themselves. Revelation chapter twelve says how this came to be. However, without a deity, religions cannot legitimately exist being void of a willful and personified intelligence to petition or appease and the authority to transcend this world to do so.

Apostleship Is a Franchise

A franchise is summed up as the source of completely delegated authority. It speaks to operational independence, special privileges, and a charter entity with full authority. Related much to the word *plenipotentiary*, discussed later in the book, it identifies an entity with full power and authority granted by a higher one. That authority is not only uncontested, it is largely unconditional and unrestricted. Such an entity is permitted near constitutional powers to self govern by the franchise agreement. Other words relate it to Christendom.[6] These are citizenship, deliverance, salvation, and redemption, emphatically linking it to the church. Lastly, it speaks to a representative government exercising a sovereignty that is protected by immunity. Meanings include the sphere, territory, authority, and business of an embassy.

When God presents Himself to apostles for His service, He does so by way of spectacular celestial drama to annex them to His heavenly franchise. See Luke 22:29, 30: "*And I appoint unto you a kingdom, as my Father hath appointed unto me; That ye may eat*

---

[6] From Rogets New Millennium Thesaurus, by Lexico Publishing Group, LLC

and drink at my table in my kingdom, and sit on thrones judging the twelve tribes of Israel." Also, in second Corinthians 10:13-16, the phrase *measure of the rule* is used for what God gives His specially commissioned messengers. The apostle, according to these scriptures, is *enfranchised* by the King of glory for some pervasive purposes. To *enfranchise*, Random House Webster Collegiate Dictionary ©1995 says, is "to admit someone into citizenship; to endow with a city, constituency with municipal or parliamentary rights." Once enfranchised, a person is liberated by the conferred privilege of government to work in or rule a territory with legal immunity and exemption to carry on specified business. That is characteristic of ambassadorship.

The word *annex* refers to being added to what is existing and *franchise* refers to being free to function or act in a given city or town as a municipal or parliamentarian leader. [7]

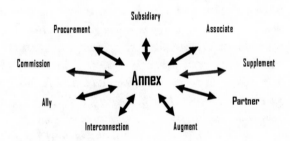

This revelation says that apostles are distributed a franchise portion of God's kingdom, particularly of the kingdom of heaven to monopolize for Him. In the way, a territory is annexed to America to enjoy all its privileges, authority, and prosperity, so it is with the apostle that receives his or her

---

[7] The Barnhart Concise Dictionary of Etymology; the Origins of American English Words, Robert Barnhart, B. H Wilson Company, 1995.

sphere (measure of rule) from the Lord Jesus Christ. That dramatic encounter mentioned earlier delivers to apostles what they are sent to do, the power they are delegated to do it, and general outcomes they are expected to achieve for the Lord Jesus Christ. The concept is enfolded in the Lord's Parable of the Minas in Luke chapter nineteen. Let us review the parable for its connections to these thoughts.

The Parable of the Ten Pounds—Minas

Luke 19:12-27

> He said therefore, A certain nobleman went into a far country to receive for himself a **kingdom**, and to return. And he called his ten servants, and delivered them ten pounds, and said unto them, **Occupy** till I come. But his citizens hated him, and sent a message (ambassage) after him, saying, We will not have this man to **reign** over us. And it came to pass, that when he was returned, having received the kingdom, then he commanded these servants to be called unto him, to whom he had given the **money**, that he might know how much every man had **gained by trading**. Then came the first, saying, Lord, thy pound hath gained ten pounds. And he said unto him, Well, thou good servant: because thou hast been faithful in a very little, have thou **authority over ten cities**. And the second came, saying, Lord, thy pound hath **gained** five pounds. And he said likewise to him, Be thou also over **five cities**. And another came, saying, Lord, behold, here is thy pound, which I have kept laid up in a napkin: For I feared thee, because thou art an austere man: thou takest up that thou layedst not down, and reapest that thou didst not sow. And he saith unto him, Out of thine own mouth will I judge thee, thou wicked servant. Thou knewest that I was an austere man, taking up that I laid not down, and reaping that I did not sow: Wherefore then gavest not thou

my money into the bank, that at my coming I might have required mine own with usury? And he said unto them that stood by, Take from him the pound, and give it to him that hath ten pounds. (And they said unto him, Lord, he hath ten pounds.) For I say unto you, That unto every one which hath shall be given; and from him that hath not, even that he hath shall be taken away from him. But those mine enemies, which would not that I should reign over them, bring hither, and slay them before me.

To begin, this parable, despite its similarities, is not to be confused with the parable of the talents. Reread that one in light of this and compare the glaring difference between the two. One of the most prominent differences is the outcome of both. The rewards are simply indicated as things rather than territories leaving the actual substance open for the Lord to decide. Still, rulership over some part of the Lord's goods (what was entrusted) is the aim of the message. There is much to be learned from this parable spoken by the Lord Jesus. Weeks of study would fail to unseal it all. However, the emboldened words make our points. A few of them are listed below:

1. The parable was really all about a kingdom, Christ's kingdom, which when He receives it, will return to divvy up its material portions to His faithful servants. This is a veiled carryover of Isaiah 53:12.

2. *Occupy* meant more than just doing business. That an ambassage, delegated embassy, was sent after the nobleman departed says much power and prosperity were up for grabs at his leaving. It also suggests that the ten he left in charge had to war to increase their money and retain the cities left in their care.

57

3. While absent, Jesus expects His apostles to retain and expand His holdings, enriching His kingdom in the process.

4. God expects apostles to engage in warfare to defend His territories and in business to enrich it.

5. The Lord sees profitability in entirely different terms than we do, especially the traditional church. He desires an increase on all He bestows in the planet and those that do not render Him an increase, He judges harshly in the end.

6. Burying the seed money for selfish and critical reasons can be fatal to an apostle.

7. The pounds represented land, territories. Another word for cities is municipalities.

8. Jesus, by His delivering (symbolically) the unused mina to the one that had the most, says that He gives the greatest reward to those that bring Him the highest rate of return.

9. Once He sits on His throne, the Lord will dispose of those that refused His reign over their lives, viewing them as enemies.

For sure, there are more intriguing points to be gained from this parable but these suffice to justify the "apostolic annexation" principle introduced in this discussion.

The franchise piece gives the apostle the license to monopolize the jurisdictional sphere delegated to the mantle for the sake of creating a divine stronghold for the Savior. It also explains why apostleship and entrepreneurialism go hand in hand as seen for instance in the Lord's push toward apostolic marketplace dominance. Apart from this revelation, the idea of a marketplace apostle is definitely suspect. In the classic sense, it may still not be quite prudent when one thinks of how God ordained the office of the apostle to function. However, there are secular apostles that do not serve Jesus Christ. Therefore, there must be of necessity those of the light that do the same on His behalf. Calling them apostles may be a stretch, but the fact remains there are non-ecclesiastical apostles assigned to handle the Lord's affairs outside the church, that is the business of the kingdom. The narrow application of the word marketplace may well be a stricter way of saying "world apostles" in which case the Great Commission's "go ye into all the world…" does apply.

Nonetheless, the phrase "apostolic annexation[8]" best defines the Lord's extension of His apostles into His world with the authority to act on His behalf in this one and transact business that includes exchanging natural and supernatural elements between the two. Nothing better distinguishes the Lord's appearances to His apostles from others in His church than this explanation. It is what Jesus intended when He gave Peter the keys to the kingdom of heaven. During their induction encounter, the apostle is brought into the Lord's world to know that it is real and then systematically taught how it works. Apostles are introduced to the invisible world's powerful citizenry and made to understand that he or she does not work alone in this world. The very requisite of apostle's induction produces these events.

Preparing to Face Off with Other Gods

A vivid life-changing encounter with the resurrected Lord Jesus Christ provides the platform for apostles' ministries and assures

---

[8] *Christ's authorized apostles already seated in heavenly places in Christ Jesus to function, serve, and profit the Lord and His church on earth as heavenly citizens. See Ephesians 3:15 and Revelation 19:10.*

them that the Risen Lord, the Lion and Lamb, really controls of all His created worlds. Apostolic faith is energized by their intimate and tangible interaction with the Lord Jesus Christ. It is indispensable when the trials of their calling become overwhelming, because they will face off with the gods of this world. It is what apostles do, which is why apostolic faith does not rest upon what is seen. The sight unseen impresses them more deeply than it does the rest of the body of Christ.

Eternal kingdom realities persuade apostles to emphasize in their ministries that the entire religion and humanist conflict is not about people's faith in a dogma, ritual, religion, or spiritual ideology. It is emphatically, God convinces His apostles, a question of whose god is God, and who belongs to what god in the world; and what god takes possession of their soul in the hereafter. That the entire campaign is about divine beings is seen in Jonah 1:6 and in Elijah's penetrating challenge to Israel in 1 Kings 18:21. More than sixty times, the Lord admonishes His people about serving other gods. His entire combat with Egypt was about their gods and their rivalry with Him over His people. (See Exodus 12:120) Repeatedly, scripture records the Lord as distinguishing Himself from the gods of the people or the nations. Deuteronomy 31:16 even warns them against showing interest in or being snared by the gods of the strangers that visited or sojourned in their land. From Genesis to Revelation, the Lord's issue has been other gods and idolatry. He declared in Exodus 20:3 that they should have no other god before (in front or instead of) Him, reiterated in Deuteronomy 5:7, 6:14, and many others. The Bible records God's acknowledgement of the gods of the following:

- People
- Nations
- Countries

- The earth

- The people of the earth

- Gold and silver

- The works of men's hands

Religion as used in Paul's Acts 26:5 and Galatians 1:13, 14 quotation referred strictly to Judaism. By then the unique nativity supernatural event that brought the Jews into existence is long forgotten fused with other religions concocted by gods and humans over the centuries. Their special status, or as the Yahweh called it, peculiar heritage from His divine lineage is more mythological now than a cherished legacy. The word religion is found in one other New Testament reference, James 1:26. There it speaks to "ceremonial observances motivated by fear, fright, or trouble."[9] There is no question in God's mind that His conflict with humanity has always been and will always be the miscegenation of fallen gods with His creation. Genesis 6:1-5; John 8:44; Judge 1:6, Revelation 12:12 make this truth unquestionably plain. The Old Testament discusses the gods of the peoples, nations, countries, and such by name. There are the Amorites, in whose land God's people dwelt, in addition to the following:

Egypt	Syria	Zidon	Moab	Ammon
Philistines	Sepharaim	Hamath	Arpad	Hena
Ivah	Seir	Edom	Damascus	

---

[9] Extracted from Strong's Concordance

61

The Eternal Truth about Religious Freedom

The ultimate religious decision is not concerned with a person's pet faith or beliefs, or with their favored rituals, ceremonies, or observances. Nature, for instance corrupts as seasonal cycles show, but nature deities are subject to their Creator. Psalm 82:1 says that God, Israel's God, stands in the congregation of the gods and judges among the gods. Review also, Psalm 86:8; 138:1; Daniel 2:11; Zephaniah 2:11; Acts 14:11. All these show that religious decisions are invariably about a personal deity to whom a worshipper opts to surrender his or her will despite the eternal consequences. That is, if they declare any god at all. The atheist by default lapses into what may be called a divine lottery where the deity that most influenced their life, known or unknown wins the soul at death, even if it is never announced. When a person dies intestate, that is, without the will of some god on record, they are simply escorted from the world by whatever camouflaged deity seduced them in life. This reality is alluded to in Jude 1:9: *"Yet Michael the archangel, when contending with the devil he disputed about the body of Moses, durst not bring against him a railing accusation, but said, The Lord rebuke thee."* The value of this scripture to the discussion lies in the statement *"**contending with the devil ...about Moses' body**."* The body in question is apparently not Moses' natural body without its spirit of life (James 2:26) because that was promised to the dust and decomposition, rendering it utterly useless to earth or the afterlife. Beside this, Deuteronomy 34:6 says the Lord personally buried Moses in the valley of Moab and no one ever found his body.

All this notwithstanding, the devil would also have no use for Moses' physical body. Being a spirit, he knows those he takes must complete their tour in their clay bodies. No, the argument between Michael and the devil was about Moses' soul because that is the only part of him that either of the two mighty angels would have been interested, or could even take to their respective worlds of heaven or hell. Evidently, the two angels, Michael as the watcher over Israel (Daniel 10:21 and Revelation 12:7) and Satan as the doomed god of this world (John 12:31; 2 Corinthians 4:4), had authority to retrieve the deceased Moses and escort him to his eternal resting place. Having met death, Satan felt he was due Moses' body—soul and looked forward to eternally enslaving the Lord's mightiest prophet forever. The Old Testament's account of Saul's visit to the witch of Endor represents the spirit of Michael and Satan's conflict because He told to the witch of Endor to call up Samuel from the dead. She was able to do so because Samuel, although he was a mighty prophet who died faithful to the Lord, nonetheless went to hell. That is how the witch could summon him and why her sorcery could compel him to prophesy something to Saul that he would have never told him if he were still on earth.

Having served Yahweh faithfully except for the Meribah incident (which caused his physical death in the first place), Moses remained overall diligent in his calling, something the writer of Hebrews asserts. Michael was thus dispatched to bring Moses' soul to the Most High. Matthew 17:3 and Luke 9:30 say that Michael won the contest as Moses' appearance centuries to Jesus and His three closest apostles, later on the Mount of Transfiguration attests. Jointly, these passages all affirm that the god entitled to a deceased in the afterlife is the one the person served in life. The decedent then becomes the deity's everlasting possession.

Religion in the Creator's divine cosmogony is a matter of where a worshipper will live forever because of their deity decision. God honors their choice and allows them to risk damnation and serve their chosen deity throughout eternity. Jesus' shed blood bought them the choice of rejecting Him as much as it liberated the Father's chosen to accept His redemption. Until Jesus paid the price to buy God's people back from hell all went there, which is why He did too according to the Acts 2:27 in fulfillment of Psalm 16:10.

However, God's punishment of Moses' single indiscretion was that he would die, that is they would see (face) or taste (experience) death, instead of immediately arriving in the Most High's presence the way Enoch and Elijah did, by translation from heaven to earth. Nonetheless, since the Lord had no intention of banishing His powerful prophet to hell forever Michael was sent to preserve Moses, to prevent Satan's kidnap of his soul and deliver Moses to the Almighty's throne.

Another illustration is Elijah's contest on Mount Carmel with Baal and Asherah's prophets. Not unlike Moses' face off with Egypt and its gods in Exodus 12:12. It too was unquestionably based upon a clash of the gods. Israel's progenitor God Yahweh and Baal to whom they constantly defected in their ceaseless rebellion against Him had come to redeem His people. Egypt's pharaoh was not interested in letting them go. Pharaohs back then considered themselves offspring and personifications of the gods of their land, and so Pharaoh considered Moses' demands a contest between himself and who Moses' claimed was the God of the Israelites. Elijah staged the challenge to provoke Israel to abandon Baal and his worship and return to their covenant God Yahweh. These examples all scripturally ground the teaching in the Almighty's wise eternal protocols.

As part of their training, new apostles are brought into this consciousness under Christ's apostleship, as He makes sure they understand that it is always about His redemption. Apostles are taught why the struggle is never a matter of a world religion or assimilating His passion and its fruit into those that dominate it. Apostleship then and now is concerned with separating, the

Jesus calls it sanctifying, the elect from the rejected, or rejecting souls of earth. Despite how much the deluded church alleges that none can perish, the truth is that God wants the best of the best. To Him, the goal is not repeating Lucifer's revolution after the blood of Jesus purged His eternal altar. This information and the corresponding experiences from which it comes, imbeds the proper "sent one's" conscious as they become Christ's apostles.

The Sent One Consciousness of Jesus' Day

When one is dispatched as a sent one, a delegated official on assignment, the people of Jesus' day knew the act committed a trust and communicated a corresponding measure of authority and power. Higher senders delegated greater authority and power depending upon whether or not the dispatch was an errand, a task, or a commission. No doubt, our Savior understood this and, based on His eternal commission and standing Apostleship as a Sent One of the Godhead, was fully cognizant of what He ultimately transferred to His body, John 13:16 and Luke 11:49. Remaining with eternity's pattern of first the spiritual and then the natural, first the heavenly and then the earthly, the world then, with its religions and governments, understood apostleship existed before Christ invoked it into the New Testament church. That is why those He chose did not need to ask Him what the term meant or how they fit it; they only needed the Lord to demonstrate how it would apply to them in His service. His initial apostles quite understood the Lord Jesus Christ represented a government: eternity's government. What they did not grasp was that He was sent to found a universal faith, and to host all spheres of humanity in His divine service in the name of God's kingdom. Hence, when the Savior approached the world as its heavenly apostle, He began with the words "the kingdom of God has come near you, or is at hand." His words underscore that Jesus knew

65

exactly what He was instituting when He renamed His twelve chosen disciples' apostles and why He did so.

Chapter Summary

1. Subject knowledge is strengthened by history.

2. Apostleship is in scripture more than 3,000 times.

3. Apostles are essential to the church, its strength, wisdom, revelations, and perpetuity.

4. Apostles of Jesus' day saw the mantle radically different from today. Their view emphasized religion, politics, and militancy.

5. **Shalach** is the Old Testament shadow of apostleship. Moses' commission to deliver Israel from Egypt typifies this.

6. **Apostello**, the word used by Jesus to describe Himself as a sent one, designates His visit to earth as an apostolic commission.

7. Redemption, not religion, is the goal of true apostleship.

8. The Bible is written to God's present and future rulers.

9. Spiritual conflicts between God and His creation are always about deities rather than faith or religion.

10. Apostle's campaigns pit them against Satan's kingdom on God's behalf.

Chapter Four

Tradition Religion & Apostolism

Chapter Discussions

Root of the Church's Escape Mentality • Pseudo Christianity
& Scripture Twisting • The Difference True Apostles Make •
Why the Church Fears Apostleship • Analyses of Apostolic
Authors • Kanon, the Sphere of Apostleship • How Tradition
Misdefines Apostles

O ne disturbing truth overlooked by those attempting to impress apostleship upon the church is the reality that the world and the traditional post apostolic New church has never met or interacted with Jesus Christ as the Great Apostle. Although, many Christians know God the Father as the Creator and Jesus as Savior, they have little or no knowledge of them as the founder and sustainer of apostles' ministries. Most of those presently occupying or entering the apostleship have never encountered the Resurrected Christ in His Apostle's Office and so find it difficult corresponding their ministries with the Godhead's vision for it. Christ's body does not know the Holy Spirit as the Almighty's apostolic administrator.

Another unsettling truth is that the God of the Bible has yet to be revealed to His modern church because He does so best with and through His apostles and prophets (see Ephesians 2:20; 3:5). So what does this mean? What is it saying to the church today? It means that the church's view of God and His work in the world is largely confined to Sunday morning services and its spiritual exploits. People pick up the Lord somewhere between Saturday night and Sunday morning and honor Him for a few hours on their Sabbath. Besides that, the majority of them are largely disinterested in God's involvement in their lives after the last amen and do not want to think about His activities in the world again until the next Sunday. If they need the Lord before then, people are generally taught to call upon Him to intervene in their situation or resolve whatever crises they may encounter in the world. Afterward, like a good teraphim (idol), God is sent back to His place and left there until Sunday comes again, or until another calamity forces them to call upon Him. Outside of these occasions, much of the church is satisfied with knowing little, or does not seem to care to know their God as He is. They are unable or refuse to see God, Jesus, or the Holy Spirit as involved in world events, despite His Bible saying He is over, and the cause of what happens in all His creations.

Such a mindset did not come from apostles. The mantle immediately obliterates such ideas upon taking up the ministry if for no other reason than that the Lord personally meets them to install them into His service. The attitude was born from the medieval church's escape theology that has persisted down through the years. The apostle's franchise annexation makes them take it more as a personal collaborator with the Lord in His affairs on earth. They know it to be the hindrance it is and that it aims to bring about the outcome it has in the church and the world. To begin to blast away at it, some deep-rooted beliefs about what Jesus has in mind for His church must be removed. The one most prevalent and perhaps most damnable is the escape mentality that permeates most theologies and sermons downplaying Christ as Creator and sovereign.

Root of the Church's Escape Mentality

During the New Creation church's formative years, the Holy Spirit's presence in the world though pervasive in the planet, had yet to spread to the multitudes of souls that it occupies today. Initially, He was confined to the few people, relatively speaking, that received the new birth at the apostles' preaching. The world had yet to be covered with the gospel of Jesus Christ. Consequently, it took time for God's Spirit to reproduce throughout the world in people's souls. Until that happened the powers and authorities in control then were antagonistic toward Christianity as history shows. Those that were saved were often excluded from the ranks of the elite and lived for the most part in fear for their lives. They met, often underground, and precious few dared to publicize their faith in Jesus Christ. It is still that way in many places on earth, especially those where the gospel has ceased, or is yet to be preached or where Christ's faith is unknown or trivialized. Many of those that dared voice their faith in the true and living God, being martyred, paid for it with their lives. Obviously, being nurtured in such a fearful environment no doubt incubated all sorts of defenses to protect believers at risk for their lives from death, and motivated them to seek to minimize their persecution. One of the most effective means of doing this was through doctrine.

Pseudo Christianity & Scripture Twisting

Paul warned his churches to beware of the mutilation. Before the apostle completed his course, he met Satan's damage control already in motion to recover his losses caused by Jesus' success. Paul included in his writings a phrase that depicts what has happened to God's words over the centuries. The phrase in Peter's second epistle about their twisting the scriptures explains it. To this end, a counter theology was formed to soften the church's stance and sermonizing. What came out of it was a desperate desire to diminish the church's exposure to government censure and martyrdom. The unavoidable answer was to remove itself as a threat to the powers that be; it became for many the primary objective. The method was simple, just persuade believers that their inheritance and the liberation in Jesus Christ and subsequent world domination were for a much later time, perhaps even after their death. God really meant it to be bestowed in eternity, for now the plan was to keep a low profile, and circumvent conflict at all costs. Thus, the escape mentality that grips the church today took shape and hold; devised to counteract persecution and fend off the brutality that stalked their lives daily.

Seeing the success of the strategy promoted another tactic of streamlining scripture and church dogma until it largely revolved around morality and salvation. "Get saved and live a good life until you die," was the message. To stay out of trouble with the authorities, and to avoid antagonizing any other religion sanctioned by it, never hint that Jesus is the only true and living God, and if one said so, do not imply that He lives and reigns today. A plethora of afterlife doctrines took hold, as Christians were seduced into ignoring this world, and in some cases refusing it, in favor of the day of their death when Jesus would come and take them away from it all.

Today, the damage wreaked by this defense is immeasurable to Christ and His faith. Both are ridiculed and shut out of the kingdoms of this world that rightfully belong to Jesus through His church. The fallout has been that the average Christian only knows, pursues, and serves God in the context of what He can, has, or should do for them. The self-defense that molded how they see Him has turned to selfishness where they do everything possible to offend no one, and resolve not to force their faith on the world. As you can see, that eliminates evangelism and witnessing altogether. Most believers are encouraged to quietly, live out their lives in the catacombs of society.

Numerous theological and philosophical contrivances were invented to support this understandable defense of the Christian life and faith. All of these are suppression tactics in themselves. Each one disseminated error and heresy to support their true objectives. Today, polished to a perfect implement, the motives are unmasked; they are to launch a full-scale attack on Christianity by dismantling its core persuasions. These include denying Christ's deity and incarnation and casting aspersions on His death and resurrection. In addition, they mock His eternality and intimating that He is no more than a moral prophet slain for His radical beliefs. At the same time, the truth and its vehicles were also being submerged. Significant among those vehicles were God's apostles. An entire move was launched to prove that their purposes and functions in the early church were fulfilled and not needed in future generations. Commentaries were written to support this argument, apologetics were devised, sermons preached around it and if they failed to make the case, mockery, persecution, and ostracism were employed.

Apostles were targeted for the reasons we have been presenting in this book; because they alone could refute the

71

errant heresy that the machine (doctrine) of unbelief was incessantly churning out and disseminating to the Church. Omitting them from the church's leadership staff, especially as its head locked the church in a multi-millennia time warp where a vicious and endless cycle of ancient worship modes supplant God's truth and keeps the church from moving on to perfection. Old songs, old sermons, no power and stale testimonies delude people into thinking they are pleasing God. Scripture is shut, as archaic revelations are recycled for each succeeding generation. Over time, the veil of Isaiah 25:7, that God initially removed covers their eyes, hearts, and minds as worshippers and seekers struggle to find out if God and Christ are dead, real, or alive.

The Difference True Apostles Make

True apostles know that God is alive and all-powerful, that Jesus truly rose from the dead. Wisdom characterizes the true apostle. He or she is known for an uncanny ability to bring eternity's wisdom in the now through astounding revelations that make practical sense. Apostles can do this because they know firsthand that there is a spiritual world backing this one and that the devil is not a figment of an over religious imagination. Christ's apostles know that Satan is as real as the Creator that made him and that he is deviously occupied with frustrating the Lord's word and work in the earth. True servants of the Lord Jesus Christ in general are persuaded that God's testimonies concerning these are true, and labor to erase the insinuation that scripture is entirely metaphoric and that nothing on earth is either concrete or absolute. Finally, their doctrine is based wholly on 2 Timothy 2:16.

Modern church doctrines, being largely para-scriptions of God's word, extrapolate His truth from contemporary human experiences or perceptions about spirituality and religion. In short, doctrines today respond to people's reaction to the

72

church and its ministers. It rarely originates from the Lord in answer to what He knows the world truly needs to hear from Him. Hence, popular doctrine and theology hawk secular resolutions to human affairs and often appears to mimic it. This fact alone contributes to the world's perception of the church's irrelevance in its societies. Because, religionists conclude that God is ancient, not eternal, they present a God that seems to lag behind modern issues and rely on the world for wisdom and insight. Much of the church cannot fathom their God or Savior as Alpha and Omega. So convinced are they of these faulty notions that today's religionists hold that the Holy Spirit is acting entirely separate from scripture and God's word. Often, as a holdover from the didactic/poimen ministry model, it is stated that the Bible, is to be believed but just not as complete in itself. It is, they claim, merely a pattern, a template to guide but not govern the church. The modern church government is not confined to it. For the true apostle, such a statement is unsettling, having met the living Logos themselves before entering Christ's Apostle's office. Several scriptures rebuke this contention: Isaiah 8:29; Proverbs 30:6; Luke 24:44; John 16:14; 2 Peter 1:19; Revelation 22:19. Together they set the bounds of spiritual manifestations application that provide the firewalls the church needs to stay within the precincts of kingdom veracity and biblical demonstrations.

Misunderstanding how broad and comprehensive the Bible is in its treatment of church and kingdom affairs in the world may be blamed for people's flighty, sometimes irreverent, treatment of the Lord. Handed down from non-apostolic church founders and leaders who saw theirs as a duty to make people feel comfortable with God despite discomforting Him in the process, the weight that accompanies God's word with power are therefore wanting. Apostles on the other hand, are distinguished by signs and wonders that enforce the Lord's will and inspire people to conform to it. Human adjustments to the

73

Lord's eternal truths are mostly affective. They desensitize peoples' spirits in favor of exploiting and scintillating the soul. Such affective mechanisms include theology, apologetics, humanism and psychology (*psucheology*—soulology) in all their forms and variations as they have been modified to appease contemporary Christendom. Much of what the church knows about the Almighty and His kingdom is taught based on post apostolic dogma that fosters the belief that everything apostolic has already been revealed by the first twelve, thirteen, fourteen, or fifteen apostles noted in scripture.

The controversy is that nothing more regarding the office is needful and so any apostle's ministry to the last days' church is annulled. The other three offices in Ephesians 4:11, evangelist, pastor and teacher, along with the deaconry and most importantly the bishop are thus charged by God to perpetuate what they interpret and apply from scripture for generations to come. What makes this conviction dangerous is that the two offices, apostle and prophet, that penned most, if not all of the Bible are absent among the voices of its message and doctrines. What must that say about the church and its position on Bible truth? This being the case, the very mantles that brought the word of the Lord to His people are silenced and those that received it become its executors in their place, although they are perhaps once, twice, thrice removed from the revelation as given to mankind experientially and officially.

Why the Church Fears Apostleship

Inspired by ecclesiastical rejection of the apostle's office, and subsequent propaganda denouncing it, theological teaching has ingrained people's consciousness to fear apostleship. The body of Christ today dreads apostles because the machine at work against them has been at work for nearly two thousand years. They are, as a result, unaware that none of the ministry classic mantles—evangelists, pastors, and teachers—credited with bringing the Church to where it is today, were uninvolved with God's eternal scripture as delivered to the Church. Therefore, they cannot replicate what He dispenses to His apostles. The mantles, like any other uniform of service serve entirely different, usually the more subordinate purposes and invoke a lesser rank of celestial support.

The New Testament urges the church to extend itself beyond itself and this present evil world. Only the apostles' mantle can aptly instruct them on how to do this without becoming enmeshed with occult or humanist genre. When the early apostles recorded what they witnessed of the Lord Jesus' apostleship and that of the Holy Spirit, they were moved by very real concerns. When the apostle Paul wrote the majority of the New Testament he did so with a mind toward addressing literal divine human beings eventually to rule this world and any others the Creator founded. Here is how the other apostles made their contribution to this heavenly text. Peter and John, research confirms, were key ecclesiastical legislators through whom the Lord canonized His scripture to govern His church.

Analyses of Apostolic Authors

As it happened, the apostle Peter contributed two books and the apostle John wrote three epistles, the Apocalypse and one Gospel. The Book of Acts, though perhaps not directly written by an apostle, is entirely about their lives and exploits, if Luke is to be seen strictly as a scribal author. James the Lord's brother. Galatians 1:19 says is an apostle. Besides this, he would have certainly, having grown up with Jesus fit the profile of the apostle and met the criteria of having seen and been personally taught by the Lord. The James mentioned in Galatians 2:9 does not appear to be John's brother before he was killed. That he took over leadership of the Jerusalem council establishes him as an apostle and evidently infers he saw His brother as the Risen Lord. It would seem from Jude's epistle that he too was the Lord's brother since the brother of John worthy of a Bible mention was killed. Jude was James' brother, to complete our profile. He too apparently saw His Risen elder brother, our Lord. For more information, see the following:

- *Galatians 1:19—"But other of the apostles saw I none, save James the Lord's brother."*

- *Galatians 2:12—"For before that certain came from James, he did eat with the Gentiles: but when they were come, he withdrew and separated himself, fearing them which were of the circumcision."*

- *James 1:1—"James, a servant of God and of the Lord Jesus Christ, to the twelve tribes which are scattered abroad, greeting."*

- *Jude 1:1—"Jude, the servant of Jesus Christ, and brother of James, to them that are sanctified by God the Father, and preserved in Jesus Christ, and called."*

Beyond these passages' ability to solidify New Testament scripture's authorship by apostles, they show the Holy Spirit's ways of verifying apostolic recognition for the body of Christ. Paul emphatically confirms James as the Lord's brother and an apostle. Jude's opening statement relies on James' position as a recognized apostle for his own credibility by declaring that he is James' brother. He exercises his new creation church apostle's kanonical authority in his own letter.

Kanon, the Sphere of Apostleship

Apostles of the day understood the Lord's kingdom **kanon** from Galatians 6:16; 2 Corinthians 10: 13, 15, 16; and Philippians 3:16. Jude's apostleship is inferred by his assertion to show his awareness of his apostolic dispensation to command church conduct via a circulating epistle. Availing himself of established church governmental protocol and

76

principles, he invoked their understanding of apostolic credibility. Jude knew they were conditioned to accept that only bona fide apostles were empowered by God to receive and verify scripture revelation and to impose scripture as the power canon law upon the church. Consequently, he justified his letter as one having been entrusted with affecting church behavior and conduct through Holy Spirit. His inspired scripture was substantiated as missives from the Risen Christ. It could be argued that Paul's reference to James, as the Lord's brother was a mere Christian family statement, but that would be sheer private interpretation and an obvious attempt to convert Bible truth to one's own preference. The same could be said about Jude who takes pains to validate his epistle by identifying himself as James' brother, a man that has already been recognized by Paul as the Lord's brother.

The mindset of the church back then was that apostles, and only apostles, could be trusted with their eternal faith. It was to them that the church looked to for guidance, authenticity, and correction. Apostles were seen as the most reliable guard against heresy and deception and so any letter authenticated as from them was given the power of divine law. Beside this, the Holy Spirit being present in the midst of them along with the exceptional signs apostles demonstrated to prove their genuineness further assured the churches of who was and was not part of the Savior's staff of apostles. Some of those signs included Paul's spirit traversing the Lord's invisible realms to witness what was going on in the churches, see 1 Corinthians 5:4,5.

Since mainly apostles and prophets inscribed the Bible, does it not seem strange that the spirits of the two mantles that inspired the writings and that are to usher the church into eternity are erased from its consciousness? Logically speaking, if the church still needs the evangelist, pastor and teacher to understand God in its succeeding generations why do they not still need the very mantles that wrote and initially uttered and doctrinated His words? It is because essential truths are discarded by traditional scholars that Christians do not receive or respect apostles. Lesser offices have defined apostleship for the church so those to be served by the apostle are prevented from learning what makes for apostleship or what characterizes the apostle. The spiritual and religious factions that shifted the church from apostleship to the bishopric succeeded in convincing the New Testament church that neither apostles nor prophets are valid ministries for them today. On account of this, when a Christian hears God's word preached by an apostle as it is written, they bristle at it and run from, what it perceives to be, its weighty demands. When they receive a prophecy that does not conform to what their books about the Bible say constitutes prophecy, they shun it and often fall into judgment for spurning the word of the Lord. When the Lord's, church order is imposed and its government aligned with God's kingdom under Christ Jesus, people panic at what they discover to be true divine order and their duty to it. They prefer spiritual democracy to Creator theocracy. All these are the result of the *mis*definition and errant teaching on the ministries of apostles and prophets.

How Tradition Misdefines Apostles

Tradition explains an apostle to be anyone who founds an original work. That makes any pastor an apostle; apparently, this cannot be so. Other early definitions name any one who does missionary work an apostle; for sure, this too cannot be. Additional sources teach a bishop is automatically an apostle, another error. Still, more references say the apostle is a bold leader, a charismatic personality, or a mere itinerant minister. Secular definitions assign the title to any trailblazer, pioneer, catalyst, organization starter, or founder of a new move. These meanings all fall short of biblical and historical aim of an apostle. As a result, misinterpretation has many people confused and others adopting the title at will demanding apostolic recognition and respect based on their assumptions. Consequently, this ministry field is littered with presumptive apostleship or with those having converted from their previous titles to apostleship—ordained or not. The lack of clear-cut apostolic delineations has many ministers jumping from one ministry career track onto another as church trends change. To date true apostleship is obscured in the hearts and minds of the people they are sent to serve. What is obviously lacking to rectify this is a concise unquestionable apprehension of an apostle despite how tradition and the church's extra-biblical, sources outside the Bible as canonized scripture, redefine the office and its officer.

Chapter Summary

1. The majority of today's church has never learned the Bible as written by God's apostles or Christ as the Great Apostle.

2. The Escape Mentality of the church is a product of ancient fear and early persecution of Christians.

3. Scripture twisting upstages God's truth.

4. Apostles alone can accurately, and consistently, identify and refute error and heresy.

5. True apostles treat and teach God and Christ as alive and in control.

6. Despite arguments to the contrary, and the resistance they breed, apostles will always be installed to serve the Lord.

7. Theology and doctrine fuel people's fear of apostles.

8. Church of old accepted epistles from only verified apostles.

9. *Kanon* is the name for the apostle's sphere or measure of rule.

Chapter Five

The Messiah's Apostolic Climate

Chapter Discussions

Unlocking Apostleship: All Things Divine • Polytheism, Pantheons, Idols, & Paganism Define Apostleship • Bible Principles for Divine-Apostolic Emphases • A Portrait of God's World Conflicts • The Messiah's Apostolic Era • Major Elements of the Apostle's Message • The Holy Spirit Empowers & Affirms Apostleship

What we have learned about the apostle to date is not entirely consistent with what the Lord Jesus delivered as the ministry to His church. Contemporary apostolism radically differs from what the apostle meant to Jesus' world. This era's apostolism is defined on the ground of what the Holy Spirit and the Resurrected Christ have been doing for over two millennia, not how it was when Jesus appointed the twelve, or when Pentecost empowered them to go into the entire world. When these events occurred, the Holy Spirit of God had not yet bathed the earth with His revelatory truths nor given humans the ability to access or obtain it. Back when the world was dark, spirituality was very different. Humanity and its cultures were gripped by Jude's fallen angels and ruled by the deadly princes of darkness referred to in 1 Corinthians 2:6, 8. These held sway over earth and humanity since Adam's transgression. His offense caused people to be born to devils under a world regime that combined demonism with monarchy. All monarchs then were thought to represent their deities on earth's thrones and their right to rule was seen as delegated by their paternal or national gods. The authority rulers exercised during that age was granted by subordinate spirits assigned to rule over humanity's terrestrial realms and spheres, until Jesus spoiled principalities and powers, took the keys to the heavens, and gave them to His apostles.

Unlocking Apostleship: All Things Divine

Everything in the human mind, during Jesus' time and before, centered on divinity. All civilizations were occupied with the gods of their lands; the gods of the elements; the gods of family lineages, human life and its conditions, and so forth. All the earth harked back to some celestial being's powers and authority to orchestrate its affairs. Idolatry was only idolatry to those who served a god other than the one most popular, triumphant, or who birthed the inhabitants of a particular territory. Pagan rituals were a regular practice of established religion and all major religions (urban religions that is) were major. Heathenism was tied to the ranks of divine preeminence. The ruler decreed who would serve what god whose affairs were generally delegated to its offspring. To have this privilege, a deity must earn it in combat.

The right god could say and ensure what deity his or her nation would worship, in much the same way Nebuchadnezzar did in Daniel chapter four when he decreed his imperial dominion's deity as Yahweh following his humiliating contest with Israel's God. Occultism was not demonic worship and demons were not collectively seen as evil; there were good ones, benevolent spirits as they were called and there were gods of the heavens and those of the netherworld. Magic too was not the taboo as it is today. Christianity brought it to a halt. Until then, it was introduced to early men as the secret arts of the Magi—special priests of a powerful deity.

Rooted in ancient Babylon, magic joined astrology and astronomy to see that the invisible forces backing this world had many opportunities to, ceaselessly dominate their civilizations. Magicians, as they have come to be known, had the task of co-engineering earthly events and overall manipulating the Most High's creation to suit the will and whims of their dispatching deities. Consequently, until Jesus, magic was seen good and evil despite the fact that it invariably worked through subterfuge to completely ignore and override people's God given human will in its attacks. During and before Jesus' time, no one cared. People were made for the gods (any god) and it was their lot in life to be abused, trampled upon, and enslaved by the children born of the higher powers and their superior arts. In that era, renowned gods became so by making their progeny great, greater than all the deities that ever came before them. Here is what the Most High did with Joseph in Egypt and Daniel in Babylon, two superior world powers that enslaved His people. Their superior spiritual prowess was celebrated in their lands of captivity to elevate both men to high positions in heathen lands.

In Jesus' and the early apostles' world no single sacred text outweighed every other spiritual book as the consummate religious guide, and temples could conceivably house and celebrate images and religions of several gods at once. Priesthoods were not always committed to just one god's temple service, but the better or lesser functionaries were established by the championship of the deity they served. The more forceful the god, the more kingdoms he or she led a nation to conquer, the more worshippers the divine one gathered, and so the more prestigious and powerful became the priesthood. Preaching, mysteries, miracles, and moral codes were diverse, though commonplace and one could blend them as needed to achieve a rising monarch's purposes.

It is against this backdrop that the Lord Jesus said, *"Upon this rock I will build my church and the gates of hell shall not prevail against it"* in Matthew 16:18. It is also the insight that moved Him to say, *"The kingdom of heaven suffers violence and the violent take it by force"* (Matthew 11:12). Moreover, it is in this dismal vein on earth that the apostle John heard the heavenly host declare, *"The kingdoms of this world have become the kingdoms of our Lord and His Christ and they shall reign forever and ever"* (see Revelation 11:15). These passages, though rendered ecclesiastically anemic over time, are somewhat stupefying to us today. To the early church, they were tremendous statements for Jesus to make as the incarnate and resurrected Son of God.

In proclaiming them, He announced to all creation's powers and authorities that had ears to hear that He was the one sent to destroy all godless principalities and dominions in the heavens and on earth. In uttering them, Isaiah's prophesied Emmanuel showed how He thoroughly understood His apostleship and what it meant to Creator God and the world. His understanding and application of the term *apostle* the people of Bible times recognized as a declaration of war, that long awaited ensuing battle between heaven and earth, good and evil, darkness and light, and the kingdoms of this world and the Most High. To them apostles established kingdoms, converted populaces, wrought victories and overthrew hostile or defeated forces in the name of their senders. There was no mistaking what Jesus meant by His words. He was taking over and there was no question about it. Definitively speaking, apostleship would have meant nothing to them then had Israel remained faithful to Yahweh in her own land. It would be equally insignificant to any monotheistic world on the planet today. Apostles took their supreme legitimacy from being sent by an offended, robbed, or ambitious god to a desired or defected people and land for conquest. Theirs was a call to deliver and restore all to the rightful god, or to hand it over to the most triumphant deity.

Polytheism, Pantheons, Idols, & Paganism Define Apostleship

Polytheism, for definition purposes, may be understood as the worship of many gods based on the idea that everything is essentially or potentially a deity. Pantheism is the worship of a specific group of gods as progenitors of a family into which one believes he or she has entered or one that the worshipper believes he or she belongs to by birth. Paganism identifies worship based on nature. It serves the stars or other aspects of creation. Apostles inducted and commissioned to the office by the Lord Jesus Christ become well versed in these details when He teaches them. As will be stressed repeatedly in this book, apostleship is an agency to ignite the change of divine powers and authorities in the land. The battle over apostleship is always about deities, the clash of the god(s) of this world with the God of all creation as exemplified in Exodus' record of Moses' clash with Pharaoh's magicians. The ministry of apostles establishes God's dominion in the apostles' spheres of ministry. This explanation is needful for apostles to comprehend their task of confronting, overpowering, and evicting the gods of the land to displace them with the authority of the Lord Jesus Christ.

In light of these truths, today's apostles face an awesome battle with the paganism allowed to entrench the consciousness and cultures of the modern world. The advent of modern technology broadcasts to the souls of this generation the ancient religions, alternative deities, and supernatural powers from nature and its fallen (dethroned) demons Christ overthrew. Modern or neo-pagans declare their agenda is to restore the world to the B.C. gods of the ancient world. They have vowed to return humanity to the eras and deities that ruled the world before Christ.

At first, it appears likely that they will do this, and on the surface may seem to succeed, but that is only because the Lord's Church allows it. The truth is that paganists' agenda cannot work as long as the Holy Spirit is in the world. Regardless of how much they manufacture the actions of the old religions, the plain truth is they are devoid of the original powers that once energized. The Holy Spirit in the earth since Pentecost prevents any real or lasting success that the real dark powers that preceded them achieved. Bound until the last of the last days, they must be released by the Lord, and the Revelation says that cannot happen until the Holy Spirit is taken out of the way. The resurrection of the Lord Jesus who took the keys of hell, death, and the grave sees to it. With this is the reality that He indeed spoiled, dethroned, deposed, and disarmed principalities and powers. For all these reasons, Galatians now calls witchcraft and sorcery **works of the flesh** because the Holy Spirit's outpouring is the dominant source of all spiritual influence in creation; what Joel's prophecy foretold and Pentecost fulfilled.

What humans choose to do with God's Spirit in the planet, how they draw on His energy, is according to the Lord a mere fleshly work. Occultists' machinations are simply based on their access to the knowledge of the old curious arts, even though the powerful devils that once empowered their magic and such are stripped and bound.

Biblical Premises for Divine-Apostolic Emphases

No other book expresses the Lord's apostolic sent one sentiment better than Isaiah. Look at some of the Bible's presentations of the Lord's conflict with the ancient world. God from the beginning of time was deprived of His rightful possession, the souls, and service of those He created for His glory. On the surface, appearing to have lost all control, God's powerful eternal plan began its work. With skill and shrewdness that yet stupefies the world and defies human logic, the Creator set out on a course of redemption that would once and for all settle the question of who was God and who owned heaven, earth, and all its substance.

From Noah's Ark to the Christ's cross, the plan relentlessly wended its way through the pages and stages of human history, ceaselessly progressing through every generation. Wars, conflicts, curses and blessings, judgments and atonement all became part of the plan as redemption worked its way through every family to ultimately buy back the souls of Adam's seed. Along the way, the battle was always fierce and bloody. Lives and souls were lost while those chosen were kept for the day of the cross, sealed to the day of redemption, whether on earth or in hell. And, the battle will continue until the end of humankind's time.

Constantly, the conflict centers on these questions: Who is the true Creator? What deity birthed and thus laid claim to what lineage? What god owned what land? What deity is entitled to what souls at death? God's chosen seed, Luke 16 says, went to hell, a paradise called Abraham's bosom. Key

87

questions like these determine people's religious views and choices, but it does not stop there; other questions include, "How would power be returned to human hands and what seed would eventually reign with the Almighty forever?" These questions the Lord raised and answered for Himself from Eden to the Apocalypse' eternal Paradise. While all creation knew who He was, and that He and His Son Jesus are God, those who had fallen as seeds in Adam's loins did not know, and that was the heart of it all. That Satan and his minions knew who was really the Almighty is seen in the demons that met Christ and reacted terrified to His appearance on earth, James' epistle says they tremble.

Customarily, people back then worshipped anything, but that was soon to be brought to an end. After Christ's triumph, people would be given something humanity had not had since the beginning of time: power over their own will. That is what Jesus brought to earth and made possible on the Day of Pentecost when the Holy Spirit arrived on the planet from heaven.

A Portrait of God's World Conflicts

The passages of scripture below were included to present a portrait of the Lord's world conflicts. God once said through the prophet Ezekiel that after He completed His judgment of the land and the nations that the prophet would see that God does nothing without a cause. Despite humans' contention that the Creator is irrational, attacking people for no reason, the prophets know that what He does to humanity He does for very good reasons. His judgments are unquestionably well deserved when people study His commandments, laws, and testimonies and contrast them with their own lives. Some of those reasons are listed below:

- Isaiah 43:10—"Ye are my witnesses, saith the LORD, and my servant whom I have chosen: that ye may know and believe me, and understand that I am he: before me there was no God formed, neither shall there be after me."

- Isaiah 44:6—"Thus saith the LORD the King of Israel, and his redeemer the LORD of hosts; I am the first, and I am the last; and beside me there is no God."

- Isaiah 44:8—"Fear ye not, neither be afraid: have not I told thee from that time, and have declared it? Ye are even my witnesses. Is there a God beside me? Yea, there is no God; I know not any."

- Isaiah 45:5—"I am the LORD, and there is none else, there is no God beside me: I girded thee, though thou hast not known me."

- Isaiah 45:21—"Tell ye, and bring them near; yea, let them take counsel together: who hath declared this from ancient time? Who hath told it from that time? Have not I the LORD? And there is no God else beside me; a just God and a Saviour; there is none beside me."

- Hosea 13:4—"Yet I am the LORD thy God from the land of Egypt, and thou shalt know no god but me: for there is no Saviour beside me."

- Deuteronomy 32:39—"See now that I, even I, am he, and there is no god with me: I kill, and I make alive; I wound, and I heal: neither is there any that can deliver out of my hand."

- 1 Kings 8:23—"And he said, LORD God of Israel, there is no God like thee, in heaven above, or on earth beneath, who keepest covenant and mercy with thy servants that walk before thee with all their heart."

- 2 Kings 5:15—"And he returned to the man of God, he and all his company, and came, and stood before him: and he said, Behold, now I know that there is no God in all the earth, but in Israel: now therefore, I pray thee, take a blessing of thy servant."

- 2 Chronicles 6:14—"And said, O LORD God of Israel, there is no God like thee in the heaven, nor in the earth; which keepest covenant, and showest mercy unto thy servants, that walk before thee with all their hearts."

- 2 Chronicles 32:15—"Now therefore let not Hezekiah deceive you, nor persuade you on this manner, neither yet believe him: for no god of any nation or kingdom was able to deliver his people out of mine hand, and out of the hand of my fathers: how much less shall your God deliver you out of mine hand?"

- Exodus 12:12—"For I will pass through the land of Egypt this night, and will smite all the firstborn in the land of Egypt, both man and beast; and against all the gods of Egypt I will execute judgment: I am the LORD."

- 1 Chronicles 16:26—"For all the gods of the people are idols: but the LORD made the heavens."

- Psalm 96:5—"For all the gods of the nations are idols: but the LORD made the heavens."

- Zephaniah 2:11—"The LORD will be terrible unto them: for he will famish all the gods of the earth; and men shall worship him, every one from his place, even all the isles of the heathen."

The Messiah's Apostolic Era

The era in which the Messiah came to earth and emerged as God's Sent Savior of the world was not sanctified as holy by the Creator's definitions, but entrenched in the accursed life of fallen humankind. It was caught in the grip of ruthless spirits hostile to humans and Creator. One cannot possibly grasp or initiate apostolism apart from recognizing and being governed by these truths. The apostle's office is perfectly explained and validated by the antiquitous and arcane religions and pantheons of Egypt, Philistia Assyria, Babylon, Persia, Media, Athens, Greece, and Rome all rolled into one. Natural Israel's struggle with their fetishes, devotions, and worship set the stage for the Creator's apostolism. God is offended, His possession is seized by these pantheons as a result, and His holy people perverted and defiled by the gods of this world. That is how it was then and how it really is today as the platform upon which apostles enter their ministry.

The Almighty's conflict with these nations and their deities makes occasion for and mobilizes apostleship. Reading the Apocalypse's Babylonian Whore and reviewing at the same time, the Lord's problem with the church of Thyatira and its Jezebel prophet show how things have not changed much since then, meaning under the B.C. era, except that Jesus did come into the world. The Lord of glory did triumph over Satan and his hosts; He did spoil those principalities that so bitterly assaulted His creation for eons. God through Jesus enabled Revelation 12:12 to become eternity's living reality: *"Therefore rejoice, ye heavens, and ye that dwell in them. Woe to the inhabiters of the earth and of the sea! For the devil is come down unto you, having great*

91

wrath, because he knoweth that he hath but a short time." Study also, the reign of Jeroboam and the world that rose up Josiah.

If modern apostles are going to accurately handle Christ's apostolism the way the Lord Jesus brought it to earth, then they are going to have to reach all the way back to earth's B.C. era to do so, beginning with understanding how to execute it.

The apostles of this age are going to have to understand how life, religion, and spirituality in the world today mirror the world before and during Christ's assignment. They are going to have to rewind history all the way back to before Pentecost and immediately thereafter to grasp the enormity of the messenger's post and the magnitude of the task that lay ahead. Present and future apostles will have to use God's moves from Pentecost to now only as guideposts in their journey to reconnect Jesus' time to current apostolic claims. It will not do for apostles of this and succeeding generations to identify or align their calls, commissions, message and mantles strictly by what has come to be a major world religion. Christianity was not a renowned world religion in Peter's, John's, and Jesus' time.

Christianity was an antagonistic little sect that rivaled all the gods and the religions that had come to earth until Jesus Christ. That is what made Jesus' visit to earth necessary and threatening to the gods of His land. God's vision of offspring after His own likeness and image according to His Son made the apostle's mantle essential. Jesus was sent to fulfill His Father's dream. The one that started back in Eden, was ignited in Sinai, and found its fulfillment on Pentecost. Up to then, the Most High was the only Deity with no human offspring to extend and multiply His seed in the earth; hence, the value of John 1:12, 13. See also Deuteronomy 32:17, 18 for clarifications of these points: "*Of the Rock that begat thee thou art unmindful, and hast forgotten God that formed thee. They sacrificed unto devils, not to God; to gods whom they knew not, to new gods that came newly up, whom*

92

your fathers feared not." Review also Judges 5:8: *"They chose new gods; then was war in the gates: was there a shield or spear seen among forty thousand in Israel?"* To overlook these critical facts is to undermine God's need for the mantle and to downplay the ongoing campaigns of darkness to win souls for hell that are waged in every era of humanity.

Since neither Christianity nor apostleship really lived the way it does today when apostles were first dispatched by the Lord Jesus, to use today's or the last fifteen hundred or so years of the Church Age's achievements alone to explain it in the modern contexts is insufficient. Doing so only gives the church more of the same: confusion, absent, distorted, or feeble apostleship. The key to grasping apostleship from the Almighty is in its lone power, the apostle's message. The simple sounding teaching scorned by many holds the secret to the apostle's mysterious power and authority.

Major Elements of the Apostle's Message

The starting apostles' message did not begin with church government because there was no church. It did not center on begetting sons and daughters because God's family was yet being born and those that were had a long way to go to shed their other god's roots and strongholds. Apostolism did not preach traditional church doctrine because it was unfolding and formulating as an ongoing event. In regards to doctrine, the apostles had the monumental task of divesting Christ's gospel and doctrine from Judaism. They did not concentrate on transmitting what we have come to accept as the teachings of the apostolic fathers who were yet to be born or recognized. What did exist during the early apostles' days were other gods, plenty of them. What did exist was a world rifled with demonic activity, abuse, and devilish dominion. What did exist in the Lord's and His original apostle's world were witches, magicians, oracles, diviners, and fertility cults that *religionized* immorality and ritual fornication.

The world of Christ's day was saturated with the occultic mysteries of seducing spirits and the doctrines of devils. All of creation served as the props for religion, holy wars, and ritual perversion. These the apostles of old confronted. They were well versed in the monarchs that claimed divine prerogatives, the priests of pagan high places, and the damnable pantheon of deities taking credit for creation and its offspring. The only enemy the apostles knew was Satan, his sway, his lies, and his bloodthirsty offspring, which served as their ministry targets and objects of conflict. Their target groups, however, did not know him as evil as he was; to them he was an adversary and prince of devils, but were devils all bad? They were not convinced.

The World Before Christ's Cross

Murder, mayhem, brutality, and atrocities of all kinds were socially acceptable; worse yet; these were ingrained in society's culture. It permeated every aspect of the human experience due to their demonic nativity. Rulers dictated the social and religious climate and their attitudes filtered down to their civil, legal, and political authorities from their spiritual powers. Whatever god the monarch served the significant members and servants of his or her society served. How their god wanted to be worshipped is how their world was compelled or seduced to worship. If human sacrifices, virginal or infant, were the god's demands, then special groups of people were targeted (sanctified or consecrated) to supply the demand. If pharmakeia—drug driven witchcraft or sorcery—was the standard of divine acceptance and reward, then drugs and drunkenness became the sacraments of the religion; likewise, fertility and nature worship. If reproduction of seed or transference of demons were the aim, then homosexuality,

94

rape, or bestiality was called for to presumably cajole nature to reproduce planted seed at harvest time.

Supposedly based on what the national, local, patronic, or parental deity needed to express him or her, extravagant worship and ritual systems were devised and perpetuated to comply. They assured the nation's right standing with its favored deities. It was understood that tribal, governmental, and priestly authorities made it incumbent upon national or tribal rulers to keep their countries or villages in good stead with the celestial beings that owned, occupied, conquered, or migrated into their territories. Provincial families were as important as the sitting monarch deemed them to be; conquered peoples were often enslaved and ill treated. Poor people were neglected and exploited, and women in many cultures meant nothing more than a constant inventory of flesh for male pleasures, except in those nations that venerated goddesses. Death and funerary cults were celebrated and very few civilizations were interested in life except as much as they could control it. Slaughter and any form of killing revolved around religion, executions, sport and entertainment; and when people were not killed to appease society's blood thirst or their bloody gods, they were slain for war, worship, politics, vengeance, and simple street crimes. Nothing was rational as viewed today, and the sacred or venerated was above a person's rights according to the divine world. Humans were just objects used to coax or coerce its invisible citizens and rulers to perform for them on earth.

Another constant of the original apostles' world is goddesses. Many variations of the ancient female deities circulated and reinvented themselves back then. They were redesigned as often as was their male counterparts. Women who wanted to find power and equality did so by aligning with and exalting the divinity of the female spirit. To maintain their status, they venerated martial goddesses such as Diana, fertility

95

goddesses, maternal, and judicial goddesses. Somehow, they all folded back into the queen of heaven motif and invariably birthed children by their male citizens. Sex was god, and everything about it saturated society. Children were sex objects and ritual sources. Little girls were born and devoted to temple brothels; little boys were devoted temple sodomites; the ancient Greeks and Romans referred to them as *flamens*.

Typically, goddess worship involved homosexual priests making lesbianism a logical recourse to the shrinking heterosexual male population. Worshippers were attracted to their religious fetishes by an assortment of sexually charged sadomasochistic rituals and induced to engage in their favorite ones as part of their deity's stipulated divine worship. This state of affairs constructed the real apostles' doctrine; their world and work was reality-based in the purest and basest sense of the word. They knew that the only God who opposed and could overturn these spiritual forces and practices was Israel's God. He alone condemned the death culture, the sexual perversion, the slaughter of innocent victims, and the unconscionable mutilation of His highest creation, humankind. Like the true owner of the stolen vehicle or the burglarized house, the Lord of all really had good reason to care; after all mankind because He is their Creator. His prized possessions were being destroyed, His beloved souls lost. The Almighty knows how He made every being and the purpose for which He made them. Therefore, He would be the last one to abuse, hurt, or destroy the works of His hands. That is how you know Satan is not the Creator. He is too hateful and destructive to humanity, as hateful to God's creation as the thief is to the stolen possessions he or she mistreats.

Apostolism back then began and rested on these truths, not the quasi cleaned up religious environment of today. The apostles under Jesus Christ knew that religion was not the

96

enemy. They understood the Lord relentlessly sought His doomed gods seeking and coercing human worship. They knew that Jesus pursued the overthrow of the false prophets, priests, and teachers that founded their own religions, even at the expense of perverting His true faith. Christ's apostles exposed and dismantled the deadly rituals devised to entice and trap people into covenanting with hell for eternity. These were the true apostle's enemy. Worldwide evangelicalism had not happened yet; charismatic religions were yet to be born. Pentecostalism and such were all dreams way down the line for them. All those apostles knew back then were that Jesus Christ the promised Messiah had come to earth as He said. He brought Yahweh's salvation to humanity and sent the Holy Spirit to empower twelve sent ones to let the world know about it and enable penitents to enter it.

Evangelistic doctrine did not birth apostleship back then, it was born by the message brought to the earth by the Great Apostle. The denominational names and traditions of bygone eras are not its source. Neither charismatic, faith, nor any other popular or venerated religious moves over the last two millennia could explain apostolism, mostly because they ignored or labored to destroy it. The only place to recognize and verify apostleship is in God's holy word and those later apostles scripture references that committed themselves to its pure presentation for the modern eras. Merely re-titling God's previous moves and extracting each, one's most salient points to mold doctrine to doctrine in order to mine one's apostolic commission will not ignite Christ's next apostolic age. Apostles of today and tomorrow will have to know more than, that they are called to be apostles, or that their impressive works could be construed as apostolic. They are going to have to know that they are sent and for what. Today's apostles will need to recount and revisit that dramatic encounter discussed earlier regularly.

They will need to rehearse it time and again as the standard of legitimacy that divinely backs their words and works.

As part of their commissions, apostles will need to explain and illustrate why they are sent and to whom; where they are sent; and for what reasons or purposes they are sent. Present and emerging apostles are going to have to know God's enemy well, and that His enemy becomes theirs the moment they step into the office. They are going to have to know what God condemned and cursed and what He will reverse and bless. Jesus spoke about knowing Satan's devises and not allowing ignorance to induce saints to sin. The modern apostle then will need power to cast out devils in more than just people, and comprehend what passes a soul from darkness to light and from Satan's power to God's. Skillful apostles will need to express how and when to confront the powerful seasoned demons that contend for people's lives and souls. They will need wisdom to snatch the Lord's purchased possession out of devilish strongholds. Before all this, however, they will need to grasp how sophisticated the machine of unbelief works, developed since time began, and why the only answer to its rampant tirade in human lives is God's apostle.

The Holy Spirit Empowers & Affirms Apostleship

The same Holy Spirit that empowered Jesus' ministry and that of His apostles throughout the church age cannot be activated, nor heaven's assigned force of holy angels mobilized by sheer charisma. They will not (and indeed cannot) respond to trendy doctrine, human thought, or the revival of the Lord's completed moves in the earth. The Holy Spirit confirms Jesus and everything that He does. He manifests the Godhead at work in humans and in the world with demonstrations and signs that can only characterize heaven's handiwork and initiatives. The Spirit of God will not affirm flesh for flesh sake no matter how eloquent the rhetoric or enticing its imitations.

God confirms God and His miraculous signatures evidence His holy commission; the Messiah's delegated authority to His sent ones so powerfully represented in His victorious works of old. Seriously undertaken, it constitutes a solid dispatch to a specific field of humanity to transform on the Almighty's behalf. Here are but some of the immutable rules for reinstating apostleship as the Lord Jesus delivered it to His church.

The work of previous ministerial flames cannot set the stage for defining the work of this apostolic age except they blatantly authenticate Christ's mantle. Apostleship is the equivalent of warfare and demonic clashes, so it is vital for apostles to accept that theirs is a confrontational, militaristic, and combat ministry. The majority of Jesus' language supports this.

New Testament apostles are sent ones of the Godhead and cannot be identified with anything outside of what Jesus the Messiah brought to earth and assigned His church. They do not blend or extend prior spiritual initiatives but break with them to reintroduce what the Lord taught and demanded in the sixty-six books that best define them. Apostles transform lives and thereby change their worlds. They do not exist to govern, but govern what they cause to exist; they emerge to restore God's rule in the earth and abound with special grace to rededicate to the Almighty His stolen or abandoned dominions. Apostles teach God's kingdom because all that earth's people know, until encountering them, are the kingdoms of men and darkness. They demand holiness because Satan's deceitful liberties profane the Creator's righteous laws and customs.

The apostle meticulously teaches about the Holy Spirit to revive and establish God's true, pure, and godly supernatural acts; perverted and exploited by the demon spirits of Satan's army. These activities Christ's real apostles pursue, while explaining them saturates their language, messages, and methods. If they do not, the Lord Jesus' words to the

Ephesians church in Revelation chapter two apply and they will eventually manifest as false apostles.

Christ's apostles discern theirs is not a mantle to reconcile the kingdoms of darkness or of this world with God's; because of this, apostleship to them cannot help but spar with worldly kingdoms. Daily their agenda cataclysmically restores successive spheres and realms to the will of the Creator and His Redeemer Jesus Christ. That is what apostolism means to those who have "been with Jesus." The effects of their efforts are always summed up in a collision with the gods of this world vying for people's souls and their afterlife. Jesus' apostles always seek to get the Creator's Spirit into human souls, a goal of other deities for destructive reasons. However, the Maker of heaven and earth, the God of all flesh, is the only Spirit not inherently born in or authorized to enter or possess human beings without their permission. The Creator is so confident of His excellence that He can afford to let people choose Him for themselves; and even accept their rejection as the best choice for their souls. Unlike the devils that deceptively seize control of people's lives, the Lord wants people to want Him so He sometimes makes them strive for His goodness. The same is not true with the spirits of darkness whose motive is to destroy people's lives, something the Lord Jesus said He did not come to do for that would be redundant to Him since Satan was doing that already (Luke 9:56). That is why apostles are commissioned, empowered, and authorized to go into all the world, to preach the gospel to every creature, and to make disciples of the Lord Jesus Christ. Theirs is a mandate to birth and establish offspring of the Godhead and not of themselves alone.

Chapter Summary

1. Contemporary apostleship radically differs from that of the early church.

2. The apostles' world of Jesus' day revolved around all things divine.

3. Ancient monarchs dictated the worship of their chosen gods.

4. Magic, hedonism, paganism, and such were commonplace and culture before Christ.

5. Polytheism, pantheons, and pagans define and ignite apostleship. These entrench worldly consciousness to prevent people from knowing or understanding Creator God's truth and way of life.

6. Before Christ, people were victimized and destroyed by villainous spirits that dominated the world.

7. Christ's apostleship was launched in a wholly perverse world devoid of His Father's Spirit, light, and life.

8. Ancient apostles' words attacked the agents of death, darkness, and destruction of their time.

9. Without the Holy Spirit, true eternal apostleship is impossible.

Chapter Six

God's Apostle as Sent by Jesus Christ

Chapter Discussions

God's Twenty-first Century Apostles' Clean Up • How & Why Apostles Will Be Needed to the End • What God Has In Mind for Apostleship • Eternal Principles & Practices of Apostleship • Apostleship Before and After Pentecost • Why & How Apostles are First • Christ Recommissions the Eleven • Apostles Legitimize the Church • Jesus Understands Apostleship from God's Mind • The Apostle Peter's Kingdom Keys • The Ecclesia • Confirming Ecclesiastical Citizenship • The Prototype of Peter's Position • The Apostle's Commission Agenda • The Apostle's Ministerial Dispensations • God's Eternal Apostolic Agenda

This chapter takes the student deeper into the study of the practicalities of apostleship. Attention shifts the focus of the discussions to the dynamics of the apostle and their purpose to the Lord's ministry. Here the apostle's work is tied to God's mind, eternity's premises, and principles for the office. The change in the world caused by Pentecost initially affected apostleship. What made Jesus give Peter the keys to the kingdom of heaven is important to this revelation as the powers, authorities, and rulers of the heavens were changing to enable what the Messiah accomplished to occur. Peter's receipt of the keys and the sweeping license and command that go with them was more than a symbolic gesture on the Lord's part. It was a staggering sign to the invisible powers, spiritual protocrats who had dominated the heavens and the world since winning it from Adam back in Eden. Giving a human the keys to a spiritual realm executed a promise the Lord made to the devil long ago. More than having to contend with the Almighty's legions of righteousness in eternity, Satan would now have to contend with a new force of divine agents that occupied the earth and somehow had means of entering and exiting his territories as well.

If you are seriously intimate with God these days, you know He is relentlessly raising up and instating His Son's apostolic mantle in this generation. It seems the Lord has been in the process of doing so for decades; yet with all that, His Church sits only on the cusp of what will go down in its history as a most powerful move of God. What makes it so powerful? The next move God launches will bring enlightenment from His empowered apostles, the mantle that began and begins it all and has been mostly ignored for centuries. It means this generation of New Testament Christians is in for the most extraordinary time in its history. The mantle of His apostle the New Testament says upholds the entire New Creation church is being brought back into the Godhead's service on an unprecedented scale. Due to the sophistication of demonic enlightenment in this era of humanity, the world will once more be turned upside down by the one ministry that confronts the darkness and overturns its darkness. For all this to happen, much preliminary work is to be done, a great work that cannot begin until a massive spiritual, doctrinal, and ecclesiastical clean up takes place.

God's Twenty-first Century Apostles' Clean Up

With decades of erroneous teaching on the subject to wade through by mainly good-intentioned evangelists, pastors and teachers (Jesus scholars), what informs today's church about the apostle goes from vague to heretical. Assuming early teachers and expounders of the apostle's doctrine did not aim to discredit or dismantle this office we must conclude that well meaning naiveté was at work. Regardless, much of the error has served to obstruct the church's ability to receive apostles and thus frustrated the destiny of many of its members.

From the tone of most of the teachings and writings on the apostle, one is led to conclude the well-meaning efforts of church leaders under the auspices of the offices of the evangelist, pastor, and teacher minimized apostleship to protect Christ's Church. The church leaders of old used the abuses of self-serving autocrats exaggerated or not, to create a case for eliminating the apostle's ministry from the New Testament church. The reason given was to prevent their mistreatment of the Church, something that did not happen anyway, considering the documented record of historical abuses perpetrated by the remaining three accepted ministers of Ephesians 4:11. In addition, early leaders further sought to prevent what they saw as redundant church founding (or planting) deduced from their conviction that the church having already been established had no further need of apostles or apostleship. What was done to rectify what was seen, as the problem, was to pass the apostle's torch to the bishopric. Later, this tactic is dealt with head-on to restore clear lines of distinction between the apostle of Jesus Christ as a sent one and the bishops that apostles appoint and empower to act in their stead once their churches are established.

Consequently, the passing of the apostles' torch brought the church to its present conflict between apostleship and the bishopric. If you read the writings of some of the apostolic fathers, you will find they reinforced this decision by circulating letters that announced all the founding and initial apostles had died. Subsequently they admonished, and in some cases demanded, that the church respect and obey in their stead the bishops[10] as the God-ordained authority over His Church until the Lord Jesus returns. While these noble intents may have been pure in motive, their outcomes were anything but because God sees it all very differently. God meant the apostle's office to be a perpetual function in the church according to 1 Corinthians 12:28, 29; Luke 11:49; and Ephesians 4:11 that the doctrines of men eventually wrenched from His service. The Great Apostle meant for apostolic wisdom and doctrine to keep, teach, and uphold His Church throughout all future generations, constantly dispensing the revelations appointed to their generations. On the other hand, the Lord ordained the bishopric to serve an entirely different purpose, which is why all apostles are inherently bishops, though the opposite is not biblically founded. Apostles bring the bishopric of their mantles into existence and authorize its function over the works the apostle founds. Perpetual apostleship rests on the Church's appreciation of the minister's ongoing service to God.

---

[10] The Epistle of Ignatius to the Ephesians, ch.1, The Lost Books of the Bible & the Forgotten Books of Eden, LB Press, Cleveland, Ohio. ©1926 & 1927.

How & Why Apostles Will Be Needed to the End

Since the Lord is still bringing people into the world, they must be saved. The same message that won thousands of souls in the church's beginning, the very apostolic fervor that ignited it, is yet needed to win the souls of every century. The same is true with the development and transformation of those souls into the image and likeness of Jesus Christ. The task requires the same apostolic wisdom, doctrine, commandments, and injunctions the early founders possessed and dispensed for the Lord to harvest from every generation born into His world ordained to eternal life. Take the following as an example.

Just because the people who first entered and founded a country are gone and their initial or constitutional founders dead, it does not mean that later generations should or need to do away with their founding structure, citizenship criteria, or governing institutions. Newborns may not have to declare their citizenship at birth but their parents do. Some native of the country must prove that the infant was born in the land, so it is put upon the authorized institution that witnessed the child's coming into the world to vouch for its inherent citizenship in a nation. In doing so, the witness must submit proof that the birth indeed took place on their country's soil. For centuries, countries have fought to retain what brought them into existence, and to, continually fulfill what they consider their founders' vision for citizenship to guarantee the benefits, provisions and protections its perpetuity affords.

Jesus Christ, the Founder of the Christian Church, feels the same way. His Church is not a religion but a nation, the new creation offspring of Him and His Father by the Holy Spirit. As the Progenitors of a nation, they too have guidelines for entry into their nation, and the subsequent citizenship that legitimizes one as a child of God. The new birth gives the Godhead parental rights, authority, and responsibility over

106

those that are filled with Christ's Spirit. In the same way that countries have rigid requirements for entrance into their nations, birth, or adoption, the Lord has the same standards. One does not *join* Christianity in the same way the neighbors' children or your child's classmates cannot simply move into your home with your child and thereby jump into your family's line. Official and legal criteria must be met in order for someone's offspring to change his or her family line. The same is true with Jesus' nation. The Lord's vision for a family includes and rests upon specific criteria for populating His and His Father's kingdom by the Holy Spirit. According to Romans 8:9, those filled with the Spirit of Christ are citizens of His nation, God's kingdom.

The requirement for becoming an offspring of the Godhead is either birth or adoption, not much different from what it takes to become a citizen of an earthly country. In the case of the Lord Jesus Christ, it is both. The penitent is adopted into the Lord's family because of being born again by His Holy Spirit. This required process remains in effect for all believers of all generations until the end of time.

Therefore, the Church of the Lord Jesus Christ should not use single dimensioned shortsighted reasoning to dismantle its own ministry organization, to do so is to disintegrate its eternal nation. As surely as such notions would be foolhardy to a natural country, nation, or family, it has proven just as foolish and reckless to the New Creation Nation of the Lord Jesus. And do not forget that the apostle Peter identifies Jesus' New Testament church, the New Creation church, as Creator God's chosen generation, royal priesthood, holy nation; His peculiar people called out of this world's nations of darkness into His world's marvelous light. For any apostle of the Lord Jesus Christ, 1 Peter 2:9 is a passage of scripture that drives their ministry. Any worthwhile apostle seizes it as the solid ground of his or her ministry's right to exist because it proves the eternality of the apostle's office.

The Lord Jesus says in Matthew and Revelation about apostles that they will rule and govern His world to come with Him throughout eternity. Obviously, from this statement God's wisdom for this officer escapes the Church even today. That wisdom the Lord appears to have injected into one mantle, the one office that scripture does not plan to abolish at the commencement of Jesus' reign. What does that wisdom desire His Church to understand about apostles and apostolism? Perhaps the answer may be found in an applied study of Matthew 19:28, Luke 11:49, and Revelation 21:14 as to the purpose and function of perpetual apostleship in the church and the world. Next is the discussion of God's mind on apostleship, something very critical to its success.

What God has in Mind for Apostleship

Fortunately, for us today, God's global church plan for apostles goes beyond the original twelve. They began their ministries as Jesus' transitional team, as His mantle was initiated under the Old Testament. The first apostles operated under the Law of Moses, so did Jesus. More interesting is that they started out as John's disciples, meaning their start was as prophets. John's Gospel's first chapter implies this. For them to lawfully preach the gospel and the message of grace to the world, they had to shift from their Old Testament sphere of service into the new. Often this obvious fact is overlooked in the controversy over the validity of apostleship.

In order for the first apostles to be legal representatives of the Godhead once Jesus' ministry on earth ended, the remaining eleven had to be reinstalled into the office under the dispensation of Grace that the Savior ushered into the world. That can only come from the Holy Spirit's dispensation, which is why Pentecost is vital. The law having been fulfilled became, for all Creator intents and purposes, obsolete. Had the Lamb of God not reinstituted their apostleship during His forty-day training period under the Holy Spirit, the original apostles would have had no God-ordained basis to continue. If they were not sent, how could they be sent ones? In addition, without a sender how could they go and to where would they go? The reason the original apostles were summoned in the first place was to carry the Messiah's message throughout Israel, not the world. Remember, in their first commission they were confined to only the house of Israel (Matthew 10:5-8):

> *"These twelve Jesus sent forth, and commanded them, saying, Go not into the way of the Gentiles, and into any city of the Samaritans enter ye not: But go rather to the lost sheep of the house of Israel. And as ye go, preach, saying, the kingdom of heaven is at hand. Heal the sick, cleanse the lepers, raise the dead, cast out devils: freely ye have received, freely give."*

For Jesus to authorize His apostles to go into all the world required another dispensation; a new commission had to be conferred, what Matthew 28:18-20 discusses. Its commission replaces the Mosaic one given in Matthew chapter ten. The second commissioning coming after the law was fulfilled, being rendered obsolete by Jesus' crucifixion and ascension, revitalized the apostles' mantles. It paved the way for an entirely new, unlimited complement of apostles called by the Holy Spirit to join those installed by the Risen Lord. Based on all these details, it is safe to say that what they did to bring the first century church into existence did not end with the early apostles or their congregants' death because their work had yet to span the globe and reach every creature to disciple all nations.

Spanning the globe, reaching every creature, discipling all nations— none of these articles of the Christ's commission could be accomplished by just twelve men or the twenty or so recognized in Jesus. History says that the world as it is today did not exist at the time of the first church, nor did it by the time of its founders' deaths. The absence of all the nations God inseminated in the planet means that His "every creature" article of the Great Commission could never be fulfilled by any single generation, and still cannot. Beyond this, the command to disciple all nations could not occur until all ordained nations have been born to populate the planet. Then the Lord's full end-time harvest can be reaped. Confining what the Savior and His Father had in mind for humanity to any one generation is rash and a bit selfish. That kind of narrow-mindedness traditional scholars devoid of the insight modern technology provides concluded what they wrote those commentaries bound what God said to one person in their time to their own era. Such errant suppositions motivated all those false "Jesus is coming" moves and other false prophecies that arose to embarrass and discredit the church.

What the Creator set in motion in the beginning, His "seed within a seed bringing forth after its own kind" principle was never limited to just one era of God's dealings with His creaturehood. God always thought to advance His creation from its archaic to everlasting roots until it reached His level of eternal life as the very seed of Jesus Christ. At the time of the initial and early apostles' work, none of this was the case, as history shows.

Christ's Old Testament appointment of the original apostles in Matthew chapter ten being under the law is why the apostles had nothing else to do but consider returning to their previous occupations and sit in the upper room upon Christ's abolishment of the Judaic institution they had served. There just was nothing else for them to do until Pentecost came. Everything else about what Jesus did while He was in the flesh on earth is understood theologically to have begun under the Law of Moses; Jesus' conversations make this clear. After His departure, an eternal priesthood had to be reinstated; Jesus had ended the decreed method of serving God is now in the Spirit and no longer in the flesh, as His Son said in John 4:23, 24. How to pray, where to worship, and the acceptable sacrifices to God all had to be re-instituted under the Holy Spirit's dispensation. Jehovah's sweeping changes opened wide eternity to the world and made the Redeemer's invitation to the Gentiles possible. Collectively these all establish that the Lord God was doing a new thing; Isaiah's profound prophecies were being brought to pass. New heavens and a new earth have arrived and the former things truly are no more.

The prophets under the Law were finished (see Matthew 11:11 regarding the Lord Jesus' comments about John the Baptist). The whole purpose for all the features, functions and elements under the Law were expired and required renewal by the resurrected Messiah the carnal, earthly man; now the eternal, immortal and heavenly had to be installed in its place. Therefore, it should not be surprising to learn that even apostleship, initially inducted by Christ under the Law, was transferred to the law of the spirit of life in Christ Jesus. Thus, apostles' authority to extend beyond Israel and the Jesus demanded restoration after the Lord Jesus' death and resurrection for Him to continue to serve and have world power. All these concepts show apostleship as Christ delivered to His church has its roots in eternity and not time. It was not the twelve that launched Christ's apostleship, but the dispatch of God's Son for eternity to this world and His return to eternity that started it all.

111

Eternal Principles & Practices of Apostleship

For apostles to act legitimately in a remote or foreign land, the principal ground of the office, they must first be rendered active by being sent by a country, monarch, or religion to the foreign land. Jesus' completion of His apostolic mission concluded the final stages of God's long-standing (eternal) covenant with Israel under Jacob. Thus, the country that He was sent to ceased to be what it was to Yahweh. Jesus' return to life as the eternal God-Man and triumphant King David transferred all natural Israel's economy from Abraham, Isaac, Jacob, and Moses to the everlasting kingdom of David. Now Christ Jesus, the Son of God Almighty is King of kings and stands as world monarch with all other rulers subordinate to Him. As David and Messiah, Jesus is both Man and God: the Son of God and Son of Man. This entitled Him to receive His Father's entire kingdom and forever rule over His dominion.

Since Satan, the god and prince of this world was cast out, there was a call for a new spiritual ruler to cover the realms of creation that he vacated. What needed to be occupied required an eternal and not just a supernatural ruler. Every era of humanity, creation, and eternity, itself was stripped of the old and left void until the Holy Spirit came and filled all with and by the resurrected Messiah. The Savior's forty-day sojourn on earth after pouring His blood on creation's altar established Him as the new Lord of the world; His is its government as foretold by Isaiah 9:6. His Melchizedek Priesthood became the only order of priests the Creator acknowledges and His body of new creation humans the only beings the Most High finds acceptable for eternity. Jesus' church became the new and eternal ecclesia to replace the old Athenian-Graeco-Roman assembly. Instead of a secular and mortal kingdom, it governs the heavens and the earth. See Matthew 16:13-19. Much has been taught on these verses, but here is an apostolic view:

"When Jesus came into the coasts of Caesarea Philippi, he asked his disciples, saying, Whom do men say that I the Son of man am? And they said, Some say that thou art John the Baptist: some, Elias; and others, Jeremias, or one of the prophets. He saith unto them, But whom say ye that I am? And Simon Peter answered and said, Thou art the Christ, the Son of the living God. And Jesus answered and said unto him, Blessed art thou, Simon Barjona: for flesh and blood hath not revealed it unto thee, but my Father which is in heaven. And I say also unto thee, That thou art Peter, and upon this rock I will build my church; and the gates of hell shall not prevail against it. And I will give unto thee the keys of the kingdom of heaven: and whatsoever thou shalt bind on earth shall be bound in heaven: and whatsoever thou shalt loose on earth shall be loosed in heaven."

In the same way that Jesus knew what He was referring when He named (summoned) His twelve disciples *apostles*, He also understood intimately that His body—assembly—of called out ones that would replace the Roman Ecclesia; an integral part of their society for centuries. This body of believers would now take on world dominion and eternal authority. That is why its authority is exercised in heaven and in earth. Peter's authority is extended to all of the Lord's creation as the rock. *Petra*, the feminine of Petros (Peter's name), became Jesus' church. She is the woman of Revelation chapter 12, Israel of the eternities. The everlasting woman was to rule forever as the Lamb's body and bride on earth. Thoroughly endorsed by the Almighty this feminine-type of a body would collaborate with the Savior as His spiritual spouse forever. The spirit of the Man that empowered and sustained it was that of the Man Christ Jesus. Hence, what happened in Eden is repeated post Pentecost. The woman is taken out of the Man and that process made her His wife. In this way, the woman shall compass the man as Jeremiah prophesied in Jeremiah 31:22.

The people of the world from every generation must be persuaded of the truth that God's invisible forces all know to be correct. The ministry is constructed to grasp and elucidate the world on God's otherwise unfathomable achievements that is revealed in His message to His apostles. What He planned for the first twelve to introduce to His covenant people now had to be carried out worldwide within His eternal ecclesia until His return. To do so, their Mosaic mantles that expired with Jesus so to speak, had to be revived and upgraded after His passion. Jesus' leaving the planet meant the divine power and grace that sustained the initial apostles left with Him. Kingdom apostleship's revival during the Lord's forty days on earth prior to His ascension began in the form of a re-commissioning of the original twelve, discussed at length elsewhere, minus Judas Iscariot who was ordained the son of perdition. Jesus' necessary re-commissioning sent the apostles into all the world when the church was born by the Holy Spirit. The Pentecost dispensation, unlike the first commissioning, was pervasive and everlasting, which is why it required the Spirit of God that is unlimited by time and space to assure the earth and all its inhabitants were covered. The Holy Spirit guarantees that what is intended for multiple generations is sufficient until the full number of the Gentiles is harvested from the earth. The Holy Spirit's residence in the planet configured the foreseen sweeping technological explosions overrunning today's world. Many of the inventions and advancements developed over the last millennia since Christ's ascension were included in the second apostolic commission. They help explain passages of scripture the B.C. world could not conceive (see Isaiah 65:16). The Holy Spirit's commissioning inducts people from every nation on earth, transforming specially chosen disciples into His foreordained apostles.

Apostleship Before & After Pentecost

The power the apostles received at Pentecost remains in the planet until the Church's time on earth is fulfilled, signified by the completed number of souls to be redeemed and indwelt by Jesus' Spirit for eternity. Their government and administration expanded the concentrations of the Father and His Son to include the Third Person of the Godhead. In doing so, it became the immediate task of the Holy Spirit to enlarge their reach globally without the limits of the Lord's first commission. Before His new dispatch became effective, in order for it to become effective, the Lord told the reactivated apostles to tarry in Jerusalem until they were endued with His power from on high.

Since God cursed futility, it makes sense that provisions were made for apostleship before Jesus or the Holy Spirit came to earth. For all these reasons, the Lord predestined His church to be staffed with apostles until the end of its earthly assignment. Perhaps that is why the Holy Spirit inspired the apostle Jesus to write 1 Corinthians 12:28, 29. It says the Lord "ordained, appointed apostles" in the New Creation church first. That means before all else, they are the legitimate head of His church. The word *proton* used for *first* is a significant choice. It means first in time, place, order, or importance; appearing or acting before all else. *Proton* pertains to that which constitutes the beginning of something and so establishes its founding order and primacy. It refers to what is first or the head of all else, chiefly. The Greek term identifies a first, primary, initiatory, primitive, even primordial element, feature, or event predating or operated before anything else.

Why & How Apostles are First

Derived from the Greek term *protos*, *proton* identifies that which is foremost in time, place, order, or importance. The use of the word *foremost* speaks to that which is chief, leading, principal, and primary besides being the start of something. What is before and/or thusly the source of the beginning of something is what makes it the best or chiefest. Luke 6:13 explains *protos* (proton) well when it recalls how Jesus named His apostles first. He not only titled them His special messengers but also, in designating their professions, commuted to them the authority they needed to execute their offices. However, there is much more. For example, in Acts 1:2-3 Jesus re-commissioned His apostles, the passage that further explains what else makes apostles first: "*Until the day in which he was taken up, after that he through the Holy Ghost had given commandments unto the apostles whom he had chosen: To whom also he showed himself alive after his passion by many infallible proofs, being seen of them forty days, and speaking of the things pertaining to the kingdom of God.*"

The account records Jesus appearing to His apostles, those who could accurately identify Him as the Lord, their resurrected Mentor and friend. The eleven apostles He left behind could say with certainty that they indeed witnessed Jesus, who rose from the dead as He said. The event taught them that their calling and commission transcended time, space, culture, and human eras. It manifested what empowered them, the same Man that had summoned them to His heavenly calling when He walked the earth. He was alive forever and would augment their first commission by exceeding the communication of their service resources. This time He would literally transmit via the Father's spiritual insemination what supplied His advantage over sin, death, disease, darkness, and death to them. The Creator's eternal Man proved He could, and would, sustain their unique strength and uphold their ministries from heaven by His Holy Spirit throughout the earth.

Christ Recommissions the Eleven

Due to the expiration of His commission, upon which theirs rested, the eleven apostles like Jesus Christ had nothing to apostle and nowhere to be sent after His departure, not to mention that they also had no legitimate sender. Thus, their apostleship like His had effectively ended. In order for them to fulfill His work in the earth with the Gentiles, Jesus appeared to dispatch them, not to the lost sheep of Israel as before, but to the entire world. Resuming His emphasis on the "kingdom of God," begun while in the flesh on earth, the eternal Man inherited the authority to resend His apostles to finish what He started, having paid the price to live forever. Notice the timing of His commission. It comes before any other office of the ecclesia. The Messiah formally reinstated His original apostles **before** Pentecost and **before** the Church was born expanding their initial apostleship from Judea and Jerusalem to the world. At the time, the Risen Lord commissioned the eleven; the twelfth one to replace Judas had not yet been selected. That means apostleship predates the birth and needs, or criteria, of the ecclesia and as such, disqualifies it to define apostleship. In fact, it is the other way around. Christ's church finds its true definition, expression, and application in its apostles as God's kingdom, more than ecclesia representatives do.

The Lord installed apostles in and from God's kingdom into which Christ's Church was born. When Peter preached his first post Pentecost sermon, he did so as a representative of God's eternal kingdom, not at the time as the head of the church. It was not until after the first thousands were saved that the church was born **under** the apostles that he and the others could legitimately occupy the position as its head. Accordingly, the Lord keeps to His pattern of installing the leader and then assigning his or her following.

Because eternity is before time, here is another reason why Jesus understood the Lord's divine order to be kingdom first and then ecclesiastical establishing first apostles. The first apostle to be inducted by the others, to complement their authority to replicate themselves, and dispatch their own apostles is Matthias, selected before the Holy Spirit's outpouring. The eleven chose him to assure all Israel's tribes would be represented at the Holy Ghost's coming. He was installed after the Lord returned home. Beside all this, the apostles coming into existence directly under the Lord Jesus as His kingdom ambassadors before the church is born makes theirs the only office the Lord Jesus formally or directly installed, and once again prior to the church being born.

The record shows that after the Lord reappointed the eleven He authorized them to install every other office in the church. Until the church grew to need bishops, pastors, and such, the apostles handled all its ecclesiastical details and identified all its officers and later its installations. That established the office of apostleship as the only one to authorize and legitimize all the others. No book of the New Testament shows that Jesus exhibited express interest in any other office in or out of the church because He commuted His authority as the Great Apostle to them to implement His will and ministerial choices. Here is why the church flounders and fails to apprehend its destiny when it ignores apostles.

Apostles Legitimize the Church

To prove that apostleship is not bound or legitimized by the church, that the reverse is true, scripture refers to them repeatedly all the way up to Revelation 21:14 as the foundations of the Lamb's eternal city. Four times in the New Testament, apostles are paired with prophets. The first time is in Luke 11:49 where the Lord, before His departure, promises to reinstate the two offices once His heavenly commission is fulfilled. This statement goes along with John 13:16: "*Verily, verily, I say unto you, The servant is not greater than his lord; neither had he that is sent greater than he that sent him.*" All this is to say that the apostles' exclusive relationship with the Lord serves as the impetus for the mantle, energizing apostles' ability to confidently face off with the Lord's enemies, knowing within they win because of their communion with Christ. Interestingly, the word for *sent* relates to the word used for **apostle** to place the statement's context squarely in apostleship. An apostle would understand the aforementioned verse to say, "*Verily, verily, I say unto you, the servant is not greater than his lord; neither the apostle greater than he that dispatched, or apostolized, him.*"

The second use of the word *sent*, being *pempo* rather than the familiar *apostolos*, changes the intent of the message; whereas, the first *sent* is the literal word the Greek uses elsewhere for **apostle**, the noun. *Pempo*, you will remember, differs from the verb for "to send," which is *apostello*. It situates the Lord's object of discussion as His apostles. To the mind concerned about translations that support doctrinal conclusions or deductions to deny the authenticity of apostleship, the passage has enormous implications. Reading the passage as the Lord spoke it brings into question the His perpetuation of apostleship and refutes traditionalists' contention that apostleship is expired forever for reasons discussed elsewhere in this text. The Lord, on the other hand, appears to say that He intended to and does dispatch them beyond the initial twelve. In the passage, He appears to be preparing the twelve to expand their initial college and recognize those yet to join them. Jesus is assuring them that He will dispatch other apostles that complement and succeed them. In doing so, He therefore sets the office in proper proximity to His own in respect to reach, authority, and perpetuity.

The next time the first and second officers of 1 Corinthians 12:28 are mentioned together is in Paul's epistle to the

Ephesians (Ephesians 2:20 and 3:5) and the last time the pair appear is in Revelation 18:20. Twice the kingdom duo is distinguished from those of the world by the adjective *holy*. The first is Ephesians 3:5: *"Which in other ages was not made known unto the sons of men, as it is now revealed unto his holy apostles and prophets by the Spirit."* The second is in Revelation 18:20: *"Rejoice over her, thou heaven, and ye holy apostles and prophets; for God hath avenged you on her."*

The New Testament apostles were installed by the Risen Christ, the heavenly Man who was spiritual and eternal when He inducted them into His everlasting kingdom apostleship. That makes most arguments about their sole purpose being to found the church two thousand years ago irrelevant. What Jesus did as the incarnate word of God, before His heavenly dispatch to earth is meant to be a guide for the church to follow. It was not meant to set the limits on apostleship forever. To rightly evaluate and apply the mantle one must resort to where it began in heaven with the Almighty, not just based on the three and a half years of His ministry. Apostleship began in eternity and will culminate in eternity as the apostle John understood. It can only be identified and somewhat shaped by its ancient expression since it, like all the Lord's technologies, must continue to develop and evolve until its fullest potential is experienced by the earth.

Jesus Understands Apostleship from God's Mind

What is plain to Jesus, who was not physically present at the time of the original twelve's' calling or their re-commissioning, is the order in which Christ named His ministers, apostles first according to Luke 6:13. Jesus' appreciation of apostleship as His day understood it, would dissuade him from equalizing apostles and disciples. He would have no doubt understood the danger of assigning or downgrading the Lord's view of an apostle to a mere disciple since disciples by definition lack a dispatch, a message (over a testimony or witness), or a delegation. They are learners, as was common knowledge in his day. Apostles, on the other hand, are sent ones, the equivalent of ambassadors as opposed to disciples' distinct learner classification. [11]

Traditional attempts to downplay apostles' authority or their legitimate place as head of the church by restricting the word *proton* to a lateral or sequential station in the church's ministry order is erroneous. It also has the effect of dissembling the office and its vital position in God's service. The word *named* used in the Luke passage identifies who apostles are to the church and what God calls them. The word rendered *name* there includes an appellation, assignment, profession, authority, and character. Compare it with 2 Corinthians 10:8: *"For though I should boast somewhat more of our <u>authority</u>, which the Lord hath given us for edification, and not for your destruction, I should not be ashamed."* See also 2 Corinthians 13:10. Before Jesus named any other officer of His church, He called and installed the apostle first as founder, and logically head of His everlasting ecclesia. Matthew 10:1, 2 adds that He gave them power that extended their dominance into His governmental sphere (see Matthew 16:18, 19, where Christ gave the keys of His kingdom to Peter as the church's first head).

The Apostle Peter's Kingdom Keys

In the understanding of those on earth at the time of Christ's delegation of apostleship, giving the keys to one's kingdom was not only pivotal, but it was exclusively authoritative. Jesus performed with Peter what the authorities of the ecclesia practiced for decades. When a high power gave the keys to his or her kingdom to a subordinate, it was to induct the recipient

---

[11] Study chapter on ambassadorship for a broader view of what the original apostles and Paul understood to constitute apostleship as ordained by the Lord.

121

into governmental service. The ceremony in which the keys were given equated to an initiation rite.

Keys to kingdoms speak to dominion and authority and invariably represent emblems of official service. Generally speaking, in the practice of the Graeco-Roman ecclesia of Jesus' day dating back to around 300 B.C., high state powers delivered their keys to the state's archives, military, and government (and sometimes the treasury). What Peter inherited from Jesus at His departure amounted to God's kingdom seal of state, explained by previous discussions on apostolic annexation. It was the very authority the Lord Jesus held while on earth and exercised in His ministry that His apostles received upon His departure. He was leaving the planet, and so the control and power Christ wielded in the heavenlies while on apostolic assignment in earth would be vacant if the Lord did not transfer it to another. That other was Peter, giving him the status of a divine key holder to heaven's archives, treasury, and arsenal. The act was more than a simple statement as to his lateral authority in the Church. Jesus empowered Peter as a principal stronghold and those to follow his type of apostleship, to handle the governmental, administrative, financial, and martial affairs of His Church in their respective spheres of heavenly and earthly assignment.

While the modern world believes what Jesus did with His apostles in Matthew 16 amounted to a wholly spiritual event, that the Lord interjected a spiritual anomaly into society that had no natural basis before, the truth is He stayed with eternity's pattern. Heaven has long since followed the pattern of allowing earthly replicas of eternal truths to explain to humans what eternity is doing in their world. Such was the case with the ecclesia briefly introduced above.

The Ecclesia as God's Satellite

Apostles receive revelations and insights from the Lord directly on the order of that which His Old Testament prophets and all the New Testament apostles received to deliver their fresh manna to His church in the world. Apostles are inducted firsthand by the living, incarnate Logos and absorbed into what has become the Creator's holy word and eternal world. They experience God's kingdom citizens and revelations directly and dramatically as His first ranking agents. John's Apocalypse and the record of Zechariah 3 demonstrating Joshua the high priest's induction both make this statement.

In addition, apostles, because of their extensive interaction with the Risen Lord, see the new convert and indeed the Church at large in more serious and sometimes somber terms than do the other officers. This ambassadorial agent recognizes the ecclesia's call to mirror the Lord's eternal kingdom. He or she approaches Christ's ministry pursuing a reflection of God and Christ's everlasting kingdom, they seek to reflect their God's world in the same way that the moon reflects the light of the sun to shine in the darkness when the sun's light is hidden. Another way of expressing this, aside from the use of the word *embassy* mentioned elsewhere is to say that the ecclesia on earth is ordained to serve the Lord as a massive satellite of His eternal world. It is created to work in tandem with His spiritual world and its institutions as tributaries mirroring the activities of the unseen spheres. That is why and how this planet is perpetually cared for, and governed by the Almighty's celestial beings, and why it is inseparably tied to their existence and influence. Also, this says how those born to darkness, sin, and death gain even a modicum of insight into the Creator's everlasting orders.

Apostles then seek to illuminate the otherwise hidden aspects, agencies and powers of eternity's sovereignty and dispense their logic in a way that vivifies the heavenly schema that portrays immortality to mortals. This is innately part of their dispensation, what the naked eye and veiled heart cannot fathom what the world of light and life looks like or does. That is what the Lord Jesus meant when He said in John's gospel that one must be born again to see the kingdom of God. The ecclesia's chief purpose, beyond this is to illuminate the darkened, human mind with its Creator's wisdom and ideally reconnect the unsaved to their eternal creaturehood as children of light rather than offspring of the supernatural darkness they pursue. Their call is to sanctify for Him the body He prepared for His eternity existence by collaborating with His Christlike dominion. Apostles start out grasping fully the Lord's reasons for propelling His Church toward its everlasting destiny. They instinctually comprehend its vast purpose as eternity's long awaited cohabitant. Apostles however, outpace the others in this objective by acting as Christ's catalytic agents; increasingly unfolding the mysteries of God's hidden worlds to those born into Christ's body. They alone are ascribed the privilege and duty in scripture as <u>stewards</u> of God's mysteries, see 1 Corinthians 4:1,2. Apostles are privy to the secret and silent workings of the Lord's invisible world and are given aspects of it to dispense to the body of Christ in their seasons.

Apostles keenly and skillfully deliver to God's Church the single power that is able to save their souls and challenge them to transform into Christ's image and likeness. That is God's unadulterated word. Apostles bring the Lord's truth home to the Christian's heart and soul, incisively influencing every area of life, directly or not, to motivate living Christ's life every day. Vague disconnected preaching and teaching will generally not come from these two officers. They know all too well how severe and glorious the Lord is. The nature of the apostles' and prophets' induction to the Godhead's service make them privy to His kingdom, tasting it sometimes personally in order to persuade people of God's word of truth put into their mouths. They learn from their divine intimacy not only that heaven and hell are real but also how God's holiness prevents Him from giving eternal life to those that reject or pervert His way of life.

Actions of the Ecclesia

The institution called the ecclesia existed at the time Jesus gave Peter the keys to the kingdom, so Peter knew what was handed to him, as did the others. That institution having its origins in ancient Athens was still functioning during Jesus' earthly ministry. Some of its functions and authorities in Greek times were as follows:

1. Legislation

2. Military decrees

3. Finance

4. Convening and conducting public court

5. Criminal investigations

6. Deciding and meting out penalties

7. Judicial functions and decisions

8. Public works

9. Official elections

10. War and peace declarations

11. Ostracism

Handling and deciding along with the senate matters of state of supreme importance included the following:

1. War

2. Peace

3. Treaties

4. Alliances

5. Military regulations

6. Acceptance or rejection of proposals from various other councils and authorities

7. Finance and economy

8. Imports and exports

9. New religions

10. Rites, observances, celebrations and festivals

11. Commendations and honors

12. Conferring citizenship

From this list, it is easy to see what Jesus Christ thought of His eternal assembly of *"called out ones."* It explains His words to the eleven in John 20:23: *"Whose soever sins ye remit, they are remitted unto them; and whose soever sins ye retain, they are retained."*

Confirming Ecclesiastical Citizenship

In regards to the Graeco-Roman Ecclesia's membership, citizenship was a mandatory requirement. Considering the empire's vast conquest of other nations, the wisdom of the requisite and its political expediency are evident. To assure only genuine members entered the gathering and participated in its officiations, a six-member board of the Ecclesia verified the right of a person to attend its meetings.[12] This board, once called the *lexiarchi*, registered all persons that became citizens of the state. The record was checked against all approaching the hall to enter the meetings and those not registered were prevented from attending. How much does this mirror the

---

[12] The Dictionary of Classical Mythology, Religion, Literature, and Art by Oskar Seyffert; Gramercy Books, New York-Avenel; 1995; pp 202,203.

work of the five-fold in its authentication of those genuinely born again by the Holy Spirit?

The Lord Jesus refers to heaven's policy of confirming legitimate citizenship with those approaching His kingdom and attempting to gain entrance into its proceedings or access to its privileges. In the ancient ecclesiastical model, non-citizens had no right to enter ecclesiastical conventions and were subject to bodily expulsion if they sneaked in without the necessary approval, attire, or credentials. Considering the size of its assembly, being called to this duty required diligence, vigilance, and dedication to the pure integrity of its proceedings. According to the *Dictionary of Classical Mythology, Religion, Literature, and Art*, there was also someone over the Ecclesia called a president and a higher institution over it called a Boule or Bule or Curia (the word used for royal court). The pattern broadens typical explanations of Peter's initial apostleship and intimates the vision Jesus had in mind for the church about to be born on earth.

The Prototype of Peter's Position

The higher council that operated above the ecclesia was chaired by persons exercising judicial, martial, governmental, civil, and administrative powers with typically royal and divine authority. In various forms and complexions, it has existed since about the late third century BC. The council chair was given the keys of the kingdom for the duration of his service. Those keys were to the fortress, archives, and seal of state and were held as long as a single council was in session chaired by the same person. The duties, authority, and tasks of the council that either convened in chambers together or dispersed proceedings to their respective assignments in other offices or domes included these:

1. Ecclesiastical business

2. Daily business of state

3. Various political, judicial, and military decrees

4. Reports from generals

5. Reports from ambassadors

6. Foreign affairs

7. Superintendence over all public business

8. Interacting with or supervening over other councils

9. Administration of civil and public works

10. Civil, local command

11. Administration of the military

12. Building, staffing, and maintenance of the armaments

13. Special supervision of the cavalry and navy

14. Administration of finance and expenses

15. Agricultural taxation

16. Temple treasury

17. Court of justice

18. Qualifying new archons

19. Assessing fines

20. Judicial decision making

This group worked with the **archons** (chief leaders usually directly under royalty and typically formed as a tribunal) though they were normally accountable to the emperor or other monarch. The tribunal was immediately answerable to the senate. When it comes to the New Testament ecclesia, the monarch is Jesus Christ and the senate is Heaven's Sanhedrin, the twenty-four elders in John's apocalypse. The archons may be seen as His holy apostles and prophets.

To continue, three scribal officers were assigned to this group that were also assisted by a number of subordinates that served as their functionaries. Jesus entrusted His Mount of Transfiguration experience to Peter, James, and John. In light of these truths and His apostles' definite awareness of secular law and community, scripture clearly amplifies what Jesus meant in his Corinthian ordination of the church and what motivated him to record it. The passage conveys that the church's administration, dispensation, and government be supervised by Christ's apostles, prophets, and teachers respectively in every era so that each of His kingdom ecclesia's generation benefited from His divine as and the foreordained spirit of leadership.

It seems that whatever God placed in apostles, however He constructed them, best suits them for their jobs. In God's mind, apostles' fundamental attitudes, made up of their life experiences and perspectives on His kingdom, arise from the Creator's predetermined will and life orchestration. These enable Him to shape ordained and installed apostles' inherent sentiments and volition to incline them to His predestined ends. The apostle Paul, very cognizant of this truth, readily spoke of an inner constraint, compunction, or compulsion that drove Him to submit to His apostolic commission. One passage of scripture that defines apostles' perpetual commission to the New Creation church is Acts 26:16-18:

> *"But rise, and stand upon thy feet: for I have appeared unto thee for this purpose, to make thee a minister and a witness both of these things which thou hast seen, and of those things in the which I will appear unto thee; delivering thee from the people, and from the Gentiles, unto whom now I send thee."*

129

This passage of scripture is pointed. God inducts and Christ's dispatches apostles to accomplish specific objectives.

1. Open their eyes

2. Turn them from darkness to light

3. Turn them from the power of Satan unto God

4. They may receive forgiveness of sins

5. They may receive an inheritance among them, which are sanctified by faith that is in Jesus Christ.

The passage lays out a five-step agenda for the apostle's commission.

The Apostle's Commission Agenda

Beginning with "opening their eyes," the apostle enters the job knowing that people are inherently blind to God and the truths of His kingdom[13]. Once their eyes are opened, apostles understand that people are born into the world outside of God and entrenched in spiritual darkness, the culprit behind all their sins and woes. Progressing from symptom to cause Acts 26:18 then identifies the root of it all: people are inwardly blind and steeped in spiritual darkness because they begin life under Satan's power and not God's. The absolute consequences of their sin condition come into view next. People need God's forgiveness to receive their inheritance from Jesus Christ's redemption, bequeathed only by a sanctification achieved strictly by entering and remaining in Him. In a single statement, the apostle's commission and its tasks and functions are described. The five steps equate to the apostle's job description

---

[13] This very different from evangelists, pastors, and teachers, who are meant to receive the apostles handiwork (revelatory mysteries) after they have somewhat oriented converts to them as Christ's way.

and double as an apostolic assessment as well. That is not, however, the end of the matter.

Another serious question arises regarding the apostle and his or her role in the church today. It is how to know the difference between the staff in 1 Corinthians 12:28, 29 and those listed in Ephesians 4:11. In order to make a solid distinction between the two verses of scripture, just think government (**head** in the Corinthians passage) and administration (**hands** in the Ephesians staff). Ephesians 4:11 presents its officers as singularly having been given to various types of congregations; some apostles are given to some people; some prophets are given to others and so on. The passage reads, *"And he gave some, apostles; and some, prophets; and some, evangelists; and some, pastors and teachers."* When rereading the passage, pay attention to what is written to note the use of the word *some* to designate how God employs His Ephesians 4:11 officers. The word *some* as used there speaks to portions or groups, numbers of people or congregants, various groups, types, of believers. The Lord dispatched apostles in some places (or cases, or to some people), prophets were sent to some people and places; evangelists, pastors and teachers in others as needed. No particular group of the ministers was ever sent to just one type of members in the body during any single era of Christendom. Each officer's assignment addresses how God ordains him or her to execute the respective ministries of these five servants within their disparate spheres and/or territories. It is what characterizes their ministries as God's hand at work in the Church.

The Apostle's Ministerial Dispensations

The pastor can only surface after the apostle has apostled and the evangelist has evangelized. Otherwise, there is really no need for the *poimen* since people must first be converted before they are interested in or even need to be shepherded. The same

131

is true with the evangelist; this mantle is how souls are saved and enter the Lord's body. Neither one of these two offices appears to be delegated comprehensive governmental authority over the body aside from, in the case of the pastor, his or her assigned congregants and the evangelist's sphere of ministry as indicated by the Ephesians reference. It seems the apostle is how the pastor and other New Testament ministers come into existence since all Christ does begins with a message that, once preached, attracts followers who become the Church. The apostle's message and doctrine once disseminated births the apostle's church out of the delegated commission and mandate, whether or not the title is donned by the minister so endowed.

Peter, Jesus and the early apostles by no means finished the job. They may have done a great work converting their generations during their tenures, but other people have been born into sin since then, leaving each generation's apostles to replenish Christ's Church. They are ordained by God to recover all that secularism took from Him and release the flames of redemption that win the lost of their era. Matthias, for instance, replaced Judas; and Saul/Paul, not an original apostle with Barnabas, went to the nations. This makes one wonder what the cutoff point of Jesus' apostles really is.

God's Eternal Apostolic Agenda

At present, every sphere of humanity is under the sway of the wicked one and the children of darkness control and occupies them on Satan's behalf. Styles, trends, customs, and culture of today reflect this sad reality throughout world history. Fashions glorify prostitution, sin, and death; secular family values are humanist, pagan, and demonic; immorality and sexuality are now social norms, while entertainment practices pervert society's cultures. Lewdness and obscenity are prized aphrodisiacs and witchcraft and magic their inspirations.

Tragically, today's Christian Church, unaware of the relentless satanic barrage against their society, cannot discern what is, or is not Christ. The average Christian is unaware of how his or her government is aggressively voting in witchcraft laws and voting out Jesus Christ. Spirit-filled souls that love the Lord are oblivious to the devious plans at work that enable business to manipulate world economies in order to drive the world into a dark financial caste system. Devilish music and entertainment drench society with pagan thought and godless rituals mediated by occultic priests. For an ancient example, read 1 Chronicles 11:14, 15: *"For the Levites left their suburbs and their possession, and came to Judah and Jerusalem: for Jeroboam and his sons had cast them off from executing the priest's office unto the LORD: And he ordained him priests for the high places, and for the devils, and for the calves which he had made."*

War and conflict exist on every continent in some way or another as world leaders position themselves for the antichrist's platform. Millions of souls lost or sacrificed to pagan liberty are convinced it is better to be alive to demons, wizards, witches, and devils than being bored serving Creator God. To them hell is not a threat but a chosen destiny. Ancient tales of human supremacy in the afterlife promise liberty from righteousness and holiness, and everlasting fun instead of God's way of life. Satanic lies seduce wandering souls into choosing an eternal party in the abyss, their chosen paradise. Demons are their friends and their higher powers; witches and spiritists their access and conduits to the netherworld's privileges and powers in this life. Christianity is dead, and Jesus is a punk; sin is good and naughty is fun, decadence is delightful. That sums up the apostolic landscape of today and it is the one that true apostles will confront if they intend to fulfill ministry.

Collectively, these events speak to apostles differently than they speak to others. The state of the world always justifies their existence and provokes their labors. Rampant devilish activities insistently urge apostles to tackle what other ministers reconcile. For all these reasons, apostles must turn their attentions to Christ's message over pop theology and traditional ecclesiastical methods. They must bring Creator God's doctrine to bear on the humanist philosophies, the carnal wisdom of their age. Each apostle must discover the revelatory message of his or her commission; the mystery to be revealed; and the redemptive words that really set the captives of their eras free. For this move to catch on, to advance Christ's agenda, doctrine must be purged and unified and ministry emphases clarified and focused. Apostleship is not just a clash of the will of men to amass followers after themselves. It is not even sparked by restructuring the church to obey the office or its resultant new or perceived restoration of God's government.

The Godhead's apostleship is about the gospel of Jesus Christ; it is about the recovery of sight to the blind, liberty of captives, and the gathering and presentation of the purchased possession to the Father God and the Lord Jesus Christ. All that takes a word that becomes a work, not a work explained by dogma. The apostle's strength, brilliance, wisdom, and charisma can take any move anywhere the apostle wants it to go. The free discretionary exercise of the mantle is part of its strength and sadly its detriment. Being a plenipotentiary, explained later, apostles of any rank can strengthen God's authority in people's lives and the world or injure His work and image. This is possible because people of necessity are constructed to respond to the sound of apostles' voices and act on the profound wisdom from their mouths.

For centuries, millions of souls have been drawn by the indisputable power and influence apostles wield. That is what

134

makes the onus put upon them so weighty. Those not commissioned by Jesus Christ, with the inciting signs of the original twelve that their contemporaries and successors relied upon, will gather. They will order people and their lives and they will prosper. What they will not do is turn over their masses to Jesus Christ, or equip them for their eternal calling and destiny in Him. Establishing spheres, exercising heavenly and earthly dominion, and clashing with Satan's angels and offspring to overturn humanist strongholds is what apostles do. It is integral to all principalic authorities and how apostles manifest as their deity's sanctioned strongholds in the earth, the heart of their divine commissions. If that deity is not Jesus Christ or the commission one of His revolting spirits, the results as have been seen can be disastrous.

Chapter Summary

1. Peter's keys to heaven's kingdom was more than symbolism; the act was a spiritual sign to Satan's heavenly powers.

2. Erroneous teaching causes people to fear and shun apostles.

3. Some of the apostolic fathers pass apostles' torch to bishops.

4. Because people are still being born into sin, apostles' authority is needed to birth them into Christ's church.

5. Apostles are promised by Jesus a significant portion of His eternal government's rule under Him.

6. Reinstallation made the original apostles qualified to take Christ's message to the world.

7. Christ's death and departure from the earth expired the first apostles' apostolic commission because it served the Mosaic Law. A new commission enabled them to spread the gospel to the nations; something the first commission precluded them from doing.

8. Apostles are first in God's ministry ranks because they were commissioned and installed into office by the Risen King David who dispatched them to His everlasting kingdom before Pentecost and the birth of the ecclesia.

9. Peter's keys equated to transference of power and a transition of heaven's authorities. Now Satan's minions were subjugated to the Godhead's children of light and life.

10. The New Testament ecclesia is patterned after the ancient Athenian Graeco-Roman institution of specially called out citizens empowered to handle a specified measure of the empire's civilian, martial, and social affairs.

Chapter Seven

Exploring & Discovering the Truth about Apostleship

Chapter Discussions

What Contemporary Apostles Must Do to Succeed • Quality Apostolic Education is Vital • Reasons for the Apostle's Academic Imperative • The Apostolic World in which Christ Lived • Finding the Apostle's Service in Eternity • Unveiling Creation's Archons in Apostleship •Spiritual Protocratics

T his chapter delves deeper into the subject of apostleship as the New Testament ministry given the least amount of scholarship over the church's history. It seeks to fill in the gaps created by scant treatment of the office, and its rejection as a valid ministry in the New Testament church. Discussions here address the apostle, as Christ's world understood the ministry.

Its eternal origins are amplified to give a richer picture of the mantle the Savior activated and dispatched in His name. More than making and baptizing disciples, Christ's world understood its apostles' mantles to govern and legislate. Apostles as God intended are first catalysts. Previous franchising discussions establish economies kingdom enterprises. Apostles break ground and bear the King's eternal and earthly burdens. Lastly, they direct His creation-wide affairs, founding and upholding their institutions.

What Contemporary Apostles Must Do to Succeed

The dearth of information and training on the apostle requires today's apostles to do more than answer the call with sermons, decrees, and demands. It requires them to define, establish, and exemplify the mantle's action as it performs in its world and times. Modern apostles have the arduous task of etching their place in contemporary ministry to fill the void left by ignoring traditionalism. The task calls for current apostles to describe who they are, what they do, and what legitimizes them. It asks prevailing apostolic organizations and communities to shape themselves practically, classify their mantles, and categorize their core functional operations. Once completed, apostles then need to emphatically institute and coordinate the fundamental commissions, callings, and ministries that designated office's impact in every sphere of life.

Beyond this, apostles must collectively draft and publicize their unique approach to Christianity and its ministries because people unfamiliar with them need something tangible to consider when comparing them with the ministers they have known for so long. For this reason, apostles need to explain and typify the distinct rationale of their policies and how their unique, often shocking government is enacted. As chief officials of the New Testament church, apostles should construct accredited learning programs and institutions that uniformly spread the uncommon wisdom and knowledge inseminated by the office. The importance of having apostles clarify their actions cannot be overstated. It is crucial to overturning the inadequate explanations and overarching regulations teachers and other ministers currently and historically use to explain apostleship. As it stands, what they have inculcated before our recent reappearance confines and subjugates apostleship to Christ's subordinate ministries. These ministries, though they were never remotely acquainted with apostles, did the ministry a great disservice and the church, as a result, much harm. Far too much effort has gone into implementing unauthorized views of apostleship, with newcomers to the mantle attempting to regulate it as others see and react to it. If true apostolic reinstatement is to occur, then what authenticates and drives the ministry must be clarified and rightly understood. These activities are most essential to apostleship since its office has not functioned in the forefront of the church as Christ ordained for millennia.

Quality Apostolic Education is Vital

The next stage of the mantle's reinstatement calls for quality apostolic education and academics. Learning and teaching materials that facilitate its instruction and equipment beyond the classic gift applications or casual local church settings are the only way the ministry can earn the respect scripture decrees it deserves. Apostles are going to have to annotate their own Bibles so Christ's apostolic mind and theology may be disseminated. They will need to write commentaries and study aids that divulge the mantle that authored the scriptures, going beyond the anemic cache of material generated by the post-apostolic church. Apostles are going to have to establish their own learning institutions and take up the task of accrediting Christian educators as God appointed, that is as the ones entrusted with Christ's ecclesiastical mandate.

Furthermore, for credibility's sake, apostles must dominate every one of creation's seven spheres, of which education is chief. Therefore, they must begin with it. In every society since the dawn of civilization, educators have been the one profession to cast their cultures often decades in advance.[14] They alter mindsets, shift societal views, and manipulate social trends with their beliefs, ideas, and preferences. Combining gnosis, philosophy, theory, and religion into practical disciplines, they have had the unrivaled opportunity to field test, correct, and embed their ideas in generations. Apostles, although they are the founders and grounders of the New Testament church, have never had such advantage, desiring to be regarded as if their wisdom is normalized among the rest nonetheless. It is no wonder then that the second half of the Great Commission commands us to *disciple*, that is teach, all nations. Teaching is the lynchpin of all civilizations, including God's entire conversion process.

Academic institutions supply the whole of society with its present and future thinkers and human resources. These thinkers shape public sentiment. As present and future politicians, they sway government; as religionists, they mold and mentor those that design spirituality. As entrepreneurs, they market the world's humanist agendas under the guise of commerce. Postsecondary educators particularly maneuver their star learners and staunchest proponents into jobs and careers that permeate their views and sustain their dominance of profession for decades. Their protégés dictate a nation's domestic and world policy, family and community life, and values and legitimize their moral and spiritual persuasions. To see that all spheres of humanity are engaged in the campaign, entertainment joins the plan by making it appealing and fun-

---

[14] Now is the Dawning of the New Age New World Order, Dennis Cuddy, PhD, Hearthstone Publishing, OK.

140

loving to all ages. These integral facets of every culture are all decided or approved by educators that rarely have God's interests or government at heart.

In contrast, the Church's present leadership is powerless to stop the tide of wickedness, humanism and demonism gripping the earth since being shut out of the fundamental task of communicating its wisdom to the learners of the world. They lack, consequently, the range of kingdom and creation insight needed to render God's value judgments on these matters and cannot impact their world in any appreciable way. Many of those that attempt to counter Satan's rampant campaign against Jesus Christ merely declare something as wrong but are unable to give prudent reasons for their stance. Often ridiculed, such defenders feebly conclude with "because it is not God," or "it is against the Bible," or "it is a sin." Lacking, the wisdom skills to argue intelligently their cases, they are regularly mocked for attempting to defend their faith and God's righteousness. For apostleship to be well trusted and attain its ordained influential stature, seizing the mien of academia is the best way to do so. As long as those called to the office cannot prepare for the call the way much of society does, apostles will continue to be disregarded as a serious or credible force in their worlds. They will continue to be seen as power hungry preachers with no respectable hold on the church or its culture.

Reasons for the Apostle's Academic Imperative

What makes apostles' obligation to develop scholastic and intelligent academia an imperative is the absence of uniform apostolic educational programs in the church's schools of postsecondary education. While one can go to a Christian school, college, or university to prepare for the offices of the evangelist, pastor, and teacher, one cannot enroll in a dedicated apostle's course. The best those called to this field of ministry can hope for is a general minister's education program tailored to one or all of the familiar three ministries of Ephesians 4:11, namely the evangelist, pastor, and teacher. Usually enrolling in a supposed apostolic program or course, besides failing to adequately prepare their learners for apostleship if such a course is real, learners must endure chronic educator ridicule and mockery of the very office to which they are called. After spending thousands of dollars on an irrelevant education, these apostles graduate from their contra-apostolic educations unprepared to answer God's actual call on their lives to continue the long history of the mantle's perceived incompetence and illegitimacy. Their routine neglect perpetuates the confusion and fundamental ineptitude generally ascribed to its ministers. Together these factors leave the sphere of apostleship open to abuse and disrepute.

The last discrediting factor in this discussion is the lack of an apostolic accrediting agency to approve, standardize, or give criteria to its education as a profession. A college of apostles and apostolic peers yet do not exist to qualify the learning and specialized competence of those claiming apostleship. To incite the esteem needed to mainstream into the strongest of all spheres of influence, education, the earliest influence in everyone's life, apostles must organize, standardize, and systematically verify what it judges is vital to certifying its specialized expertise. It will not do for apostles to leave this to other study fields and disciplines to do for them. Adopting without distinction, the legitimacies of traditional academia if apostles aim to distinguish the office as God's divine agency to accredit all the others is counter productive to the goal. An interesting note on the subject of apostleship is an unusual synonym given for a **commission**. In the Roget's Thesaurus reference mentioned throughout this book, a synonymic word for it is *accredit*. That in itself says much about the standing of God's apostles among the ranks of His ecclesiastical ministers.

On its own, it suggests how Christ's world received and interacted with apostles.

The Apostolic World in which Christ Lived

Apostles as society knew them in Christ's day understood His New Testament transference of the ancient ecclesia revealed a mystery hidden before time began. As previously shown, those Christ named His apostles perceived His act to invoke (better yet transfer) the office of apostleship from natural Israel to the cosmic kingdom housing the New Creation church birthed on the Day of Pentecost. Capturing how Christ inducted the mantle and dispensation of the apostle into His body is important if their successors will effectively occupy and execute the office. So far, how and why the Lord set the apostle as His church's head ministry and number one official has been the object of hot debate and much contention. Plenty has been said so far to explain it. However, for present controversies to subside, a change people's in historical perceptions of ministry is indicated. Only by these can we overturn the disservice that has been done to apostleship over the last thousand years or so.

One place to begin to unclad the matter is with Creator God's typical way of acting in the earth. Touched on earlier, it requires discovering where and when the apostle occupied a place in eternity, since for the Lord all things earthly have a heavenly origin and counterpart (see Hebrews 9:23 and 23). The New King James Version of the Bible renders the word used for *patterns*, *copy*. In any case, the fact remains that earthly materiality finds its structure and substance in eternity's spirituality. Think about, for instance, the sperm that fertilizes the egg; without intense magnification it is assumed invisible. This is debatable since no one can discover the tiny life charge that gives it its potency. So it is with the Creator's eternal resources. Spiritual only means invisible to us in this world. To those occupying or elevated to that sphere, their world, and its

143

contents are more real than ours since theirs is the machine that manufactures and energizes all that manifests in ours. The premise having been laid let us return our attention to apostleship.

Hebrews 3:1 calls apostleship a "heavenly calling." To reiterate, for the Lord the pattern is first the eternal then the earthly, while for those in the flesh it appears as the reverse: first the fleshly and then the spiritual. A spiritual prototype of all God's handiwork predates the physical form of everything that happens on the planet. Remember Christ's words in John 6:63. He said, "*It is the Spirit who gives life; the flesh profits nothing.*" James the Lord's brother, echoes this truth in his epistle by saying, "*The body without the spirit is dead*" (James 2:26). Therefore, of all the tremendous wisdom presented in this book, the apostle's place (like everything else the Lord ordained) being etched in prehistory, history, and eternity is most profound.

Finding the Apostle's Service in Eternity

To see the Spirit of the Lord's pattern of revelation to education, look at the extra biblical book of Enoch from the Apocrypha.[15] While some of its later adaptations may be questionable, the fact remains that the Bible does mention Enoch and traces him in the Messiah's lineage. Hebrews 11:5 especially commends Enoch's faith in his perverse, antediluvian generation. Genesis 6:1-7 explains their wickedness and God's response to it: most of humanity would be destroyed from the face of the earth. (To learn why, read Genesis 6:1 and compare it with Jude 1:6). Enoch's Hebrews commendation says his faith

---

[15] A collection of religious writings omitted from canonized scripture for various reasons, although they are included in some sacred Christian texts such as the Catholic Bible. Most of them were rejected in canonized scripture because of their spurious treatment of the incarnation, Christ's cross, and most notably the Holy Spirit sent to earth to verify and administrate it all. Enoch is one of those books and is valuable in its expose of God's invisible world, its government, agencies, and citizenry.

in the Lord grew through his constant communion with the Almighty and it eventually qualified him to escape death and enter God's realm to live forever.

The last mention of this mystical character shows Enoch's interactions with the Creator were more than devotional. Enoch did not just hang out with God all day aimlessly roaming around His world; the man, Jude 1:14 explains, was a prophet. Demonstrating God's faithfulness and righteousness, Enoch brought back to his world what the Lord showed him and preached it to his decadent generation that God finally destroyed. There is much in this apocryphal book to debate, but one thing is sure: its description of the eternal structure, staff, and operations of creation is amazing. This is especially true when one reads the man's glimpses of God's world order that in due course became part of the Bible today.

In addition to all the Prophet Enoch brought back to earth, regarding the Almighty's dominions is his revelation of the seven archons of creation, alluded to in the Bible every time the Old Testament commanded Israel to perform a certain rite for seven consecutive days. These heavenly beings are understood as the embodiment of the angels of the New Testament church. They surface and dominate monarchies as assigned powers over specific dominions. The archons' identifying function is hidden in the revelations of Christ's Apocalypse, where He represents those of His light and life as the seven angels of His seven churches synonymous with the seven spirits before His throne sent out (dispatched and apostolized) into all the world (Revelation 4:5; compare it with Hebrews 1:14).

Unveiling Creation's Archons in Apostleship

Before Christ, the book of the Prophet Zechariah discloses seven eternal creation powers symbolically as seven eyes in the stone that symbolically designate Him. Later they are established in the world as the candles in Creator God's heavenly candelabrum, supporting its prototypical premises as representing Christ's church, hence their apostolic symbolism as the seven spirits before the throne of God in the book of Revelation (see Revelation 1:4; 3:1: 4:5: 5:6). Mentioning them in this context validates their eternality in the latter days of Christ's earthly history. All this shows how Jesus knew exactly what He was instituting when He renamed His twelve chosen disciples, *apostles* and dispatched them to the four quarters of the earth. His doing so returned the dominion of apostolism to His Father God's kingdom. Scripture disseminates the apostle's ministry from the perspective of the officer and the office in relation to its interactions with eternity's powers that have been before time began. It justifies the continued officiations of the apostle in the modern church that Christ declared would never end. The apostle's commission is fulfilled in eternity under Christ's multitudinous government His world without end that begins terrestrially with His thousand-year reign, His church being under the headship of His apostles.

As you can see, the spirit of the apostle always existed and will rule throughout eternity under the headship of Jesus Christ and His everlasting government. In the beginning of His earthly ministry, He understood His first major act was to return this powerful officer to the work, business, and rulership of His Father's interminable kingdom (see Matthew 19:28 and Revelation 21:14). Apostles today need teaching on how to cooperate with this mandate and in understanding, the terms, and conditions of its appointment that is how God qualifies a minister to serve in the office. Modern apostolic orders, authority, decision-making, and operations should know how Christ's eternal kingdom works above and within the earth as demonstrated by their predecessors. Only their dispensed wisdom and insight can give today's apostle a sound

146

appreciation of the call and what the Church of the Lord Jesus is to become through its labors. Think of the Church's enhanced possibilities and its members' world impact when such knowledge of this officer abounds.

The centuries' long stagnation of the apostle's mantle begs for these explanations. Too much time has already been spent at the debate table arguing over the validity of perpetual apostleship. Here we are at its earliest stages of reinstatement and a spiritual chasm in the body and the world has already been created. Numerous useless texts, lectures, and sermons dispute its validity in the modern church, and without grounds stigmatize its action in the church and community. The cost of this attack to the Lord is monumental. Just considering the hundreds of centuries of ignorance, blindness, and resistance to apostolic leadership and service brings the tally of lost or jeopardized souls into the countless billions. Of course there were pockets of apostolic fervor and activity that the Lord ignited periodically, but if apostolism were as consistent in the church as the pastorate, evangelist, or the teacher, where would the body of Christ be today in terms of Christianity and its global impact and respect? A better question might be what would be the state of the world right now if this were the case?

Spiritual Protocratics

The word *spirit* speaks to what is immaterial, ethereal, otherworldly, and supernatural. Spiritual authority comes from above, as the people of the ancient world thoroughly understood. Reading Titus 3:1 with this enlightened perspective sheds light on the old world's understanding of spiritual order and divinely delegated authority. Visitations from otherworldly creatures were commonplace. They helped them establish their world and its governments. Usually these were arcane cultures denounced by Israel's God in Deuteronomy 32:15-18. The practice however, erased any ancient beliefs about humans inherently possessing the authority to rule the outside world from within themselves. Consequently, spiritual authority has its origins in the immortal and eternal, not the earthly and temporal. Authority coming from above then means it comes from the eternal Creator who decides to speak through a human vessel and exercise His sovereign powers and authority to enforce His words' and manifest His will in due time.

Founding rulers invested their positions with power and authority before they invested the officers to occupy them to assure their corresponding measure of rule. Human attributes and aptitudes are endowed by the Lord in anticipation of such life's calling. These create the attraction that fuse predisposition with installation in those installed into the office. A person's vested authority releases their attributed authority by virtue of being placed in a position. Without a position invested with authority, one's strengths and powers have no lawful outlet, and cannot operate to effect change, provoke behavior or achieve improvement.

God, Celestial Rulers & Law

The ancient idea of law was not some philosophical ideal of territorial or tyrannical control during Jesus' but it was rather an unseen realm populated and administered by spiritual citizens. These beings are charged with keeping God's creations intact and His presence among them at peace. Humans way back understood this and felt that God's sphere of law was independent and above earth's. All scripture writings point to this belief.

Although words are used to mete out their celestial rulers' judgments, the actions that triggered them were not seen as violating some abstract cryptic code or indifferent behavioral script. Offending God's creature government literally meant offending those immortal beings delegated overlordship of His kingdom. Thus, personhood and not just edicts were affronted by rebellious humans. Here is a biblical example, *"Beware of him, and obey his voice, provoke him not; for he will not pardon your transgressions: for my name is in him. But if thou shalt indeed obey his voice, and do all that I speak; then I will be an enemy unto thine enemies, and an adversary unto thine adversaries. For mine Angel shall go before thee, and bring thee in unto the Amorites, and the Hittites, and the Perizzites, and the Canaanites, the Hivites, and the Jebusites: and I will cut them off."* Exodus 23:21-23. See also Ecclesiastes 5:8. All God's invisible creatures are active in His superintendence of this natural world. The Bible calls the name of two angels that God appears to rely on repeatedly in the dispensation of His plan for humanity, Michael and Gabriel.

Why Jesus Remains Forever the Eternal Authority of Creation

Gabriel's and other angelic visits to Daniel, for instance, paves the way for clarifying why and how Jesus became the head and end of all Creator God's authority and power. The Bible says that Jesus came and reigns today because He has an endless life in Hebrews 7:16. Living forever means His laws and government, as Head of the new creation church never need change, revocation, or revision. His laws fit because they are more for the eternal world and its citizenry than the ones whose government the Lord entrusts His temporal spheres. That is why Jesus could say to those of His day that Moses' law governed the old creation, and will govern those outside him because they are flesh, dead and alienated to the Creator's life. Those not born again into Christ's kingdom remain under the curses attached to Moses' law because it is prescribed expressly for them. The only way to come from under Moses' law is to become a member of Christ's eternal kingdom whose government is for the immortal and eternal.

149

To best understand this, Apostles should be well trained in government and spiritual protocratics. Apart from an appreciation of what makes God do what He does and how He enacts His laws and commandments, Apostles make poor representatives of Christ's eternal kingdom. They must understand that God instated and relies on His governmental laws to preserve, prosper, and perpetuate His creation. Apostles can never think of becoming able or accurate authorities on His behalf under any other conditions.

For the apostle, spiritual authority begins from eternity and weaves itself through the temporal requisites of this life to direct its objects to eternity. A complicated statement for sure but nonetheless key to the weighty demands put upon those who would bear the Lord's word and take up the task of legislating it in His name. Both comprise the first place of beginning for those entrusted with the Lord's spiritual authority. For this to happen, they must be made fully aware of His governmental plane of existence. Shaping young Apostles to conform to the mind of Christ begins their arduous journey of learning and experiencing firsthand His embedded creation laws, statutes, judgments, and the Creator testimonies that glorify their success over the year. See Psalm 19:7-9 and Psalm 119 in its entirety. Its exhaustive study gives any devoted Apostle a broad understanding of the various elements and effects of God's powerful word.

By now, it is obvious how spiritual authority is integral to all creation not only from ancient times but also from before time began. It cannot be dissolved or disengaged from earthly existence because those on earth desire it to do so. Humans die and when they do and whatever authority positions they may have held must always be replaced. That makes for a changeable leadership. That is the best reason for the Creator to place the perpetuity of His kingdom into the hands of immortal beings. In doing so, God assures His prototypical judgment remains unchanged throughout the life of this creation. Humans, largely unaware of this are simply shut out of what is really governing them. Believing they are really in charge of this world, they are oblivious to the authority exercised over their lives from eternity. From the highest heaven to the lowest parts of earth, authority that is more spiritual than carnal exists and dominates.

Creation is divided according its Creator's design that is patterned after God's divine order that we are only given glimpses in this world. Based on creation's design, the Lord after dividing His worlds set about assigning spiritual agents and authorities to care for and defend it for Him throughout all time. Specific custodial and perpetual replenishment instructions were given to see that what He made endured and prospered for every generation to be born to enjoy it. To assure those given charge over His handiwork are empowered sufficiently enough to enforce His will and vision, and effectively carry out their rescue and preservation mandates, our Maker created positions of authority for them to do so.

God's protocratic authorities, initially unseen though frequently felt long after being set in motion, are invested with His power and wisdom to assure their authority is not vain. Potent governmental constituent are dispensed to them mete out the Creator's laws, prescriptions, proscriptions, commandments, warnings, and judgments. God also assigned weapons, armaments, arsenals and treasuries, from which those in authority can draw for their rule's equipment and implements, see Jeremiah 50:25.

The main tool of the Lord's government is His word. Mainly unknown executors of that word are the multitude of angels that stand around His throne waiting to fulfill His that word. Study the following passages of scripture for a richer

151

understanding; Amos 5:13; Amos 9:6; Deuteronomy 32:8; Job 25:2. See also Psalm 104:1 and 103:19-22.

Spiritual Protocratics and the Apostle's Spiritual Authority

Embedded throughout scripture is an eternal government that is imperceptibly carried out by God's seven ruling powers of creation. That the seven spirits are angels oversee all creation, dominating it is seen repeatedly throughout scripture. From Revelation 1:4, *"John to the seven churches which are in Asia: Grace be unto you, and peace, from him which is, and which was, and which is to come; and from the seven Spirits which are before his throne; to* Revelation 3:1, *"And unto the angel of the church in Sardis write; These things saith he that hath the seven Spirits of God, and the seven stars; I know thy works, that thou hast a name that thou livest, and art dead."* It continues with Revelation 4:5, *"And out of the throne proceeded lightnings and thunderings and voices: and there were seven lamps of fire burning before the throne, which are the seven Spirits of God,"* to end with Revelation 5:6, *"And I beheld, and, lo, in the midst of the throne and of the four beasts, and in the midst of the elders, stood a Lamb as it had been slain, having seven horns and seven eyes, which are the seven Spirits of God sent forth into all the earth."*

By now it is obvious what all these scriptures have in common, but is it as obvious to see their underlying truth in relation to the New Creation church of the Lord Jesus Christ and His Spiritual Protocratics? However, as rule, for any New Testament revelation to be valid it must be substantiated by an Old Testament prototype. Substantiation for this is seen in Zechariah 3:9 in its discussion of Joshua's the High Priest's coronation in Jerusalem's restoration. The passage reads, *"For behold the stone that I have laid before Joshua; upon one stone shall be seven eyes: behold, I will engrave the graving thereof, saith the LORD of hosts, and I will remove the iniquity of that land in one day."*

A review of Revelation 4:6 and 5:6 shows its fulfillment in the work of the Lord Jesus Christ and His dispatch of the seven spirits into the world to carry out His everlasting ministry. These seven spirits reach back to eternity as collaborators in God's eternal government of His worlds and were poised from Israel's inception to become His protocratic rulers throughout the church age and beyond. These spirit that once stood before God's throne have been sent (*apostolized* is the word scripture scribes understood) into the earth as the perpetual stationary rulers of the new creation and its progressive development on earth as the manifest sons and daughters of God. As such, they represent apostolic angels that assure the church's stability under God's eternal governmental order remains intact until it is removed from the earth. Consider what these powerful never changing beings do for the church as a heavenly layer of spiritual apostles under the Great Apostle Jesus Christ. Consider as well what their station in the heavenlies on the Lord's spiritual staff means to the apostles God ordained to emerge until the end of this dispensation. What type of profile would you draft of spiritual government and the church's obligation or abdication of it in the world's present eras of existence?

That dispatch further makes our point when one thinks of the seven angels that oversee the New Creation church introduced by the Lord Jesus in Revelation's early chapters. By now, it is apparent that the revelation of the seven spirits as God's prototypical archons and the seven angels of His seven churches reintroducing us to their ecclesiastical Spiritual Protocratics. What has been said so far unveils mystery of the church further? In essence, they constitute creation's seven principalities and their rule and government are encoded throughout scripture in the Old Testament repeatedly.

We find out how these powerful never changing agents regulated many of Israel's rituals and observances, as the determinant time code of creation. A thought back to Genesis 1:14 in view of Psalm 19:1-4 shows their impact. From time immemorial, these seemingly inanimate lights have ruled the earth since it began, outliving everything ever born on the planet, and evacuating all that the Lord wants out of it. In relation to Spiritual Protocratics and their actions on behalf of the Godhead, the revelation is that the church has always existed. First hidden in the being of the Lord Jesus Christ before time and the world began, then in natural Israel according to Revelation chapter twelve, and lastly upon its unveiling in Christ who was hid in God. A mystery of the ages, the eternally submerged church that was hidden until the last Pentecost is brought it into being by the Holy Spirit. Upon its entrance into the world, it became the source and substance of God's human divine government to span the church age.

Chapter Summary

1. Contemporary apostles must answer their calls with more than sermons, decrees, and demands.

2. Reinstatement of Christ's apostle calls for quality education and academics.

3. The absence of specialized apostolic tools and programs makes the above an imperative incumbent upon all apostles.

4. The society alive in Christ's day knew Him to transfer more than a religious title or spiritual ideal to His ecclesia.

5. Valid apostolism is patterned after eternity's prototype, the only thing the seven angels of the

church, which are the seven spirits before God's throne, upholds.

6. The seven angels of the New Creation church are the very spirits the Lord dispatched into all the earth. These uphold and govern the Lord's church according to His heavenly structure, protocrats, and guidelines.

Chapter Eight

The Apostle's Relevance

Chapter Discussions

Manifesting God's Truth by Our Fruit • Returning to True
Foundations • Comprehending What Advances God's
Kingdom • Apostles & Prophecy • Apostles Deliver
Apocalyptic Prophecy

I f asked the question, "What makes the apostle
relevant?"—what would your answer be? The world
and the church are all clamoring for the significance
that can only come from being relevant in life. When
it comes to the church, the pressure is on for it to
prove its relevance to its world. That is what this
chapter covers. It probes and answers the question of spiritual,
apostolic, and Christian relevance.

Relevance is a term that is rapidly becoming an indictment
against the modern and postmodern church. It speaks to

significance, weight, importance, consequence, and application. Relevance refers to being pertinent to a given subject or matter and germane to it existence or advancement. In relation to the discussion, web statistics, commentaries, sermons, literature, newspapers, magazines, and radio talk all pose the word as a question or criticism. "Is the Church relevant today?" Decide on the answer yourself with a little personal ministry exercise. Put present apostolic views, beliefs, and actions to the test with the synonyms for *relevance* and personally judge the present apostolic move's relevance, its germaneness to the world and the church. Apply the major elements and impact of known ministry works to their meanings and see if their fruit (outcomes) reflect a reliable grasp of world and societal affairs sufficiently enough to achieve Acts 26:18, a chief apostolic objective.

Manifesting God's Truth by Our Fruit

There was a time when parenthood's work was judged by the children raised. If a family of several children produced only one or no fruitful children while the rest were collectively scandalous or delinquent, the first place causes were was in the home. For a time, this practice may have been challenged as resentful parents resisted the notion that perhaps they could have done more, or less, for their children. Over time, though, decades of problematic youngsters filling courts and prisons forced society to rethink its lenience and so authorities became less inclined to relieve parents of all responsibility for their children's misconduct and mischief. If the Bible's position on natural affairs holds true, as is the natural so goes the spiritual and vice versa, questions concerning church relevance and its reasons for not being so has to look back to its prior leadership.

If the church's effectiveness is questioned today, then one must return to where society resorted for its answers to parental questions, home base. For Christianity, that home base would be the local church and its leadership the pastorate. If natural parents' work is brought under scrutiny for answers to why their children are delinquent, destructive, and counter effective in society, then in all fairness spiritual parents too must investigate any role they may have had in the church's current state of inconsequence today. It is, the only way the repentance that releases God's restoration can happen. The outcome of such introspective probing may supply the answers to the Church's relevance today and unveil some of the causes of its lapse into irrelevance.

Sadly mirroring the world's problems like for like, the New Testament church birthed just over three thousand years ago is rendered largely impotent and contemptuous in the eyes of non-Christians for the second time in its history. This time it is despised for its ineffectiveness in the world, completely different from the reasons earlier Christians were martyred. Herein lays the root of the problem. Unwittingly, the Church has fallen into the trap of professing godliness and denying its power. Despite vehement spiritual disavowals of preacher responsibility and denials of worldliness and carnality, the Church to solve its dilemmas is going to have to shoulder its share of blame for its societal anemia, at least as much as those it hopes to reach with the gospel.

The New Testament church is going to have to face the truth, and perhaps the fallout, about its labors, its fruit, and itself (see Romans 2:24). As the Godhead's mass representation in the world, Christians will have to accept that people today are not largely prospering from the gospel preached for decades. Their offspring are no better off, and in some cases are worse off for having been raised in God's house, and not all the blame can be placed on the devil. Ministers heretofore and those to come must begin to accept their share of the responsibility. If people are not impressed with Christianity it is because it has failed in their eyes to affect them where they need it most. In short, they have not seen captives set free. They have not experienced the blessings of the Holy Spirit, God's Spirit of truth by which captives are set free, and have been saturated with human doctrine. If there is no evident freedom for those outside of Christ who have earnestly tried to enter it, then it is sure that many in Christ are bound as well. Perhaps all this reflects the fruit of an inaccurate gospel preached.

Returning to True Foundations

Returning to God's truth begins with how or where the church of Jesus Christ lost its way on God's highway of righteousness. Hard questions are going to have to be asked by those tough enough to hear their answers. Serious seekers must be integrious and mature enough to consider fairly appraising the answers. Keeping one's head in the sand and refusing to see the pathetic state of the world that emerged under Christianity's dominance will not do. To once more win people's attention, affection, respect, and conversion, the Church will have to resolve to become relevant, and that takes realistic awareness of how it got where it is and how pop culture and world affairs point back to the ministry's ineffectiveness as it has been done to date. Church leaders and ministers are going to have to see their part in the sinister influx of paganism, witchcraft, and idolatry that has taken hold of every strata of society, even in the New Testament church over the last several decades. For example, how can a Christian support magic in any form, even under the guise of illusion? What on earth, or better yet in heaven is a Christ illusionist? To delude anyone requires deception, which means having him or her believe a lie. Second Thessalonians 2:11 and Revelation 21:27; 22:15 all condemn this. How then can Christians celebrate what the Lord Jesus clearly condemns? Jesus said, "I am the way, the truth and the

159

life." What can that statement mean but that His way is truth? Taking synonyms for illusion at face value (delusion, fantasy, and deception), how can Christian leaders promote the misleading sleights of illusion as representative of Jesus Christ? This is just one very troubling example of what is creeping into the body of Christ. Frank answers to concerns like these must be sought for how Christless nations and their gods invaded and overtook the Christian consciousness. Honestly looking at fashions, entertainment, legitimized immorality, and the ruthless business sectors that once pursued godliness, morality, and the fear of the Lord is the only place to begin. To sincerely work to displace the ancient deities resurfacing today in all industries and echelons of society with Jesus Christ and the message of the cross means igniting great change.

The Church is going to have to cease envying the world and stop Christianizing its demonism overlaying it with humanism. Christian identity must be restored and Christ's excellence shown to outstrip the dark carnality of the world. Nothing less than a word that inspires redemption can succeed in this hour. Old church versions under new veneers will not work; neither will new modifications of stale rhetoric get the job done. Today's church will not be replenished with pop theology, retrofitted doctrines, and linear ministry shifts. A back-step apostolic commission to advance to God's next place cannot make it happen, says Jeremiah 7:24 and 5:6. The converted apostle will not bring God's same life-changing power to the world that His commissioned ones will except they thoroughly abandon the old. Satan cannot and will not cast out Satan and so nothing belonging to him will restrain the darkness swiftly overrunning this world. The true apostolic commission must take God's family, world, and kingdom forward and not backward. Retrogression will only reenact God's most serious charge against His people uttered through His Old Testament prophets' mouths. His judgment will activate the former curses as He censures the nation that changes its god and turns to what can only hurt them.

Comprehending What Advances God's Kingdom

Kingdom advancement does not mean allegorical applications of obsolete moves and methods. The apostle's mandate is to manifest truth, multiply the Godhead's offspring, and enlarge Jesus Christ's kingdom. It is to manifest the powers of the age to come and equip Christ's bride for eternity. If today's apostles respond to world issues by returning to archaic molds and missions then once more it will fall into the grip of the old wine skin and wine it claims to replace, no matter how well remodeled or renovated its efforts. What drives apostles should stem from receiving answers from the Lord to pressing questions that ignite their commissions.

If apostolism today is to become relevant, it must answer these and more than a dozen critical questions concerning its initiatives. Indisputably, their answers must reflect what early church founders ploughed through at the beginning; what moved them to obey the Great Commission and go into all the world and make disciples of Jesus Christ. God's eternal wisdom and knowledge is how His Church achieves its relevance and accurately manifests the Godhead and its kingdom.

According to the pattern the Great Apostle left behind, those He commissions, aside from manifesting His truth to their generations, are to unseal the next collection of heaven's mysteries veiled in the scriptures. They are to propagate the next volume of biblical *apokalupsis* assigned to their eras and be occupied with recovering, restoring, and reinstating the sovereign preeminence of the Lord Jesus Christ as head of the Church and Lord of the world. The only thing to rival these ongoing apostolic mandates is today's apostles confusing their subsequent missions with their divine commission, promoting isolated methods to assimilate apostolism in the world rather than disciple it to Christ.

Apostles & Prophecy

The single resource that upholds the church is prophecy. That is God's voice actively and continually communicating His will, thoughts, and actions to the world. The church, according to Joel's prophecy fulfilled on Pentecost is God's lone prophecy center of truth in the world. The head quality controller of its divine communications network is the apostle. Frequently, you hear apostles say, "I am not a prophet, or I don't really prophesy, but I just tell people what the Lord says." First, there is no better explanation of prophecy than "I just tell people what the Lord says." Secondly, for the apostle to fulfill the range of duties attached to the call, especially apostles of a new move, prophecy is inescapable. What the Lord is doing with them, how He sent them to execute His will, and the distinct way the apostle affects the church and the world according to God's plan are all confined to His revelatory sphere until they are uttered in this world.

To be heard, apostles are inseminated with the message of their commissions and are generally the first to hear the changes God is about to make and how He will accomplish these in their generation. That alone makes them the prime candidates for saying them to the world. Consider Jesus' words to the world when He was dispatched to Israel. He started with a stunning prophetic statement: "The kingdom of heaven is at hand." For us today it is old news, but to those that heard Him at that time, it was ominous. The kingdom of heaven is at hand? Why, it is invisible, it is eternal, and it is greater than this world—how can it be a hand or near? Yet that is what Christ said, it is the single statement that catapulted His ministry. All this is to say that apostles launch their ministries usually with prophecy. It may not be with the personalized prophecies today's Church has grown accustomed to, but it is with prophecy nonetheless.

What apostles prophesy is God's actions during their ministries. Usually these are presented as imminent fulfillments of those of the Old Testament. For an apostle to recognize how God is doing a new thing is the prophetic test of the commission. The word for the distinct type of prophecy apostles are specially known for is *apocalyptic*. That is a technical term for *revelatory*. Apostles are as a force world impacting. They more than gather a following; they marshal heaven's forces before doing so to prepare the planet for what the Lord sent them to do. If you will recall Jesus' and the apostles' ministries were marked by high celestial events where angels assigned to work with the apostle step into humanity's theatre of life.

To assure they are heard by those affected by what is happening behind the scenes on earth, apostles voice the portion of God's word that best annunciates what they are sent to do. They begin with how the very things that frustrated His work and hindered His hand in human affairs gained control of society again. The apostle, endowed with exceptional wisdom and revelatory insight, links God's historical conflicts and conquests in scripture with what He faces and is poised to resolve through their ministries. These are triggered by revelations of divine judgment, world power shifts, and end time signals. They join long-standing promises of relief for the chosen and oppressed and restoration for those victimized by the world's overbearing callous humanists. Apostles realign the planet during their seasons of kingdom occupancy no matter how short that period may be.

Apostles Deliver Apocalyptic Prophecy

The gospels are saturated with the apocalyptic words of our Great Apostle, the Lord Jesus Christ. Remaining faithful to them, He foretells the end times and how His Father's will and visions are accomplished. Humanity will grow worse, despite His ushering its new age of the Creator's light and life. People will continue to turn on God's people for their righteousness and the powers of darkness will intensify their attack on humanity. God's name and character sustain relentless persecution because His truth is routinely buried beneath the will of the flesh. Dysfunctional families and doomed marriages usurp His destinies for people's lives and the Holy Spirit's presence in the planet effectively empowers it, all just as His Father foreordained.

Apostles are persuaded that regardless of what the darkness does, God will continue injecting His light into the earth and establishing Himself and His reign in people's souls. Christ's kingdom will explode as the one that shall never die and while it will cost some fervent worshippers their lives to learn, that after death it. Basically, that is how the Savior foretold the coming world events. Later when He reappeared to John on Patmos, He defined and enlarged these saying so they would become the property of His apostles and Church. The entire Revelation is no more than an extensive prophecy that covers the world and its end times. For apostles to say that they do not prophesy or are not prophets is for them to be out of touch with the expansiveness of their mantles.

Revealing God's mind, deeds, and predeterminations is what apostles are called to do as they communicate their message. It continues to show God's long history of working His will in and through people. Apostles must receive a potent revelation on what the Father said to the prophets of old and what Jesus delivered to John personally to mark humanity's race toward the end of the world. As the world grows more technological and its citizens more devious, prophecy is a critical piece of the apostle's foundational architecture. That apostles prophesy and must do so is seen in Revelation 10:11: "*And he said unto me, Thou must prophesy again before many peoples, and nations, and tongues, and kings.*"

The word *again* that is used in the verse suggests a continual action reflective of a fan's oscillation. The Apostle John must repeatedly tell the world what His Savior says. He must reiterate his prophecies incessantly the Lord's end of the world calendar to mobilize its advance to the Almighty's destined future. In doing so, he moves the world toward its destiny and renews God's will in their eras. Here is why the book urges, admonishes its readers to read and keep. The Revelation must be constantly read, taught, and applied in every era until the end. If no other minister of the new creation church understands this, the apostle does. One most efficient way of doing this is for the apostle to write the prophecies. That is precisely what John does, attaching a warning and an incentive to them. Those that read, keep, and propagate it are blessed; those that do not are cursed. Revelation 1:3 starts the action: "*Blessed is he that readeth, and they that hear the words of this prophecy, and keep those things which are written therein: for the time is at hand.*" Revelation 22:19, 20 adds, "*And if any man shall take away from the words of the book of this prophecy, God shall take away his part out of the book of life, and out of the holy city, and from the things which are written in this book. He which testifieth these things saith, Surely, I come quickly. Amen. Even so, come, Lord Jesus.*"

The messages and prophecies about end times, judgments, and calamitous world events, along with those of church dominance and kingdom supremacy, were written in the New Testament by apostles and not prophets. Perhaps the apostle may not know the answers to life's mundane affairs and people's everyday lives, but they should know about God's apocalyptic plans for it all time.

Chapter Summary

1. Apostles are what make Christ's church relevant.

2. As with natural parents, spiritual parents, church leaders, and teachers too must be responsible for Christianity's irrelevance and contempt in the world.

3. Christians must recognize what God calls and decrees is sin, like magic and illusion. The Lord Jesus and His faith must be sanctified.

4. Apostles manifesting God's whole truth are the only sure way to purge the world.

5. Apostles cannot help but prophesy.

6. New Testament prophecy came from apostles and not prophets.

7. John, Peter, Paul and Jesus were all apostles and they all prophesied; else how could the church have God's futuristic word today?

Chapter Nine

The Apostle & the Priestly

Chapter Discussions

From Confession to Profession • From Glory to Glory, Says the Apostle • Apostles of a New Move • The Purpose of God's Ministry Dispensations • Apostolic Service Summarized • Apostleship & Revival • Apostleship, Melchizedek, & the Priesthood • The Character of Priestly Service • Priesthoods Not Strange to Moses or Israel • The Church's Struggle with True Priestly Service • The Spirit of a Priesthood • Priests Were High Level Functionaries • Comparing the New Creation Priesthood of Jesus Christ • Malachi 2:7 & the Priesthood • Seven Kingdom Conditions Apostles Treat in Office

T his chapter emphasizes a little recognized aspect of apostleship. It covers its priestly connection, and official meanings that distinguish the office and wisdom of positive apostolic interrelations. Apostles are called to order, structure, and govern the Church. They mediate its interrelations with Jesus Christ and His body similar to the pattern the early priests used. The apostle John well understood how this came to be. He wrote in his gospel his understanding, *"That which we have seen and heard declare we unto you, that ye also may have fellowship with us: and truly our fellowship is with the Father, and with his Son Jesus Christ"* (I John 1:3). Paul in Romans 1:11 shows his grasp of this aspect of the office's duty in divulging that what he delivered to the church transcended sheer theology and religion: *"For I long to see you, that I may impart unto you some spiritual gift, to the end ye may be established."* The whole of Hebrew's priestly recollections are transferred to the church, including its officiations that are not applied to the heavens. The same Levitical preparations that were performed by the ancient priests on animals are now spiritually accomplished by God's word on souls and hearts of the redeemed. Life for like, act for act, they mirror each activity perfectly.

The apostles' unique fellowship, *koinonia* in the Greek, with the Father and His Son Jesus Christ, is the centricity of the mantle's entire work. It is empowering, impartational, and solidifying to explain why many of today's Christians are unstable and flighty. The absence of apostleship in their development is tantamount to a child being raised by teenage parents. Basic care may be rendered with attention and provisions given, but what nurtures and unlocks the child's wisdom and insight are lacking because these are acquired and transmitted after life has been lived. Parents cannot give their children what they never received no matter how much they love them and yearn to do so. It is the same with the pastor and nurtured Christian that is locked in a strictly evangelical world. Fundamental lessons are taught, Bible knowledge delivered, and the rudiments of the faith explained, but invariably Hebrews 5:11-6:3 are the result, what we have today.

The apostle's capacity to kindle true fellowship between the Lord and His people speaks to mediation that distinguishes itself by restoring relations between Him and wayward worshippers. Encounters with true apostles challenge the doubtful, heal and revive the fainthearted, and buttress the faith of the disillusioned. They inspire trust and renew waning reverence for the Lord. Apostles induce concentrated Bible study because of their normally superior scripture wisdom and insight; challenging believers to revisit God's truth. They, through this mechanism, encourage repentance to release God's promised forgiveness. These are what Acts 26:18 has in mind and what the Lord Jesus infers in Matthew 10:11-13: *"And into whatsoever city or town ye shall enter, inquire who in it is worthy; and there abide till ye go thence. And when ye come into an house, salute it. And if the house be worthy, let your peace come upon it: but if it be not worthy, let your peace return to you."* What a statement for the Lord to make. In it, He grants His apostles the privilege of embodying a commutable peace that may be sent forth or even more amazingly, retracted from those that refuse it. Such a potent though intangible quality suggests much about the inimitable side of the apostle's authority.

From Confession to Profession

The object of this discussion is seen in Hebrews 8:1-6. It discusses Christ as the High Priest whom Hebrews 3:1 also identifies as the Great Apostle and High Priest of our profession. From it, much may be understood about the spiritualities of apostleship ordinarily overlooked when the office is explained in favor of its more carnal elements:

> *"Now of the things which we have spoken this is the sum: We have such an high priest, who is set on the right hand of the throne of the Majesty in the heavens; A minister of the sanctuary, and of the true tabernacle, which the Lord pitched, and not man.* **For every high priest is ordained** *to offer gifts and sacrifices: wherefore it is of necessity that this man have somewhat also to offer. For if he were on earth, he should*

not be a priest, seeing that there are priests that offer gifts according to the law: Who serve unto **the example and shadow of heavenly things**, *as Moses was admonished of God when he was about to make the tabernacle: for see, saith he, that thou make all things according to the pattern showed to thee in the mount. But now hath he obtained a more excellent ministry, by how much also he is the* **mediator** *of a better covenant, which was established upon better promises."*
Hebrews 8:1-6

If Jesus meant what He said when He declared in John 20:21 that as His Father sent His, even so (implying likewise) that He sent His apostles (presumably to do the same thing), then the above passage offers great insight on the intangibles of the apostle's mantle. These verses materialize unseen often, imperceptible activities that should outweigh natural ones. Hebrews 8:1-6 rationalizes Paul's language, as do Romans 15:27 and 1 Corinthians 9:11. Thus, the case is made for the apostle's priestly duties in ministry. See Romans 15:16 for how well Paul articulates it as a pattern for succeeding apostles to follow. The confession-profession tie presented in Hebrews 3:1, the underlying theme of this chapter, is only eclipsed by the subtle tie between apostleship and the priestly, its dominant one.

From Glory to Glory, Says the Apostle

The apostle's call is to lift the members of God's new creation church up to their God-ordained level of interaction with the Creator's celestial and heavenly beings. Apostles resist the temptation to negate the reality that everything about the New Testament saint is to accomplish Ephesians 3:10. However, in the true apostle's mind, the Church's seat in heavenly places along with Peter's receipt of its kingdom keys epitomize what the Lord sends them to do for Him. The Christian is no longer a citizen of this world but of heaven.

170

As an immortal being, the Spirit-filled saint is now a member of the Father's family of human divines constructed like His Son, which is why Jesus took upon Himself flesh in the first place. He did so to authorize divinity to occupy humanity legally and enable humanity to be elevated from the dregs of mortality. These key truths are integral to all apostles' temperaments dictating how they execute their ministries. Their mindset is that believers actually reside in the heavens where Christ is seated on the throne at His Father's right hand. What born again Christians—those born of God from above— obtain and fulfill are the direct result of their heavenly standing and divine stature as members of the Godhead. Jesus implies this in His response to the rich young ruler that wanted eternal life the worldly way. He told him that if he sold all he had he would have treasure in the heavens that was impervious to theft and deterioration. To a person who had amassed great wealth on earth, Christ's words were agonizing and inane. The rich young ruler certainly thought so because he could only see life according to this world. Any idea of another one being better than his or enriching him more than what the earth could give was just plain preposterous to them. Still the Savior maintains that all we cherish in this world is pitifully inferior to His, but one has to become a citizen of heaven to discover it. Paul contributes the following insight to the subject from 1 Corinthians 5:1-4:

> *"For we know that if our earthly house of this tabernacle were dissolved, we have a building of God, a house not made with hands,* **eternal in the heavens.** *For in this we groan, earnestly desiring to be clothed upon with our house which is* **from heaven:** *If so be that being clothed we shall not be found naked. For we that are in this tabernacle do groan, being burdened: not for that we would be unclothed, but*

171

clothed upon, that mortality might be swallowed up of life."

Apostles of a New Move

The ongoing goals of apostleship entail restoration, catechism, governance, revived worship, and holiness. They are all fundaments of the apostle's work to transform God's infant children into His mature sons and daughters. Together they infer apostleship brings about the Christ's Melchizedek mandate on God's New Creation priesthood. Here the extraordinary union between the apostle and the priestly surfaces their heavenly marriage of ecclesiastics and divinity, both of which are essential to purposeful apostolism. According to one reference source, the apostle is a mediator of Christ's new covenant mysteries and revelations. Mediation is a common theological term that immediately calls to mind the priestly.

Christian ministry, for the above reasons, began solely with the apostolic commission of Jesus Christ, providing later apostles no better model after which to pattern their ministries. He establishes the "new move[16]" apostle's comprehensive commission. Jesus as a prototypical, new-move apostle began as His own messenger. His apostleship required He serve as His own prophet, until those He converted were established. In line with scripture, He knew this to be according to the prophecies concerning Him. Deuteronomy 18:25 foretold of this moment in His life in Moses' prophecy about the Great Prophet that was to come.

---

[16] **Note**: Some apostles are called to attach themselves to those that found more than buildings and enterprises. New Move apostles are catalytic change agents that spark shifts in God's kingdom with a new word, deeper wisdom, profound revelatory doctrine, and usually displacement of the status quo. With this type of apostle, the message rather then the methods distinguishes the "new move" apostle from his or her later attaches.

Beyond this, to ignite His commission, the Lord came as the first herald of Yahweh's good news. True to His word, the Almighty performed the prophecies He spoke through Isaiah. Jesus' evangelical word was bold and uncommon: "The kingdom of heaven has come near you; repent and believe the gospel—God's good message." In doing so, He recalled the pathway that John the Baptist had paved for Him. The Messiah in this context served as His own new move's evangelist and because Israel had no shepherds of His move, He pastored them too. As the mediator of the New Covenant, the Lord's apostleship instructed God's impending ecclesia in His eternal ways. In His diverse functions, the Lord Jesus occupied and executed the entire five-fold ministry, classically depicting what constitutes the Bible's New Move Apostolic Commission in meaning and mission. The Great Apostle's foundations and actions establish His true Church more inescapably more apostolic than anything else does. Due to the nature of His work and its origins, Jesus is established in scripture as the Great Apostle. He is the first apostle of the Gospel of the New Birth, and according to Hebrews 3:1 the first professional minister to exercise its ministries.

Based on these unquestionable truths, to claim personal prerogatives over one's ministry gifts and calling received from the Lord is errant and perhaps reckless because it presumes Christ as an incidental party to the venture. Those doing so are in danger of treating Him as no more than a marketable commodity in what they are called to do. To prevent this trap, those ministers that come behind Him in any way, regardless of the offices, must remember they are the called *by heaven's Sent One*. Although it has been said that the New Testament church is prophetic, it is actually both apostolic and prophetic. More accurately, because of the work the Lord Jesus initiated, His Church is to remain within the framework of 1 Corinthians 12:28,29 and Ephesians 4:11. Its use of the phrases "gave some," or "gave some to be," relate to modern usage of ordained or appointed. They refer to the following:

- ◆ Apostles
- ◆ Prophets
- ◆ Evangelists
- ◆ Pastors
- ◆ Teachers

That makes the church structured administratively as follows:

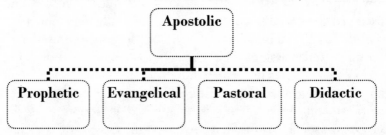

All these appellations aptly identify the New Testament Church, designating it accurately a comprehensively five-fold Church. Consequently, all the officers, operations, and authorities belong to Jesus Christ and exist solely to execute His apostolic mandate in the earth. Do not get confused by the above chart and think that it presents the headship of the Church, because it does not. That order looks entirely different and does more to establish the apostle as God's head. These are shown in 1 Corinthians 12:28, 29 as the fundamental headship of the Church:

The above chart depicts not only the headship of the church, but reiterates the apostle as first in the line of God's leaders and administrators. It further shows the stages and streams of the minister dispensation.

Classic Definitions of a Minister

A minister was viewed quite differently during the Bible's formative eras than today. More definite than what today's democratic church would want to classify its ministers, the word to the early church referred to:

1. A person authorized to conduct religious worship.

2. A pastor or other clergy

3. A person appointed to a high office in submission to another; ranks below ambassador.

4. The job of a head of a government department

Key Synonyms for Minister:

In addition to the agent and ambassador terms used below, synonyms for minister also mean, anointed, apostolic legate, attaché consul, divine ecclesiastic, elder, legislator, magistrate, messenger, minister of state, officiate, preacher, priest, servant of God, shepherd, supervisor.

Seeing every entity birthed by a divine being as the injection of a new kingdom and thus government in the earth, those that represented their progenitor deities were seen as agents of both worlds. On the one hand, the minister served his or her deity as an agent of the other world. On the hand, the minister functioned as an official intermediary between the two worlds assuring the citizens of the god's territory learned, understood, and obeyed their celestial monarch.

Below are some of the terms that were applied to this responsibility. After reading them, observe how well they establish the work, duties, scope, and influence a minister hand before secularism ruled.

The Title **Minister** Encompasses the Following Synonyms

Dean	Agent	Aide
Ambassador	Envoy	Diplomat
Executive	Official	Plenipotentiary
Premier	Prime Minister	Chief of State
Governmental Head	Chancellor	Administrator
Steward	Governor	Judge
Leader	Overseer	President
Negotiator	Operator	Operative
Subsidy	Consul	Priest
Shepherd	Lecturer	Missionary
Ecclesiastic	Delegate	Official
Statesman	Legate	Chairman
Emissary	Commissioner	Functionary
Servant	Captain	Commander

Twenty-five terms express what earlier eras understood to be a minister. The words listed above shed light on the authority inherent in the offices people enter upon being installed in God's service. It is difficult to overlook in the list the common thread of secular titles that it contains. The question is, in comparison to traditional theology, what really classifies as a minister? This is because in ancient times there was no division between the sacred and the secular. A minister always began as an agent of the god of the land, a go between that handled his or her affairs and mediated relations between the divine world and its secular satellite (earth). If you studied each word carefully, you will see every sphere of official service is represented, from the leader to the executive, from the official to the authority figure. Government, religion and foreign affairs all characterize the spheres of ministry. The words above show the title minister originated in the sphere of the divine initiated and established by celestial beings. Its service was understood as being first and foremost to the divine ones. That is before the earth turned to secularism. Nonetheless, in ancient times, having a ministry is impossible apart from a government.

A commonly accepted definition of the word minister is, "an official ranking just below the status of the diplomat; one politically appointed as the head of a ministry within a government."[17] Historically, officials representing their countries abroad were termed *ministers*. However, this term was also applied to diplomats of the second rank. Together they explain the logical reason for attaching governmental inferences to the work of minister as seen in the following definition:

---

[17] The Diplomats Dictionary

> "A minister is a true diplomat (not merely consular) accredited by one sovereign state to another who ranks below an ambassador."
> *Dictionary.com*

Ambassadors[18] are ministers of the highest rank, with plenipotentiary authority to represent **their head of state**. The term plenipotentiary comes from the Latin, *plenus* and *potens*. Together they define an agent deputized with 'full power' to act on behalf of a sovereign sender as representative. Plenipotentiary refers to a person with "full powers" to act in another's stead or on their behalf. The word commonly refers to a diplomat or ambassador fully authorized to represent their government as a *minister* in an assigned ministry.

A *ministry* is a department of a government. It defines all those appointed as ministers under the leadership of a prime minister in or out of a cabinet. A cabinet, for the sake of definition, is a body of high ranking government officials that represent the executive branch of a government. Cabinet members' duties and influence range from policymaking, tactics, and legislation to advisory council to the head of state. Those occupying cabinet positions are typically given the title of <u>minister</u> that seems to be akin to a secretary in many countries.

From these explanations, it is clear that a minister cannot exist apart from a government's authorization. In addition, the above meanings establish that the idea of casual and freelance ministries on behalf of a deity or sovereign were virtually unheard of in Christ's day. Ministers were representatives; they represented their governments and their gods. This information alone disturbs if not undoes traditional thoughts and theology on the subject of individual ministries. Among all

---

[18] Discussed at length later in the text

178

the inferences to be derived from the above, one glaring fact stands out, ministers must be appointed by a sovereign authority to fit the classic definitions of the word. Furthermore, ministers must have an organization that backs them and authorizes their intrusion and actions into people's lives. Without a legitimate entity to authorize the minister, those practicing "their" ministries are devoid of legitimacy, and are acting on their own without dispatch or delegation by a higher power. This truth is born out by the Lord Jesus in John 7:18 and 13:16. Both passages say that servants must be *sent* and that servants elevated to the status of minister must have an authorizing entity to which they answer that fills the vital role of a principal that is essential to a minister's influence.

That ministers are officers of Christ's church a legal entity recognized by any society's government is to be seen in the following:

An Officer is:

1. One who holds an office.

2. A person lawfully invested with an office, whether civil, military, or ecclesiastical.

3. Any person who holds a position of authority or command.

4. Someone who is appointed or elected to an office and who holds a position of trust, officeholder

5. A member of a force; authorized to serve in a position of authority in direct charge or command as an officer

Try as we might, the church would have to go all the way back to the root origin of official words and purge all language's vocabulary and application of them to achieve its goal of eliminating words like *office, authority* and *titles* from its **minister** definitions. Of course, that being impossible, its next prudent course of action should be to do what our somewhat successful secular counterparts have done. We shall reevaluate each word's purpose and intent in the context it was originally employed. Afterward, we analyze and refine their functions and applications to correct any deficiencies that surface in the process. Lastly, apostles should restructure the church according to what the Lord has in mind. Such a process would not only be prudent it would be responsible and intelligent, worthy of apostles' and ministers' much craved respect as well.

Officers, Agents & Agencies

Officers are assigned to agencies that employ agents to conduct the duties of an agency by meeting the demands that render agency services effective in their principal's public business. Agents represent their principal's in:

1. Their principal's agenda

2. Offerings, services, alliance, and collaborative negotiations

3. Presenting and clarifying their principal's views

4. Authoritatively persuading their hosts to cooperate with and accommodate their principal's vision, plans, needs, desires and strategies.

5. Pursue and achieve their principal's objectives, interests, aspirations, interests, and results

What range of abilities, skills, beliefs, and attitudes do the above five duties and responsibilities involve? Here is a summary list of the most important ones below:

180

Ministers are public servants that handle the civil affairs of their governments. The word for the authorization a minister receives to fulfill the office is called *ordination*. It is, "The process by which those called to Christian service are authorized to perform religious rites and services. The ordination process is governed by the laws and procedures of the ecclesiastical body overseeing the appointment, and the ordaining entity. Being ordained is often a prerequisite specified by many states in order to officiate in certain functions. Sometimes ordination grants a license or other official papers to certify the minister is empowered to act on behalf of the church or ministry he or she represents. The operative word here is 'represents.' A few ecclesiastical authorities traditionally typically require ordination to perform certain rites, ceremonies, and observances. These include weddings, funerals, and baptisms. Other churches add christenings and communion as well as leadership and catechism in their license or ordination requirements. Ministers preach, teach, lead, administrate, and overall preside over their assignments as appointed by the church.

Another reference that ties apostleship to an office as used in the New Testament in addition to Romans 11:13 is Hebrews 8:2, where the type of minister Jesus is classified as in the New Creation Sanctuary is meant. The word *minister* in these passages is *leitourgos*, the very word Paul uses for his office of apostleship. Prototypically, it first identifies our Savior's ministry in eternity before it names His apostles on earth. The apostle, for instance, from Paul's inferences, is a *leitourgos* minister according to the Romans reference; Paul clearly understands this to be the type of minister his apostleship makes him.

181

A leitourgos minister goes beyond our traditional knowledge of the term's common variant, liturgy. According to scripture, it encompasses political, civil, social, and religious service to one's god or country. That the term is applied to the Lord Jesus Christ subtly suggests that His ecclesia is more than a congregation, an assembly, or even a church, as we know it. To God, the church is His kingdom, a mainly abstract concept to most of contemporary Christendom. Yet that is precisely the mien the Lord's gospel seeks to convey. Nowhere does it show up more vividly than in 1 Peter 2:9 where he designates the Redeemer's New Creation as a race, a generation, and a nation. Attaching his words to the Lord's brand of apostleship as an office, Peter's epistle shows the typical apostle's polity is God's everlasting nation. In our case, it describes the Lord's community of people in his first epistle. His understanding explains the basis upon which the apostle Paul uses the term in Romans 15:16: *"That I should be the minister (leitourgos) of Jesus Christ to the Gentiles, ministering the gospel of God that the offering up of the Gentiles might be acceptable, being sanctified by the Holy Ghost."*

Spiritual Applications for the Apostle's Ministry

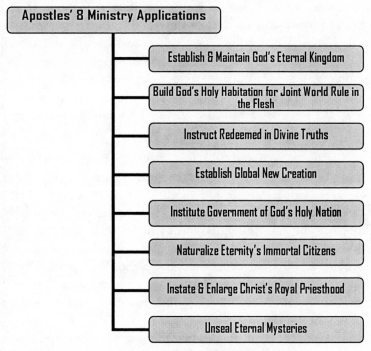

Apostles' 8 Ministry Applications

- Establish & Maintain God's Eternal Kingdom
- Build God's Holy Habitation for Joint World Rule in the Flesh
- Instruct Redeemed in Divine Truths
- Establish Global New Creation
- Institute Government of God's Holy Nation
- Naturalize Eternity's Immortal Citizens
- Instate & Enlarge Christ's Royal Priesthood
- Unseal Eternal Mysteries

The Purpose of God's Ministry Dispensations

The Bible is quite emphatic about the purposes of God's ministry dispensations. Regardless of their diversity, they share one singular end, to raise up priests that establish and express the Creator's original intent for humanity, its multiplication, and manifestation of His holiness. Look at its most concrete reason as spoken to the world from Leviticus, the book of the Priesthood: "*That you may distinguish between holy and unholy and between unclean and unclean, and that you may teach the children of Israel all the statutes which the Lord has spoken them by the hand of Moses*" (Leviticus 11:10). Enabling the Church's distinguishing faculties to know the difference between the holy and unholy, the godly and ungodly, priests are to teach others the predominate aims for the Holy Spirit's dispensations. Apostles as His sent ones are obligated to it. Abraham recognized this in Genesis 18:18, 19 as did Moses who served not only as the Lord's speaker, but also as His legislator, prophetic teacher, and inaugurating priest too. Moses, after leading Israel out of Egypt, began the unending and arduous task of educating them in the ways and will of the Almighty. As said earlier, Moses prefigured the apostle demonstrated by God giving him His Law and His Living Oracles.

Moses as an accepted Old Testament apostolic shadow was to teach God's people His word and why His is the only truth in creation. Uppermost in God's mind was His nation's ability to distinguish what He designated as holy from the unholy cultures of their day, as stated in Leviticus 10:10. Jehovah's call on Moses' life included his teaching Israel God's word so that others would do the same over the nation's lifetime. Down through the ages, Ezra captures this mandate and commits himself to it in Ezra 7:10. In this respect, God feels His servants are the only ones (by virtue of salvation, redemption, eternal covenant, and the indwelling Holy Spirit) spiritually capable of precisely declaring in His name what is spiritually clean and unclean according to Creator standards (refer to Isaiah 43:1-12 and 44:8).

Apostolic Service Summarized

Christ's ministers, to serve the Lord as He needs, must embed His qualifications in their understanding, and convey them to those they serve. In agreement with these two requisites for approved apostolic ministry service is spiritual sanctification, what the Lord sees as elementary to serving Him. Deuteronomy 4:8, 9 says why. Essentially, it sums up God's goal of disseminating His word and its product to commissioned apostles. With it, they are in turn to apostle souls out of darkness and sin. God's officers need in ministry to grasp intimately just, what makes them a discrete class of officers in God's kingdom. It is their capacity for doing what nothing else in the world can do that detaches them from the priestly staff of every other deity in creation. That is how they disconnect a sinner from his or her sin and initiate the sanctifying program that extracts sin from sinners' souls. Of all the ministers mentioned in Ephesians 4:11, the apostle is the most highly charged and endowed for this work.

Aside from the holy and unholy distinction, God's apostles have some extensive mandates to accomplish for Him to bring about His ultimate aim of people receiving His eternal life. God's primary ministry objective comes from Romans 15:16. It is to bring the members of Christ's body into His own personal holiness and purity. Apostles perform this directive by wisely manifesting God's truth; what Jeremiah 23 says produces understanding promptly accompanied by obedience to Him. Only from these come the dynamic communion and fellowship with the Godhead through Jesus Christ, that catapults believers into their heavenly station. Last but not least is the conversion to Christ's way of thinking, living, and conformance to His image that assures the soul's salvation according to Hebrews 10:39 and 1 Peter 1:9. These evidence the Godhead in all walks of life. In this process, God continuously attends and responds to our prayers and favorably grants our petitions. These reasons clarify His word's power and truth, and show how the forces performing the knowledge and wisdom are imparted to His servants and set the apostle above the rest. True apostles learn God's truth intricately as their chief ministry readiness lesson; obedience is second. Apostleship thrives on revealing truth, says Paul in 2 Corinthians 4:2.

The consummate work of apostleship is *manifestation of truth.* Apostles initiating a new move apart from His truth are not God's apostles. Genuine apostles have an edict to return the

Church to the authority of canonized scripture because it is rooted in creation's systems and infrastructure. Apostles' government allows creation's custody and maintenance of God's world. They, like the scriptures, are driven by eternal and immutable purposes and objectives. Apostles that emphasize a move without an emphatic word from the Lord or a direct commission from Him are not His apostles; apostolism is birthed from, and breeds, God's truth. It authorizes the assignment to gather those who would return to it. Here is why the Lord Jesus Christ's dispatch to earth qualified Him as God's only truth, way, and life.

Apostleship & Revival

Ordinarily, the truth of apostolism as Christ designed it is divinely founded on revival of the eternal God's word, not church tenets, or tradition. Apostolism does not seek to extend denominational mandates bur rather arises in its place as a remedy to a drastic, often heinous event that occurred in the camp of the righteous. That event was a defection to the world and its ways that thoroughly obscures the true God in the eyes of His disciples is that event that Isaiah 5:20-23 describes as the state of the Church. The cultures of the earth have invaded the New Creation's ecclesiastical spheres. To restore things to Himself, God reopens the way of salvation en masse, rather than just to a cloistered few by igniting a sweeping apostolic move. His aim includes returning pure worship and service to His household, along with reestablishing the priestly consciousness of His ministers and members. Both are vital to any revival God sparks in the land. Apostles who have been thusly groomed by the Lord understand the place and role of a sanctified, consecrated priesthood among the deity's believers. It is part in a global apostolic plan that is especially critical to their redemptive service to the Almighty.

Creator God installed His own devoted priesthood after Moses delivered Israel to Him in the wilderness of Sinai. It turned out to be the temporal prototype of what Melchizedek initiated with Abraham centuries earlier.

Apostleship, Melchizedek, & the Priesthood

Here forms the basis of this chapter's relevance to the Hebrews 3:1 passage introduced previously. It links Christ's apostleship to the Most High's perpetual orders of priesthoods. Understanding the rationale of priesthoods helps to cultivate an appreciation of the church, its ministers, and most especially apostleship.

Earthly priesthoods go all the way back to the time that Adam and his sons were to bring offerings and sacrifices to the Lord God after their fall. One would think the premise for priestly ministry today springs solely from that, but its origins really go back to eternity. That is why Jehovah already had His earthly priestly institution in place to bring Abraham into covenant with Himself; namely, Melchizedek's Priesthood. Perpetual negotiations fostering spiritual powers and earthly provisions are bound to the work and devotions of priesthood. Since the agents and citizens of God's invisible world have their boundaries when it comes to acting or interacting with our world and humanity, superseding means of overriding the normal course of earthly affairs is required. To transcend those boundaries a whole system of mediation was devised for the priesthood (ministry) that is what Melchizedek paved the way for in ancient Jerusalem.

Melchizedek was the priest-king of ancient Salem, as revealed in Genesis 14. Presented casually as if every reader knew precisely who the writer was talking about and what he intended by exposing this ordinarily enigmatic character of history to the world, this king of righteousness appears in scripture several times. He shows up twice in the Old Testament: Genesis 14:18 and Psalm 110:4. By comparison, this priest-king is mentioned nine times in the New Testament, all of which are in the book of Hebrews that devotes an entire chapter to his history. It forges the Church's connection to the priest-king. The brilliant writer of Hebrews ties it all together; the Melchizedek of long ago is the Almighty's prototype of His eternal priestly institution stationed on earth. Besides providing the fundamental pattern for the Levitical Priesthood under Aaron, he is disclosed as the eternal provision of priestly service for the New Testament Ecclesia. It served the Lord long before earth came into existence.

Going back to the writer of Genesis' casual mention of Melchizedek as a significant priest-king of the ancient world in Genesis 14, one reason for Moses, the book's author's unassuming introduction of the man is that priest-kings, *ensis* as they were called at the time, were commonplace. They were human designates installed by deities entering or conquering a land to rule it. Ensis were the human embodiment of their authorizing God that governed their territories in their stead. Much of the world then was settled as city-states. Often they were simply villages whose communal life centered on the god's temple in its midst, venerated much as today's societies esteem their state's capitol cities. There was a good amount of empires that threatened to absorb them. That made it appealing to appease the most powerful deity one could find to protect the land. When that happened, a human ruler exercised secular and sacred authority at once. It was simplistic and efficient for small, disconnected areas. The task of an ensi was to establish and/or convert a populace to the deity that possessed or took over the land. This priestly monarch's duty was to protect it from marauding invaders by a potent connection between the god and its people (see Psalm 122:1-6 and Ezekiel 43:7).

188

Based on the preceding, the title priest-king perfectly fit Melchizedek and his God-assigned purpose for being in the planet because all life back then revolved around deities. It was virtually impossible for a human to see himself or herself as godless; the concept of atheism was practically unthinkable and those that claimed it kept it to themselves. Ancient villagers and antiquitous leaders considered being without a god a curse. That is what Jesus had in mind when He stated John 14:18. The word the King James Version renders *comfortless* actually means parentless or fatherless. To be without a god was to signify that no deity wanted responsibility for a person's existence or security in life because he or she had so offended the deity (or the divine realm) to the point of being evicted from a divine family, as was the case with Cain. It could also be because the person merely rejected the notion of being accountable to any deity. In short, atheism could never have flourished in humanity's formative years. The angels and demons were too prevalent, powerful ruthless and immediate for such a belief to successfully flourish. Consequently, just as people today would not consider themselves blessed to be literal orphans, so too those of Abram's time and before would see themselves as damned if they were godless. That independence came later.

In the ancient world, it was a foregone conclusion that the chief priest in the land was its monarch and that he or she was begotten of the god to officiate the altar where he or she is to render priestly officiations to their god. On that ground, those chosen to represent their territorial deities before the people were called priests, carrying the title of 'priest of the god....'".

The Character of Priestly Service

Priestly service back then took precedence over secular functions simply because the single most important absorption for all citizens was to see that the deity in whose land he or she dwelt was appeased to guarantee success, prosperity, and

189

longevity. Hence, when God covenanted with Abraham, He promised Him long life, world acclaim, and a multitude of descendants to perpetuate his linage. To both the Lord and the man He chose, posterity was indispensable to the plan. How else could a man become a family, his family mushroom into a tribe, a tribe multiply into a village, and a cluster of villages became a city stronghold for the Lord? Moreover, priests were revered as the first line of defense against tribal or national disaster and when anything calamitous occurred, it was to them that leaders resorted for answers.

Here is a Bible example of this truth:

> *"Wherefore they spake to the king of Assyria, saying, The nations which thou hast removed, and placed in the cities of Samaria, know not the manner of the God of the land: therefore he hath sent lions among them, and, behold, they slay them, because they know not the manner of the God of the land. Then the king of Assyria commanded, saying, Carry thither one of the priests whom ye brought from thence; and let them go and dwell there, and let him teach them the manner of the God of the land"* (2 Kings 17:26, 27). Add to this wisdom the insight of the prophet Micah: *"For all people will walk every one in the name of his god, and we will walk in the name of the LORD our God for ever and ever"* (Micah 4:5).

The conflict the earth has with God and His authority is fundamental to the Lord. His mind and attitude on the matter are stated in the following:

- ◆ Deuteronomy 10:14—"Behold, the heaven and the heaven of heavens is the LORD'S thy God, the earth also, with all that therein is."

- Psalm 22:28—"For the kingdom is the LORD'S: and he is the governor among the nations."

- Psalm 24:1—"A Psalm of David. The earth is the LORD'S, and the fulness thereof; the world, and they that dwell therein."

- 1 Corinthians 10:26—"For the earth is the Lord's, and the fulness thereof."

- 1 Corinthians 10:28—"But if any man say unto you, This is offered in sacrifice unto idols, eat not for his sake that showed it, and for conscience sake: for the earth is the Lord's, and the fulness thereof:"

As the Creator, the Lord is the Most High God and therefore considers Himself the rightful owner of all creation. See how Melchizedek presents himself to Abram as *"The Most High Possessor of heaven and earth"* (see Genesis 14:18-22). Perhaps too simply stated for us today, this introduction was typical of the spiritual climate of Abram's day. The then God of Salem sent His priest to Abram who had been inducted into the Almighty's family back in Haran. It seems God's dominated the land of Salem back then, Psalm 76:1,2 says God still claims Salem as His own, even if it is presently in the context of a spherical stronghold in the spirit. Since then he had been on a collision course with a new life, deity, and destiny since defecting from Babylon.

Hence, to Abram the eternal Melchizedek's role in the planet was customary. He was the priest of the Most High God that Abram's soon to be Abraham, seed would come to know as Yahweh or Jehovah, the Self-Existent I Am. Melchizedek, the epistle to the Hebrews explains was made like the son of God without father, mother, genealogy (family tree), nor end of days (everlasting life), was not alone in the planet. The scriptures credit him with a priestly order saying that he had a force of priests and like servants that governed the ancient land of Jerusalem. Today they would probably be called aliens. Psalm 110:4 says that his was a priestly order; that means he had a staff of priests also installed by the Most High to keep the function active and viable for the human tribe that belonged to it. This information on its own establishes Jerusalem as a supernatural divine site for the Creator's Godhead. Its powers and martial forces then must have been immense.

Today's Jerusalem, then Salem, based on scripture's explanation of Melchizedek's earthly life long after he presented himself to Abram after the slaughter of the five kings, was meant to be God's land from before the foundation of the world. The Lord brought to His very town the one the book of Romans would later call the "heir of the world." God intended to fulfill His word to the former Babylonian prophet, now sojourner, to bless Abram for believing in Him. He orchestrated events that culminated in his blessing being officiated by the Most High's one and only Priest-King in the earth. No other land could have assured Abram's blessings. No other priest or king could have earned Abram's victory tithe and reciprocated by making him the heir of the world as Romans 4:13 says.

For people today, the idea is ludicrous. Many citizens of sophisticated countries often think one god is just like any other; one's favorite deity is equal to the task of any other god, if they subscribe to any divinity at all. People in this era just shop around until they find the god whose rituals and spirituality they like. Certainly, this was not Abram's mind as a former Babylonian prophet well educated in ancient divinity. He knew from his prior career the major gods populating and occupying the earth at the time. He was familiar with them because he had been ministering to them for years before

192

defecting with his father Terah. Abram also knew there was one god that never ran with the pack, so to speak. He was remote, somewhat aloof, and not impressed or enmeshed with humanity's foolishness. Appealing to Him Abram learned was difficult; He was not interested in all the machinations every other deity sought or rewarded. Instead, this God, though He made His presence and power known from time to time, put pressure on every priestly attendant to discover what pleased Him and more often than not, most never could quite figure it out. Abram would have surely met this vague, non-descript deity before encountering Him after Terah's death, which is why he could obey him without question when he was told to leave all he knew and follow the God whose only definitive feature was a voice. Ignoring Abram's history lightly esteems his destiny. The series of events that landed him in front of Melchizedek were no coincidence. Abram recognized it as another cog churching in destiny's wheel.

Abram obeyed the Most High God's call. He finally had a servant. His interactions with Abram were atypical in contrast to the myriad of deities he served with the numerous prophets and priests in Babylon. Yet he understood Melchizedek, whom the Lord dispatched to fuse heaven with earth; a priest-king recognized as the activator of the Creator's plan of redemption in and through him. This priest appearing out of nowhere declaring the name of the God that just wrought his victory was significant. Had he not met Melchizedek, Abram's subsequent meetings with the Almighty and he and his wife's name changes to indicate the change in their paternal deity would never have legitimately taken place. His dramatic encounters with the Lord thereafter could not have occurred and would not have foretold Isaac. Who having not been born into the world, would not have birthed Israel and subsequently his family. Acting as God's official priest in the earth to forge the covenant that would later transport Abram's descendents from Egypt to the Promised Land, Melchizedek met Abram with bread and wine, customary elements of communion between a human and a divine one. With Melchizedek's mediation, the covenant between Jehovah and Abraham is forged. The encounter occasions the very first yahwehic communion sacrament with God staying consistent with His principle of first practice. See creation's sixth day birth of humanity—male and female—and Noah's observance of the rite upon exiting the ark. Thus, the priest of the Most High God was sent to the vessel of the God's victory to ratify Abram's covenant with the Almighty. Here is how Hebrews chapter three could identify Christ as the Great Apostle, drawing its functional insight from ancient Israel's Levitical Priesthood. Strangely, *Moby Thesaurus II*[19] by Grady Ward lists Melchizedek's name as a synonym for *apostleship*.

Priesthoods Not Strange to Moses or Israel

Before finding its fulfillment in the New Testament church, God ordained His religious structure for Israel's offerings and sacrifices. He appointed the rites of observance for their worship, decreeing who would be the servants (temple ministers) and who would deliver up the sacrifices (the priests). The line of Aaron, Moses' brother was chosen for priestly functions, and one of them would be designated high priest. Reading the accounts of how the Lord enacted His orders and systems explains why not once the people sought an explanation of what a priest was or did. No one interrupted Moses' discourse asking him, "What are a priest, a high priest, and sacrifices?" Somehow, they knew exactly what the Lord was saying, following Moses intelligently as he outlined Yahweh's commands concerning their religious rites and officiations. Where did they learn about it?

---

[19]Wikipedia.com

Priestly service being common worship vernacular of the day, most fathers served as priests of their household and multiple households elevated them to high priest. Moses' audience may have recalled stories of Abraham's seed how he and later his sons showed them the Lord's worship. Later, during their Egyptian captivity, they were further indoctrinated as the nation was drenched in bloody; bizarre sacrifices officiated by serpent-clad priests. When Israel came out of Egypt, their call to worship something was established in that rituals were as integral to their society as the party life and spirituality are in ours today. What God faced in settling them was how to turn their internal worship appetites and impulses away from Satan to Jehovah, the God that just delivered them from bondage. That is what the book of Leviticus does for Him and us. It shows as much about how the Lord does not want to be worshipped or served as it does about what He desires from His worshippers.

The book of Leviticus gives the grounds for the Israel's apparent understanding of Moses' newly formed priestly institution. Turn to chapter 17 and it will become apparent to you as well. Look at what is written in Leviticus 17:1-9. The tone of God's discussion implies the people were already sacrificing animals and were quite accustomed to priesthoods. History records classes of priests go as far back as Abraham, and even farther. In addition, Jethro, Moses' father-in-law was also a priest in Midian when the Aaronic Priesthood had yet to be born. Moses for sure had observed Egypt's priestly functions for years as heir to Egypt's throne and later participated in them under Jethro's tutelage. Obviously, the forty years he spent with the man and his family as a member of Midian's priestly classes exposed him firsthand to a great deal on the subject. Moses' experience with Jethro served God's purposes by enabling him to establish the Lord's kingdom once Israel was freed from Egypt. That history made his Mount Sinai conversations with the Lord much easier to grasp and obey, well groomed by Egypt's and Jethro's priestly functions by the Lord anticipates his institution of the Most High's Levitical order.

When the time came for him to inaugurate Jehovah's priestly institution, it was not difficult for Moses to recognize God's concept of His new nation's priesthood. Years with Jethro and a royal life in Pharaoh's courts together paid off as a long history of godless priestly officiations were easily conveyed to the freed Israelites. The people who constituted the assemblies that worshipped at the gods' altars that the priests of Egypt officiated for these reasons needed no explanation of priesthoods or their necessity to their world.

The people's captivity experience well oriented them to the customs and practices of worship and ritual sacrifices. That left God to deal with only one thing, shifting His people's compulsion to sacrifice slaughtered animals genetically and culturally ingrained in them from Satan to God. Acts 26:18 expresses this best in an apostolic context. For the era and culture, sacrifice and worship were mostly obligatory. That was not God's issue. His objective was the object of their sacrifice. That is what the Lord opposed. Instead of to demons as Leviticus 17:7 writes, the people were now to redirect their offerings to the Lord God Jehovah who had delivered them from the house of bondage. Killing innocent animals for "any old" reason became taboo. They were now to do so to commemorate their salvation and honor their covenant with the living God. In addition, they were to continue the practice to foreshadow the Messiah's coming, who would one day take away the sin of the world that necessitated the unpleasant requirement in the first place. History shows Israel found it hard. They had no problem with the killing; it was the prescribed program of doing so that hampered them. They enjoyed ritual celebrations that called for fertility rites and orgies like those their pagan deities required. Yahweh's ordinances bored them as His restricted holiness frustrated their hedonistic passions that were never quite subdued.

God instituted the pattern of priesthood with Moses that His Son would later perfect. Along the way, though, the Levitical Priesthood was instituted to perpetuate what was initiated with Abram, later Abraham, through Melchizedek all those years ago. Being human, it repeatedly faltered and constantly failed God. The book of Malachi records God's indictment against His priests, stating they failed His most fundamental aim for their ministry: the impartation of knowledge. His priests neglected to make known the difference, a synonym for *distinguish*, between what was *clean and unclean* in the sight of God. This they did, in addition to overall violating His Creator Law, profaning His Sabbaths and perpetually breaking His covenant.

The other leaders in the passage, if you were to read on, were just as guilty in their duties. The officials were greedy and abusive; the prophets lied and deluded. Ezekiel 44 strikes this touchstone of God's displeasure again. Verses 23, 24 once more set them up as divine objects. Still, the Lord's procedure is to transact His official business through an institution called, a priesthood where selected representatives lead the way to the true and living God. That is the role of the New Testament church's New Creation Priesthood. Its continued existence blankets the earth with the official service and revealed will of the Almighty as dispensed through Jesus Christ by the Holy Spirit. Though this is what the apostle Peter meant in his first epistle, the idea is difficult for most Christians to fathom.

The Church's Struggle with True Priestly Service

What stumbles most people about Christ's New Testament church, its work, and ministers most is their obligation to the Lord's priestly service. Unknown to most people is the inescapable role of priestly service the whole of creation revolves around. Everyone born on the planet serves and draws invisible and immutable strength and benefits from creation's invisible realms in one way or another. Some human sacrifice, life, labor, or cherished possession must be surrendered by a sort of priestly mediation to coax the invisible to release its treasures to our world. To put it bluntly, everyone serves something to reap in the seen world the powers and provisions of the unseen. Romans 15:27, 1 Corinthians 9:11, Ephesians 1:3, and 1 Peter 2:5 all say as much. Whether it is money, love, pleasures, or passion, everyone surrenders his or her will, comfort, and convenience to creation's powerful concealed forces or agencies to acquire them, knowingly or not.

Another unknown factor in eternity's protocol that most people are oblivious to is what releases those spiritual forces and agencies to serve humanity, a principal Hebrews 1:14 upholds. The unholy angels (a distinction Jesus makes three times) provide their services under the guise of goodness and benefaction to disguise their true stratagems to delude and coercing people into petitioning them for favor through deception. Unlike the holy angels the Lord Jesus refers to, they demand outright servitude and eventual bondage in return for their benevolence. This is the outcome if one petitions the forces of light or darkness for special favors normally outside the range of human powers. What is released from eternity by these supernatural powers comes only by way of covenantal service. Covenant, sacrifice, and service are the core modes by which petitioners are escorted into the spiritual sanctuaries and treasuries of God's invisible worlds to acquire their favors.

Invariably, official or unofficial it is accomplished via some sort of priestly ritual. Specially authorized representatives of the deity (allegedly) exercise their agencies to act and provide for the earth. Early in life, some petitioners are taught what a particular divine being needs and how their spiritual or supernatural exactions are to be met by those seeking their intervention. To respond to the earth, some human vessel becomes an official member of a divine being's staff to represent its agencies, permit its presence, and exercise its powers on earth. These all comprise what may be accepted as the god's desire for expression and embodiment on earth and fit the category of priesthood.

The Spirit of a Priesthood

Priests mediate worshippers' approach and access to their god, who in turn, usually through the priest, responds by granting requests brought from the priests or by issuing further conditions for doing so. Conclusively, the petitioner's requests brought to the deity revolve around rescue, provision, protection, promotion, and prosperity. Priests are generally chosen either by parental (usually patriarchal) lineage, or by divine induction into the god's service. It often happens as part of the god's introduction to one marked at or by birth to enter its service. Often in return for some favor, a grateful person surrenders to the call and receives a special endowment that elevates his or her abilities above the masses. Abram's conquest in the slaughter of the five kings and his subsequent encounter with Melchizedek is an example of this method. Divine favor, granted in lieu of the ordinary relationship humans have with the spirit realm (judgment and retribution), makes the priest an agent of the god for the purposes of the priest's intercession, privileges, and action on behalf of both parties to the covenant established and maintained. It enables heaven to earth transactions. This concept Paul alludes to in Romans 15:27, 1

Corinthians 9:14-18, and 1 Timothy 5:18. It is also what the Lord means in Matthew 10:10 and Luke 10:7.

Priests Were High Level Functionaries

The above passages were included in scripture to dispel the notion that priestly service to humanity on any divine being's behalf is not gratis (complimentary), nor is it the equivalent of slavery where no thought of remunerating the slave's work is ever considered. In fact, the idea of paying a slave for labor in the mind of most ancients is ludicrous. As property like chattel, slaves are expected to work for no more than daily provisions. The same is not true for the priestly or ministerial servant. Their service rests upon their heavenly sender's uncontested ownership of everything in the sphere to which the priest is assigned. The priest is thus apportioned the intermediary's share of the god's material wealth acquired over millennia to dispense to its worshippers and to maintain its territorial stronghold. Those delegated distinct spiritual powers and abilities draw invisible blessings into the visible world. For doing so, they are entitled to reap for themselves and their deity a predetermined measure of the land's wealth from all those subsisting on the god's economy. A reputable priesthood falls within these parameters. Comprised of an order of humans who have dedicated themselves to the service of a divine being for the sole purpose of delivering once captured souls to them briefly describes their function. Priests become the mediators that transcend the archetypal mundanity of earthly existence and its human limitations to access what is normally hidden in creation from the average human being. They use their authority, enlightenment, and impartation from their god to convert lives to their faith, often by providing exceptional rewards, provisions, or services as an incentive.

Comparing the New Creation Priesthood of Jesus Christ

To succeed in his or her objective, the minister of Christ's New Creation Priesthood is also appointed to concentrate on teaching people the Lord's difference between holy and unholy, a requirement that sounds more simplistic than it is in practice. Doing so calls for study, personal devotion to the word, will, and work of the Lord, and diligent allegiance to His word. At its advanced levels, priestly instruction begins with the introductory message of the gospel to instill God's living statutes, testimonies, laws, precepts, and ordinances in the being and lives of the redeemed. To achieve this important attainment, priests must possess the wisdom to; rightly divide the Lord's word of truth and the ability to discern both good and evil. Such skill relies on not modifying scripture to accommodate popular trends. The prophet Ezekiel shows that the Lord gives His priests ability to do this by teaching. His prophet's foresight into Yahweh's revived kingdom reiterates the priests' call to discern between the Lord's cleanness and the uncleanness the world. That is the only way the serious Christian can remain sanctified.

In other words, debates over what the redeemed can and cannot do once saved are minimized as the immediate and ultimate cleanness or uncleanness of desired acts are reconciled within the wisdom-filled believer's heart. Again, making such judgment calls is more involved than it appears on the surface. The minister's qualifications for doing so are more extensive than it would initially appear from the writer's choice of words, which is why James warns that teachers will receive the stricter, harsher, judgment: *"My brethren, be not many masters, knowing that we shall receive the greater condemnation"* (James 3:1). The King James Version translates the word *condemnation* in place of modern translations use of **harsher** or **stricter** judgment. The softer terms seek to downplay the severity of errant teaching

201

that the Lord calls a crime. The word *krima* for crime is used and its meanings infer much more than abuse. It conveys the idea of a "criminal act," which the errant teacher commits that the Lord considers a condemnatory offense.

Lastly, God's aims for priestly ministers include settling controversies (Moses spoke of and practiced this according to Exodus 18:13-18, as does Ezekiel 44. Judging with the Lord's judgment, observing and enforcing divine laws and ordinances are all central to the priests' functions (see Leviticus 20:25; Hebrews 5:12-14; Deuteronomy 17:11-12; I Samuel 2:30-36). How much ore should they be to the apostle? One final place that cements this ecclesiastical missive is in Malachi's book. It records God's specific testimony against His priests (ministers) along with His aims for them as listed in Malachi 2:4-7. Let us look at them summarily below.

Malachi 2:7 & The Priesthood

To administrate and mediate the Lord's ministry covenant of life and peace is what Malachi understood to be the supreme duty of priests. One of the many difficult concepts for the New Testament church to grasp, since it is void of apostles' influences, is that ministry is administration. Fear of bureaucracy borne out of early ecclesiastical or secular mishandling motivates Christians to isolate the practicalities of Christianity and its service from what is presented as imprecise spirituality. An over-emphasis on the five senses, charismata and human intelligence, theology, doctrine, and apologetics has left the church to perceive its sole purpose on earth is to exercise intangible, often irrational acts blamed on the unseen. This largely magical mindset overlooks the difference between magic and manifestation.

The Holy Spirit in the world and in the church is to manifest the Godhead. His Agency demonstrates God's eternal kingdom dynamics at work and legitimizes the Lord Jesus' involvement in human affairs as its everlasting King David. These truths may be accurately deduced from 1 Corinthians 12:4-6: *"Now there are diversities of gifts, but the same Spirit. And there are differences of administrations, but the same Lord. And there are diversities of operations, but it is the same God which worketh all in all."* Gifts, administration, and operations all speak to more definite functions than those normally ascribed to the religious sphere, namely prayer, ritual, liturgy, and worship.

The church is a business, God's sacred business practiced on earth under the auspices of His Holy Spirit. Those noted in 1 Corinthians 12:28, 29 and Ephesians 4:11 along with the deacons, bishops, elders, and presidents mentioned throughout the New Testament are designated officials of God's kingdom with delegated authority to carry on specific activities in His stead just as He would if He were physically present. They are needed because the Lord is on earth spiritually embodied within His people. Their service expresses the underlying principle beneath the word *delegated* usually attached to authority.

As God's representatives, these ministries administrate; that is, have charge of God's affairs on His behalf in the planet. Whatever He releases by His Spirit and dispenses to earth comes through His body. It is translated and dispensed through His appointed agents in the Church. The entire responsibility put upon the ecclesia entails control, management, direction, government, operation, processing, and procedures the Savior deems necessary to advance His Father's kingdom on earth and in the flesh. The Lord Jesus by His Spirit aims to consistently and in times and situations of difficulty persistently compel creation to yield to the Almighty's end time agenda as inscribed for humanity and imposed on creation by the Godhead. Careful reconsideration of Paul's epistle to the Ephesians, other New

Testament writings, and our Lord's teachings not only enlighten Christian ministers to these realities but also empowers them and the Church to implement them. Below are seven conditions the Lord sends His apostles to treat in their offices.

Seven Kingdom Conditions Apostles Treat in Office

> **1.   *Ignite the reverential fear of the Lord in His people.***

A serious void in the New Testament church's consciousness is a healthy fear of the Lord. Over arching grace and libertine liberty perverting Christians' redemption and inspires absurd beliefs and actions that offend the Lord's holiness. His standing mandate on every Christian's life, "Be ye holy as I am holy," may only be achieved by reverencing who God is with a wholesome fear of His power and dominion over His created worlds. Paul says in Romans 11:22 that although God is good, He is nonetheless severe. The same passage adds that those who forsake His goodness will be cut off. Hebrews 10:1 substantiates this by declaring how fearful it is to fall into the hands of the living God.

A Christian's irreverence manifests a seminal disbelief of inwardly doubting God's existence, and the reality His Son Jesus' incarnation, resurrection, and eternal life. Such attitudes trigger the misconduct that treat His laws and government as worldly in origin and the God that inspired them as a statue or religious ideal humans flex as situations dictate. That God is longsuffering, wishing that none should perish, is no grounds for negating His conditions for eternal life. It remains that the Lord demands all to come to the knowledge of His truth as embodied in His Resurrected Son. Apart from that knowledge, people break all restraint, disdain truth and righteousness, and rise up against the character of the Almighty to their harm.

Isaiah chapter eleven outlines what Jesus' anointing required of and supplied Him as the Creator's emissary sent to the earth. The prophet Isaiah, long before the Messiah's coming and the Holy Spirit's outpouring, defined what a vessel of God's glory felt and exhibited as His holy habitation. Isaiah 11:1-5 says, *"And there shall come forth a rod out of the stem of Jesse, and a Branch shall grow out of his roots: And the spirit of the LORD shall rest upon him, the spirit of wisdom and understanding, the spirit of counsel and might, the spirit of knowledge and of the fear of the LORD; And shall make him of quick understanding in the fear of the LORD: and he shall not judge after the sight of his eyes, neither reprove after the hearing of his ears: But with righteousness shall he judge the poor, and reprove with equity for the meek of the earth: and he shall smite the earth with the rod of his mouth, and with the breath of his lips shall he slay the wicked. And righteousness shall be the girdle of his loins, and faithfulness the girdle of his reins."* As Christ's offspring and siblings, the Church is to exhibit the very traits the Lord Jesus became famous for on earth.

The Spirit of God in a person's life produces wisdom, invokes understanding of Creator God's divine kingdom, and explains why and how it is regulated by the godly fear of the Lord. The New Creation church is not above Jesus Christ, its founder, or outside the bounds of what was set for Him. His standards apply to everyone in God's eternal family; that is why He became human. His fear of the Father as His God and the holiness that exemplifies the Almighty is required of all who receive His salvation. Yet throughout the church world and proliferated in doctrine, the Lord's standards are at best marginalized as people revere mortal creatures more than they do the immortal Creator. Servants of the King of kings exist for the King and not for the citizens of His kingdom. The body is handled by God indirectly through those charged with perpetuating Christ's ministry in their respective generations. Where there is an absence of reverence on the part of Lord's

205

servants, there cannot help but be rampant irreverence from those they touch. Regardless of how often or vehement the disclaimers to the contrary, ministers as with all other humans are known by their fruit, and in eternity they are judged by the character and produce of that fruit. This is what Matthew 7:22, 23 have to say.

2.   *Revive God's veneration to hallow His name in their generations.*

Paul wrote in Romans 2:24, brought forward from Isaiah 51:5-6, that God's people cause His name to be blasphemed continually, or every day. What a sad statement. The good name of the Lord is not only cursed, condemned, vilified, or rendered spurious by the sinner; His saints also insult, harm, and damage by their abhorrent misconduct. Christian's rude and sometimes lewd behavior profanes the Lord's image in the world. Angry, bitter Christians and those practicing licentiousness show themselves to be faithless to God and His cause. Observers of the church's mixed signals and pagan ways lead others to disdain God's name and antagonize His presence in their world. Referring to the previous statements, the eternal New Creation priesthood after the order of Melchizedek over whom the Risen Lord officiates seems to have failed the most fundamental of its priestly duty. As God's holy habitation, the New Testament saint does not hallow His name, except perhaps as part of church service.

Otherwise, God's name, fame, reputation, and character are blighted with worldliness, humanist doctrine, worldly rhetoric, and besmudged with carnality. The world has elevated the very pagan deities Christ destroyed on the cross to His stature, and His church appears powerless or disinterested in overturning it. Decades of Christian neglect and spiritual defilement helped the godless achieve their goal: displace Christ with their versions of the old, dethroned deities He destroyed. The name of Jesus Christ and His Father are no longer venerated as anything more another religion, however distasteful to the world, and Christianity to be attacked and eliminated from the religions of the earth.

Christians themselves are ashamed of the name of their Lord, something Jesus foretold would happen. What is not readily apparent in His prophecy is the Godhead's seemingly long overdue response to it. Jesus declared in Mark 8:38, *"Whosoever therefore shall be ashamed of me and of my words in this adulterous and sinful generation; of him also shall the Son of man be ashamed, when he cometh in the glory of his Father with the holy angels."* Luke 9:26 echoes this divine sentiment. God has serious problems with being ignored, shunned, and rejected by those He made and causes to live. Venerating anything other than Him is not only foolhardy; it is juvenile. The word *venerates,* by the way, means *to worship, to adore.* The Lord's mind on this is captured in His first commandment: "Thou shalt have no other god beside me." Haggai adds that the coming Messiah that we know to be Jesus alone is the "Desire of all nations," and God told His people in Deuteronomy 13:4 to cleave to Him. To venerate is also to *idolize.* It is common knowledge by the saint and the sinner what the Almighty feels about idolatry although many souls remain oblivious to what makes for idolatry. He finds it especially anguishing when it is practiced by those who are inhabited by God's Spirit. Venerate further means to esteem, respect, and admire; something Jesus said should first be directed toward God above others. Lastly the word venerate means *to honor to the point of seeking the revered object's praise above the praise of all else* (see John 12:43). Without question, the Lord Jesus and His Father are to be the sole objects of such praise.

The cost of venerating anything except or above the Almighty is promised disastrous consequences when Jesus takes the reins of His kingdom. The only reason people refuse to venerate the Lord who deserves it is that they fear the ridicule of the natural world. Bluntly speaking, they are ashamed of Him. God decreed severe repercussions on those that are ashamed of Him and His words. But what is it to be ashamed of the Lord and His words as defined by the Savior in Matthew 10:33, Mark 8:38, Luke 9:26, and Luke 12:9? In particular, the phrase, "of Me and My words" almost makes the answer self-explanatory. Think about the insecure youth or teen that, for no logical reason, dreads his school friends meeting his parents or other unpopular or unattractive people in his life. The youngster lies to avoid having the two parties ever cross paths, and he pretends the unfavorable party does not exist, refusing to invite them to any of the pop-group's gatherings. Should the two groups accidentally meet, the insecure youth or teen ignores or pretends not to know the one he despises in favor of those he admires and strives to please. The youth's further embarrassment gives the popular group the license to humiliate the less esteemed peers or their parents because of selfish insecurity, something the Savior also spoke about in Matthew 6:24 and Luke 16:13. That is how the Lord sees those of His family that are embarrassed about Him and His words.

3. Teach God's people the Law of Truth.

Malachi 2:6, 7 says the chief duty of a priest, what enables all the other accomplishments of the office, is to teach God's law of truth. We have dealt with this extensively elsewhere. At the outset of every ministry, the task is ever present. Ministers, a synonym for priests, are not just to teach people God's laws in general, but also to identify specifically their inviolable truths in contrast to all the world's wisdom and knowledge. Following this, they are to depict the value of that truth in their daily existence. Priestly teachings answer what makes God truth and how practicing His truth translates to His life. In this vein of wisdom, the apostle demonstrates where and how the Lord's truth clashes with world systems and kingdoms. These commonplace eternal principles should become routine knowledge and conversation for any of the Most High's priests. That applies not only to the priests of Moses' law, but more importantly to the priests of Jesus' redemptive law of life now shifted to the line of Judah and Christ, God's eternal King David.

The priestly work of the New Creation is understood from 1 Peter 2:9, 2 Corinthians 5:17, and Galatians 6:16. Inferred in detail throughout Hebrews chapters five through ten, the writer presents its High Priest as Jesus the Son of God, whose order is after eternity's Melchizedek, Salem's (Jerusalem's) ancient king. This subject has been discussed in detail as well. Tying Jesus' eternal status as High Priest to Peter's royal priesthood and nation of kings and priests supports his designation of the church as God's chosen generation. The new creation is God's ultimate generation of all born of Christ's Spirit. His description establishes every believer's call to share Jesus' true message: to fulfill the Lord's law. All Christians must proficiently explain God's immutable holiness and righteousness after having lived and learned from it themselves. They are to make known His eternal (more than spiritual) laws to the earth until the end. Beyond this, God's royal priesthood is to embody, pursue, and disseminate His truth in word, thought, and deed.

God is truth, He is the God of truth, all His ways are truth, and His works are done in truth. God cannot lie and declares it is impossible for Him to do so. Those on earth under the sway of the wicked one's lie cannot know this without God's help. People are born into Satan's dark kingdom and his darkness is bred in them until Christ sets them free. When He does, He gives them unlawful entrance into His life; a reality God persuades His apostles of early in their training. God sent His truth into the world incarnated in Jesus Christ to be disseminated first by His preaching and teaching and continually by the Pentecost outpouring of His Holy Spirit. Before then, the only truth the world knew, and today can discover, was found in Moses' law, the Ten Commandments. Post Pentecost that truth became available to the entire world as foretold by the prophet Joel and articulated by Peter's first sermon. All anyone in the world has to do now to access it is to become one with Jesus Christ, the Savior.

Isaiah 43:10-15 speaks to this and the unique privilege God's people have of knowing and sharing Him in a way others do not, and cannot. Amos 3:2 agrees with this in spirit by saying that the chosen are known by God in a rare and unequivocal way, the way Genesis 18:17-19 regards God's intimate knowledge of Abraham that enlightened him to attest to the Almighty as the true and living God. For Abraham, this was, no inconsequential task considering his former occupation as one of Chaldea's prophets in ancient Babylonia.

When God permits Himself to be known by anyone, it is for the express purposes of revealing Himself and His way. He expects that revelation to transform those in his or her sphere of life. Here is what offended the Lord most about King Solomon's failure. God's intimacy with the man in his youth was trivialized as he allowed his many wives to turn his heart from the Lord to their plethora of gods (1 Kings 9:11). Solomon evidently never believed in his covenant God enough to convert to Him fully. Instead, he chose the deadly path of religious tolerance and permitted his foreign wives to station pagan temples throughout the land. Solomon encouraged them to fabricate their polytheistic worship among Yahweh's people using their husband's with royal authority to do so.

Apparently, Solomon ceased believing God's revelation and declaration of Himself. As Israel's immensely endowed king, he

210

lost sight of its God's truth and righteousness and consequently plunged his nation into the depths of depravity and idolatry. A man granted his enormous wisdom and the benefits of its profits in life reciprocated to God by growing bitter, indulgent, polytheistic, and reprobate. He rewarded God's goodness with his wives' evil. When did Solomon fall? He fell when he ceased to know the difference between Yahweh's truth and the world's lie; he ceased to believe by faith that Israel's God was true, good, and righteous and began to use his tremendous wisdom to question and doubt everything he wrote in Proverbs and to supplant it with the humanist observations of Ecclesiastes.

4.   Manifest and exemplify Jehovah's justice, peace, and equity.

Calling upon Malachi 2:6 again, God's equity and peace emerge as prime by-products of His law of truth. The angels cried out when Jesus arrived on earth that God had made peace with humanity. They declared His incarnation brought peace on earth and good will to men. The Prince of Peace had donned flesh to usher in an era of concord between God and His creation.

Prior to that, the Law of Moses emphasized justice and righteousness and peace was achieved by way of an elaborate system of sacrifices and offerings to appease the habitually offended God of their covenant. No matter how meticulous these were carried out, they failed to achieve God's peace within and His expression of that peace on earth. This the Lord Jesus brought by way of His shed blood upon the cross. Peace between God and humans is impossible apart from the cross. It is the means by which what chronically offended the Creator since before Adam's transgression and alienation from his Creator was remedied. That peace, God expects to be expressed by His ecclesia living it out as much as possible. Such authority the Lord Jesus left the ecclesia on earth, should it take

211

its power seriously to countermand the world's chaotic forces of darkness. If this happened, the New Creation church can truly establish the Father's peace on earth. However, it requires the Church to give itself entirely and perpetually to the Savior's teachings; an ideal that, because of humanity's internal schism, cannot be totally realized until the Savior's thousand-year reign. Pending that momentous event, the Lord's eternal peace, justice in all realms, and equity in all His dealings with people continue to struggle with the sin nature and humanity's appetite for the death-producing deeds of the flesh. Their passions alone will promote injustice and unfairness and only the resolute will choose to refuse the evil and choose the good.

5. Spark and spearhead God's ministry of repentance and conversion.

To be a minister of Christ's evangelism and an officer in His Church requires the same frontal approach to sin and its devastations that He used. The Lord learned from His Father that in the flesh dwells no good thing; that all the earth is guilty before God; and that there is none righteous (apart from His redemption), no not one. God is a pragmatist and His word shows that He holds no delusions about His creation, its natural proclivities, and the state of His world because of it. God as Alpha and Omega does not believe things will work themselves out in the end. He planned every beginning and acted on every end before time began. Those plans include the upside and downside of His existence. God's very prophecies show He knows things will deteriorate despite how much good news is concocted to the contrary until He ushers in the end and establishes His Son's everlasting kingdom.

The kingdom of heaven suffers violence because there is much there to be wrested away from the fallen powers that refuse to obey the cross and Christ's gospel. These must be ripped away from eternity's godless contenders on earth with greater violence than they wield. God's kingdom for now is invisible and largely imperceptible. Experiencing it and witnessing its glories are matters of individual repentance and conversion to the Lord Jesus Christ. Although the devil is cast out of the high heaven, says Revelation 12:12, he remains deviously active in the terrestrial realms, angrily slaughtering all he wills. The only way to escape his rage is to become a member of Christ's body. His ire, though venomous in the spirit, initiates its affects as momentary delights to the soul of the deceived or the damned. As time draws near to a close and the real motives of his seductions intensify as Satan aggressively reaps his world harvest. By the time people realize they are caught in his trap, they are too hardened by their sin to repent as reprobacy and apostasy take their toll.

Sadly, many of those who, like Solomon, started out with the Lord Jesus Christ will abandon Him as the worldly pleasures and pressures of Satan's machine collide to make serving the Savior a hardship. Those that succumb to his machinations will be subverted by questions such as these: "What if Jesus is not alive? What if the Christian God is not God and Jesus is not His Son. What if Christ did not come to earth or if there is, no God and I spend a lifetime trying to please Him alienating the devil? Would I be denying myself for nothing? What happens in the end if Jesus does not exist, if God is not in control, or of hell is much better than the Bible depicts?" All these speculations are mediums of impenitence and must be confronted by the work of ministry. Classes, words, and counsel should encourage repentance and righteousness for the Lord to prevail in the lives of those He receive. These are all in addition to intense teaching about the Holy Spirit and His work in the world.

6. Restore esteem for the messengers and the ministers of God.

213

It hardly needs to be said that the church's credibility and worth in the world is, at the least compromised and more accurately jeopardized. Centuries of careless dissemination of God's word brought Christianity to its current tenuous place in history. The absence of God's ordained authorities in position over the church, suppression of Bible truth, and perversion of whatever knowledge that does get through have all merged to confuse the Lord Jesus' Christianity and blur the sound wisdom and insight the Almighty dispensed to the planet since time began.

Present leaders have little idea of what is on God's heart, or of the sorrow that He feels over the lost generations, spiritual neglect and doctrinal error have cost Him. Having become so saturated with human philosophies and the commandments of men the church cannot tell the truth from the lie. Occultic teaching is passed off as spirituality and demonism as divine education while the church is enticed into paganism and polytheism. Meaningful expressions of the Creator's holiness murk as hyper-grace and selfish liberties continually discredit the gospel and entice God's people to be at peace with their sin. So long has this been going on that the Lord's people no longer have ears to hear. Lulled into rebellion and unaware of their consensual role as saboteurs of His kingdom, modern saints relish their independence from traditionalism. Much like ancient Israel, their predecessors, they want to be free to choose their own courses in life, desiring only not to be condemned to hell for their choices. They passionately want to be just like other religions, free to explore, err, and join other faiths to their worship to show their open mindedness and mold earth and heaven as their fantasies say.

Feeding too long on humanist doctrines, Christians are intolerant of God's new sound. The voice and wisdom of apostles and prophets incense them as they shout cries of legalism, witchcraft, manipulation, and control. Far too long separated from biblical wisdom and scripture truth, todays free-spirited Christian is God's greatest opposition. With the strength of self-righteousness and scant Bible insight, these people raise up against God's apostolic doctrine because it is foreign to their ears and disturbs their marginal outlook on God and religion. Initially, they appreciate the freshness of the apostle's word, but they soon turn surly when its demands invade their freelance Christianity. Too many of them have been raised in the me, myself, I, mine and my doctrine of the humanist church and know Jesus as their Savior only because they feel it or someone told them saying a prayer would make it so. Beyond that, they are no closer to the Lord or nearer to understanding His ways than the sinner in the world. Many of these people are so worldly that they have no knowledge of what God's presence in the world by His spirit means and consistently violate His holiness to follow the spirit of this world. Until the redeemed are willing to hear the word of the Lord in truth, devoid of the self-happiness coating of humanism the Lord's messengers will do them little good.

7.   *Provide the answers to life and living saints and society need to hear.*

Hardly anyone in today's spiritually charged environment can dispute that people want answers. They want real answers to the real lives they are living. Typically, they do not expect those answers to come from the Christian church, as its wisdom has long ago proven unreliable in their minds. So convinced are they, that what they seek cannot come from Christ's church that any hint of religion in a conversation shuts them down immediately. Mentally, they tune out discussions that mention God, especially Jesus Christ, because of the extreme disservice disgruntled and reckless Christians have done His name and word. Entertainment pokes fun at Bible toting Christians and movies use maniacal Christians to mock Bible believers by

215

having them avow they committed heinous crimes in obedience to God (which one is never said). They contend the Lord told them to commit whatever atrocity the movie glamorizes.

Meanwhile, every other religion is venerated by the sinner's worldly regard and respect. The causes of this attitude come from the over spiritualization of Bible truth and irrational Christians blame shifting to absolve themselves of misconduct that even the sinner knows they should "fess up". For apostles to recapture the heart and souls of their generations, they are going to have to be wiser than the world and like Daniel a minimum of ten times better at handling spiritual matters for their followers.

What all this has to do with apostles, besides the fact that they are all priests in the New Testament is that those who embody Christ are to surrender all to Him. To avoid scattering instead of gathering, their offerings and officiations are to be no different from His.

Chapter Summary

1. Apostleship has strong priestly connections.

2. Confession and profession are related but not the same.

3. Apostles lift Christians up to their ordained level.

4. Apostles of a new move restore, catechize, govern, and revive true worship.

5. Apostles have eight ministry applications.

6. Moses represents an Old Testament type of apostleship.

7. Apostles are detached from the world to penetrate and affect it.

8. Apostles must emphasize the word (message) of their moves.

9. Revival marks all true apostles' ministries.

10. Jesus as the Great Apostle cast the pattern for future apostleship.

11. True apostleship characterizes effective priestly service.

12. Priesthood is eternal, not just ancient.

13. Jesus Christ's priesthood comprises the church as His new creation nation of royal priest and kingdom from Judah's line.

14. Apostles are sent to treat seven spiritual conditions.

Chapter Ten

Apostleship as God's Embassy

Chapter Discussions

Apostles as Ambassadors & Embassies • Political Definition of an Ambassador • How Apostleship Qualifies as an Embassy • Diplomacy • Diplomatic Immunity • Diplomatic Relations • What Is an Embassy?• Embassies in the Old Testament • Consuls: Another Embassy Type • Special Consul Privileges • Ambassadors, Consuls, & Embassies • The Founding of Literal Embassies • Ambassadors Began in Religious Spheres • A Legate • God's Calculated Use of the Word *Apostle* • How Apostles See Law & Government • Snapshot of Apostleship at Work • Chart of Key Apostleship Actions • Ancient Terms Identify & Blend Apostleship with Militarism • Meaning of the Word *Tsava* in Relation to Apostleship • Apostleship & Spiritual Warfare • Angels & Apostleship

T he following information is to guarantee the perpetual legitimacy of apostleship in the minds of those called to the office and in the minds of those they serve. The nature of apostleship as discussed at length elsewhere is that of messaging. Natural and secular examples are employed somewhat metaphorically to forge a strong relational connection between the world of Jesus' day and ours. As you read this material, keep in mind that in Jesus' religion was supreme and secularism followed its lead and dictates. Hence, spirituality was not an alcove of society but more of its capstone. The aim of this subject treatment is to tie apostleship as Christ's world understood and practiced it to military actions, government and judicial legislation, and divine ministry. These four categories of ministry service sum up the essence of apostleship. Apostles are activated by an authority, their principal, the one that sends (dispatched) them as ambassadorial agents to serve in distant destinations. Today those destinations are usually foreign lands. Apostles are sent as heavenly messengers to earth's territories. They are ambassadors dispatched to act on their sender's (Jesus') behalf in business, diplomatic, ministerial, military, and political matters. Senders may be governments, organizations, sovereigns,[20] or deities.

---

[20] "Sovereignty is the exclusive right to exercise supreme authority over a geographic region, group of people, or oneself. Sovereignty over a nation is generally vested in a government or other political agency, though there are cases where it is held by an individual. A monarch who rules a sovereign country can also be referred to as the sovereign of that country. The concept of sovereignty also pertains to a government possessing full control over its own affairs within a territorial or geographical area or limit." *Wikipedia.com*

In the case of Christ's apostles, He and His Father the Lord God fits them all. Their government is in the eternal heavens, making anyone sent to anywhere on earth from heaven's station an envoy and their apostles, ambassadors, by definition. The Godhead's organization is the church of the Lord Jesus Christ; Heaven's sovereign is His Son as King David's offspring. He, the Father and the Holy Spirit are the ending principals.

Apostles as Ambassadors & Embassies

The above example explains what makes apostles ambassadors. That phrase itself is replete with insinuations that point to extraordinary nuances in the calling. As ambassadors, apostles their secular counterparts understand, occupy the highest seat in their embassies. Every other diplomatic officer is under the ambassador standing in the position of emissary, envoy, plenipotentiary, or principality. These critical functions execute the purposes for which the embassy was established in its foreign territory. Eight times the word ambassador is expressly used in scripture

1. *They did work wilily, and went and made as if they had been **ambassadors**, and took old sacks upon their asses, and wine bottles, old, and rent, and bound up (Joshua 9:4 KJV).*

2. *Howbeit in the business of the **ambassadors** of the princes of Babylon, who sent unto him to inquire of the wonder that was done in the land, God left him, to try him, that he might know all that was in his heart (2 Chronicles 32:31 KJV).*

3. *But he sent **ambassadors** to him, saying, What have I to do with thee, thou king of Judah? I come not against thee this day, but against the house wherewith I have war: for God commanded me to make haste: forbear thee from*

meddling with God, who is with me, that he destroy thee not (2 Chronicles 35:21 KJV).

4. *That sendeth* **ambassadors** *by the sea, even in vessels of bulrushes upon the waters, saying, Go, ye swift* **messengers**, *to a nation scattered and peeled, to a people terrible from their beginning hitherto; a nation meted out and trodden down, whose land the rivers have spoiled (Isaiah 18:2 KJV)!*

5. *For his princes were at Zoan, and his* **ambassadors** *came to Hanes (Isaiah 30:4 KJV).*

6. *Behold, their valiant ones shall cry without: the* **ambassadors** *of peace shall weep bitterly (Isaiah 33:7 KJV).*

7. *But he rebelled against him in sending his* **ambassadors** *into Egypt, that they might give him horses and much people. Shall he prosper? shall he escape that doeth such things? or shall he break the covenant, and be delivered (Ezekiel 17:15 KJV)?*

8. *Now then we are* **ambassadors** *for Christ, as though God did beseech you by us: we pray you in Christ's stead, be ye reconciled to God (2 Corinthians 5:20 KJV).*

9. *For which I am an* **ambassador** *in bonds: that therein I may speak boldly, as I ought to speak (Ephesians 6:20 KJV).*

The Isaiah 18:2 reference above makes the important connection for us. Ambassadors are sent with a message that equates to a task to be accomplished. Paul's Corinthian statement, theologically related to the entire church, initially concerned Christ's apostles. Read the entire passage yourself to confirm it. While every Christian can and should evangelize, witness Jesus' salvation and share the message of the gospel, not all of them are called to become kingdom representatives, as are His apostles. This is obvious by the fact that proportionately speaking, only a few Christians feel the drive to do so at exorbitant risks of their personal lives. The 2 Chronicles reference given above illustrates this. Often in the Bible, kings sent ambassadors to bring offers of peaceful surrender to a distant country with which they want to establish political relations or to achieve some international purpose. If the offer is ignored, a siege mound and troops followed.

Make no mistake about it, back then when rulers decided to invade and overtake a land they had done their homework and concluded their resources and armaments were more than able to complete the task. Here is what the Savior alludes to in Luke 14:32. *"Or else, while the other is yet a great way off, he sendeth* (apostello) *an **ambassage** (embassy-presbeia), and desireth conditions of peace."* Those not accustomed to the political and military climate of the day, could easily overlook the embassadorial (embassy over the ambassador) overtones of Jesus' word choice. To gain insight into it, just remember that Jesus is speaking as a king. He is the head of His own country on assignment in another, the earth, representing Him and His Father's world. A second illustration of the use of this word is found in Luke chapter nineteen where *ambassage* is the word used for the modern translation's delegation that was sent after the nobleman left to prevent recovery of his territory when he returned.

Political Definition of an Ambassador[21]

An ambassador is "a permanent diplomatic mission usually known as an **embassy**." The head of the mission is known as an **ambassador**. An **ambassador**, rarely **embassador**, is a diplomatic official accredited to a foreign sovereign or

---

[21] From Wikipedia.com

government, or to an international organization, to serve as the official representative of his or her own. In everyday usage, it applies to the ranking *plenipotentiary*[22] minister stationed in a foreign capital. The host country typically allows the ambassador control of specific territory called an embassy, whose territory, staff, and even vehicles are generally afforded diplomatic immunity to most laws of the host country. The senior diplomatic officer among members of the Commonwealth of Nations, are known as High Commissioners. Ambassadors are ministers of the highest rank, with **plenipotentiary** authority to represent their head of state. An Ordinary Ambassador is one heading a permanent diplomatic mission, for instance the senior professional diplomat in an embassy. An extraordinary ambassador could be appointed for special purposes or for an indefinite term; politically appointed ambassadors would fall under this category.

In some countries, the longest-serving ambassador to a country is given the title Dean of the Diplomatic Corps, and is sometimes accorded a high position in the order of precedence. In New Zealand, for example, the Dean takes precedence over figures such as the Deputy Prime Minister, former Governors-General, and the Chief Justice. The diplomatic corps may also co-operate amongst itself on a number of matters, including certain dealings with the host government.[23] Since Israel, like most countries of the day, was under theocratic rule, it was firmly Creator God's nation. Consequently, their clashes with their neighboring rulers and rivals came under the heading of religious battles, or holy wars. It was well understood at the time that whenever a nation went to war it was because the

---

[22] An ambassador is and envoy, diplomat; a deputized minister with a delegated commission; a spokesperson, politician, statesmen and tactician; a messenger, administrator, executive, official, premier, and prime minister.
[23] ibid

223

gods over those nations had engaged them. The territories that were up for grabs were spiritual and earthly in addition to being natural and heavenly in nature with angels present and active in every one of Jehovah' cosmic and international conflicts. Natural battles in reality were supernatural in origin. For them to occur at once on different planes of God's creation required the dispatch of one agency to combat another. Warnings that an invasion was imminent usually preceded the onset of battle. The angels then, along with God's chosen leaders, established all His people's wars as intercosmic battles waged by international representatives.

One biblical term from the Old Testament that expressly makes this point is, *Tsawah*. It expressly defines an ordained command, charge, and commission and infers a delegation (as an embassy and ambassadors) set or commissioned over something. A messenger; an officer charged with setting things in order. Lastly, the word refers to a superior giving a verbal communication to or by a subordinate.

The term **plenipotentiary** (from the Latin, *plenus*, + *potens*, full + power) refers to a person who has "full powers; an agent that is given full authority to act on behalf of another, especially in diplomatic matters." In particular, the term is commonly used to refer to a *diplomat* or *ambassador* fully authorized to represent his government. Diplomacy is the art and practice of conducting negotiations between accredited persons (the diploma of the diplomat) representing groups or nations. As stewards of their principal's best interests, diplomats are guardians of their security, well-being, citizens, and possessions while they are on foreign soil. Among all the ways they can do this, is by making and keeping friends to retain their principal's access to global opportunities, advantages, and influence, and enlarge their country's access to a society and its elites. Diplomacy's purpose, while largely rooted in messaging communications, and negotiations is to effectively change attitudes and behaviors to what that is more suited to their principal's best interest. The word when used usually refers to **international diplomacy**, the conduct of international relations through the intercession of professional *diplomats* with regard to issues of peace making, culture, economics, trade, and war. Since theirs is largely ostensibly a messenger ministry,[24] ambassadors, ministers, and apostles are nonetheless agents of their sender. That means the apostle must pursue the best interests and outcomes of God's kingdom, the assigner of their commission. Everything the apostle does in office must be to the end that the Lord's will is done in the earth, His rule is established by the Holy Spirit, and His interests are consistently pursued. [25] Such a responsibility places a great work upon on the apostle. As God's agent must be devoted to the Lord's way and will, as well as His word. It inspires abandonment of their own personal views and wholeheartedly adopts and promotes those of Christ and His kingdom. A major danger facing all apostles, especially those with pervasive influence and acclaim is the temptation to substitute personal, popular, or prevailing views and beliefs for those of their Sender. That is what Solomon did as he gave his heart to the many women he acquired. It is what Hezekiah fell prey to when he met the Babylonian ambassadors. The king was so flattered by the ambassadors' interest in his kingdom and what he had acquired as Israel's king that he foolishly

---

[24] See discussions of ministry elsewhere in the text.

[25] The importance of apostles rightly choosing words: "Nothing is more important to diplomacy than care in choosing and reporting words. Whether the formulations are vague or precise, other nations must assume that they were selected deliberately and with thought. That is why such care must be given to statement made during official visits and in official speeches. In foreign ministries around the world, what you say gets quoted back to you and you are expected to stand behind your words." George P. Shultz, 1993. The Diplomats Dictionary

"The word is older than the state. Words form and reform states. Thos who run states know the power of words and attempt to control them." Richard Stern, quoted by George P. Shultz, 1993, The Diplomat's Dictionary, pp. 321.

showed them all his realm. When his royal prophet, Isaiah, questioned him about his actions, he admitted that there was nothing in all his realm that he did not show his Babylonian visitors.

> *"At that time Berodachbaladan, the son of Baladan, king of Babylon, sent letters and a present unto Hezekiah: for he had heard that Hezekiah had been sick. And Hezekiah hearkened unto them, and showed them all the house of his* **precious things***, the silver, and the gold, and the spices, and the precious ointment, and all the house of his* **armour***, and all that was found in his* **treasures***: there was nothing in his house, nor in all his dominion, that* **Hezekiah showed** *them not. Then came Isaiah the prophet unto king Hezekiah, and said unto him, What said these men? and from whence came they unto thee? And Hezekiah said, They are come from a far country, even from Babylon. And he said, What have they seen in thine house? And Hezekiah answered, All the things that are in mine house have they seen: there is nothing among my treasures that I have not showed them." 2 Kings 20:12-15.*

This was a politically risky act on Hezekiah's part. Few national leaders would consider being so forthcoming with their allies no matter how extravagant the gift or lavish the attention. Apparently, despite Hezekiah's success and fame he remained insecure about stature and still needed the approval and admiration of foreign emissaries to reinforce his confidence. In an informal or social sense, diplomacy is the employment of tact to gain strategic advantage. [26] Babylon's emissaries achieved this objective for their king with the help of Hezekiah's

---

[26] ibid

braggadocios nature when he showed them all they needed to eventually invade and conquer Israel.

As you can deduce from the above, the present concept of the apostle has run far aground of that originally intended. As stated earlier, apostles are first messengers. That does not mean however that theirs is an office devoted to just verbalizing. Messengers were more than postal couriers were back humans were the only mode of message communication. Messengers were "officials appointed to perform certain duties generally of a ministerial character. They served as officers (ministers in the context of being public servants) authorized to execute the lawful commands of commissioners."[27] As officers and agents of governments and temples, messengers fell under the general heading of minister.

The Twelve Branches of Apostleship

The church's gift only mentality has done much to diminish its minister's strength for the Lord and obscure what He intends for His ecclesiastical sphere. Establishing the offices of the church on its members' gifts and talents puts responsibility for their success on humans, taking it completely out of the Holy Spirit's hands. That goes against the Savior's standard organizational and institutional order, not to mention how risky that would be for the Lord. People grow old, get sick, and die. Offices on the other hand survive them because institutions outlive the people that occupy them. That is why power and authority are installed in offices and officials upon appointment. Institutions empower the people that serve them, and yes, it is true, people are servants of their institutions. The reason is because entities outlive and thrive despite humanity's mortality.

---

[27] Bouvier's Law Dictionary Revised 6th edition (1856).

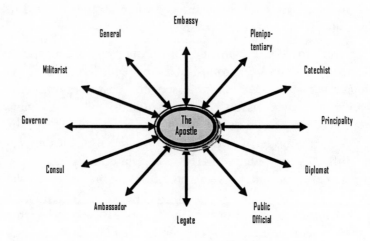

How Apostleship Qualifies as an Embassy

On all levels, the Lord God's dispatch of His apostles, beginning with the incarnation of Jesus Christ His first begotten, qualifies as an embassy and thus His apostles as His ambassadors. The presence of the Holy Spirit in the planet since the church's first Pentecost, sets the entire world up as the Godhead's embassy. Anyone dispatched by the Holy Ghost is authorized to act in the Godhead's best interests in the planet according to his or her assignment. Apostles then as the first of its representatives in its line organization are the ambassadors and they oversee the work of the remaining officers of Ephesians 4:11 as high-ranking officials of the Lord's embassies. With so much of what defines, and has defined, the apostle to date not coming from the apostles themselves, what is communicated as their office criteria—boundaries, features, and functions—distills from those apostles exist to accredit and install. Therefore, a major portion of the information on the mantle circulating to date is either incomplete, or errant, however well intentioned its assimilation may have been. For that reason, the information to come is to clarify apostleship's most salient points to enlarge the reader's concept of it as understood before, and outside, the church and Christian circles. Its wisdom seeks to upgrade present and future apostles' view of the scope and import of the office and transform their identification to what the Godhead had in mind when it dispatched and continues to dispatch its kingdom's high-ranking officials to the kingdoms of men in the earth.

The following material discusses what should be the spirit of apostleship, which encompasses:

- Embassy
- Ambassadors
- Diplomacy

Each of these words is discussed under its own heading, beginning with Diplomacy.

Diplomacy

Diplomacy is broadly defined as the art and practice of conducting international negotiations. The word *diplomacy* conveys the idea of negotiations that aid the management of international relations. Originally, diplomacy came from the Greek word *diploma*. Its English equivalent, after many different applications, came to mean "a state paper or official document granting some privilege." From there, it took on the meaning of the name for that piece of paper formally granting academic or professional recognition," its present meaning.

Diploma's usage being transferred to "the originals of such official state papers" is a later development that ties it to today's diplomatic institution. A diplomat is the body of persons that administer a government's official documents and manage its international relations. Of the numerous details diplomats handle, negotiations are a major part of them. A diplomat negotiates treaties with skill without offending the parties to their agreements. They do this by using **tact**, an essential tool for establishing good personal relations, especially with other nations. Those conducting such negotiations are generally called ambassadors or agents and are so chosen because of a unique skill in handling foreign affairs without arousing hostility. Winsome ambassadors gain impressive favor in foreign relations to their countries' advantage by employing customary diplomatic methods that influence their host countries' decisions. Through dialogues and other means, they avert war or other international violence and successfully resolve potential conflicts.

Outside of dialogues, the diplomat may use other measures of defusing volatile situations abroad and alter the landscape of nations' interrelationships so that treaties and other accords can be achieved. In addition to negotiating skills, the ambassador needs the ability to effectively, manage communications and overall forge relationships between divergent nations. To be welcomed and trusted, ambassadors expertly use their gift of tact to share thoughts and exchange ideas that present their sender's proposals and debate conflicting views. Experienced in non-offensive behavior and discussions, the ambassador's skill, integrity, and performance must be above question as the institution is known for notable persuasion technique that protect their sender's diplomatic edge.

Ambassadors, to accomplish their tasks, employ prescribed protocols that are generally well known and observed by the diplomatic community. *Protocol* is the term for the rules that govern diplomatic conduct. The word defines the range of written instruments associated with diplomatic activities, its decisions, or treaties. Examples of these include authenticated minutes of international conferences, preliminary agreements, or statements of principle—all of which are needful to forge mutually beneficial treaties and agreements between nations.

Sometimes the term *protocol* is applied to an agreement that has the effect of a treaty, especially when it sets forth guidelines for harmonious relations expressing agreed upon conduct and behaviors. Protocol shapes attitudes and forms the basis for returning accord to explosive or deteriorating situations. Diplomatic protocol codifies the international courtesies that govern the conduct of diplomatic servants or those otherwise engaged in international relations. Such a code is concerned with procedural matters of precedence among diplomats. Each foreign affairs office (or equivalent body) has an official in charge of protocol. Would not it be productive for apostles to do the same? Many discourtesies and inequities are committed in the name of spiritual liberty. Such acts are credited with divine approval although they are at times impolite and offensive. Diplomacy would not risk relationships and benefits on such carnal behavior.

Diplomacy further involves managing the ministers of a foreign court or embassy, and in previous centuries, diplomats were sent by princes and states. Wisdom and discretion are two additional skills used in international affairs. Diplomats use these subtly to handle their ambassadorial situations.

Diplomatic Immunity

A discussion of diplomatic immunity aids in the understanding of the spirit of the apostle's status in this world. It explains why the officer is such an antagonist to its gods. Diplomats enjoy diplomatic immunity; that is, they are exempt from search, arrest, or prosecution by the government to which they are accredited. If apostles were set up as embassies and recognized as such by their territorial rulers, this would be more readily practiced. To show its operation in the early church, the Holy

231

Spirit exercised the Godhead's preeminent authority by releasing His apostle's from jail when they were arrested in Jerusalem.

Immunity is deemed necessary for diplomats to properly, carry out their official duties. Thus, they may travel and communicate under autonomy, diplomatic autonomy, without interference to facilitate policy-making. Their embassy and residence enjoy similar privileges, technically called extraterritoriality. Many of these practices have been, with the advent of communications technology over time, absorbed into other means of directly contacting otherwise impossible to reach superiors. The change has made many diplomats serve more as expert advisers not as those empowered to make final decisions, though still greatly influencing the decision-making process.

Diplomatic Relations

The larger countries of the world have permanent diplomatic relations with scores of other nations, friendly or unfriendly. When a country has no diplomatic relations with each other, their interests may be represented by diplomats of other powers. This is especially so with two states at war. Their interests are usually represented by neutral states. A nation refusing to admit a foreign diplomat or demanding his or her recall to the home country requires the diplomat's government must either comply or break off relations.

What Is an Embassy?

The site of most diplomatic business is called an embassy.[28] An embassy broadly speaking is the building where an ambassador's service and assignments are stationed and

---

[28] The Columbia Encyclopedia, Sixth Edition; April 22, 2004

executed. The word *embassy* defines an organized body of agents maintained by a government for its international communications. Embassies are the offices and functions of an ambassador's service and include the entourage granted to him or her. Often they too reside and work in their embassies. An ambassador oversees an embassy and the staff of workers attached to it. As diplomatic officials, ambassadors occupy the position of the highest ranking appointed and accredited government representative residing in a foreign territory handling the sending nation's diplomacy.

Diplomacy is the official, and permanent, mission of one dispatched to another country for extended periods. Usually ambassadors are authorized **messengers** or representatives, but they can also be unofficial couriers sent on non-political, non-governmental missions, such as good will missions. At times ambassadorship is classified by two types of ambassadors, ordinary or extraordinary by some nations. Ordinary ambassadors take up residence in their assigned territories. Extraordinary ambassadors are task driven and dispatched on a special or unusual duty. This distinction between ambassadorial assignments coincides with the Lord's parable of the kingdom in Luke chapter nineteen. There the nobleman in the parable told his servants to *occupy* in their lands on his behalf until he returned. In that case their ambassadorship, and it did qualify as such, was both ordinary as they resided in the land for an extended period, and extraordinary as the task at the outset stated its temporariness. The reason the ten servants' assignments qualified as an ambassadorship is because of the language of the two words *sent* and *message*, "*apostello* and *presbeia*" used in Luke 19:1:14 for the forces that were sent to the ten servants hostile to the nobleman that left his land in their care.

233

Apostello means *sent* and often applies to an official sending rather than just an errand. Frequently as the word is presented in scripture, dispatch is meant or implied as the type of sending intended. The second word, *presbeia*, also makes the point. Its terminology pertains to the subject of this discussion. The word *presbeia* means jointly <u>embassy</u> and <u>ambassage,</u> the delegation of an ambassador and the message he or she is dispatched to deliver. In Luke's parable, the *ambassage* was militaristic as the last verse in the parable reflects. Taken traditionally to be a passive object lesson from these applications appears to be anything but. Read closely, it connotes a strong military and revolutionary meaning where conflicts are implied, opposition to assigned leadership surfaces, and a clash of the old guard and the new challenged the ten servants. Clearly, this parable is very different from the one on the talents it is often confused with, as the outcomes of both are quite different. Evidently, Jesus told it to enlighten His apostles on what they could never otherwise comprehend about His impending departure. Their occupation in the world after His ascension and until His eventual return as the triumphant Son of God, Son of Man was symbolically depicted in His story.

The nobleman, the subject of the parable, seems to have been assigning his trusted servants to maintain his hold on his territory and prosper his holdings in his absence. Those in the land must have well understood the significance of the ten servants' assignment and its impact on them since they chose the moment of the nobleman's departure to revolt against him. The excuse of the tenth servant, the fearful and judgmental one, indicates the nobleman was a no nonsense leader that demanded diligence, industriousness, or an enterprise and profitability from his agents. From the increase of the first nine, he was ninety percent successful. The fearful and lazy servant judged the nobleman's business practices, resented his success, and penalized him by hiding his money instead of at the least earning him interest on it. These three reactions signify the unprofitable servant's harbored resentment and disapproval of the nobleman's rulership. That would also make hi a party to the nobleman's overthrow.

Meanwhile, the other citizens now hated the nobleman more, establishing what would seem to be an embassy that dispatched ambassadors to confront and resist the authority and apparent stronghold of the ten. The implications of the possible events that transpired in the nobleman's absence are intriguing to say the least; they waged a campaign to hinder the ten servants. The parable exemplifies the Lord's awareness of the existence of embassies and the functions of ambassadorship that existed during His earthly apostleship.

Embassies in the Old Testament

According to *Easton's Bible Dictionary*, in the Old Testament the Hebrew word *tsir*, for "one who goes on an errand," pertains to an embassy and ambassadors. The word as they applied it equates to ambassadorship, as has been shown in Joshua 9:4; Proverbs 13:17; Isaiah 18:2; Jeremiah 49:14; and Obadiah 1:1. Another rendering of the word *ambassador*, is the Hebrew term *melits* defining "an interpreter," in 2 Chronicles 32:31. This word speaks to the interpretive function of ambassadorship where the fine points of diplomatic negotiations are interpreted to hammer out treaties. These scriptures have been explored elsewhere in this text. Refer to those discussions for a more extensive review.

Melits' use in scripture further explains the interpretative role of ambassadorship. The word's meaning includes the ability to speak other languages and understand other cultures to bridge any gaps that may hinder the ambassador's ability to form alliances or agreements. *Melits* says these become two of its ambassadors' essential requirements. It implies them, in order to forge their alliances or to build the relationships needed to transact their foreign business should be at least bi-lingual and ideally multi-lingual to increase their diplomatic worth. Accurate transmission of messages, policies, and proposals are critical if all parties to their agreements are to comprehend and unite. Therefore, valuable ambassadors must be able to communicate with the nationals of the lands to which, they are sent to win their favor at best, or at least their respect for the sake of cooperation.

Another word for ambassador is the word the Hebrew uses most frequently for *angel*; it is the word *malak*. *Malak* defines a "" and is the name used to designate those appointed by God to declare and execute His will. Its use correlates to Paul's ambassadorial references in 2 Corinthians 5:20 and Ephesians 6:20). *Malak* comes from the idea that in difficult times, angels were prone to show up to help or inform humans. Thus, those appearing out of nowhere to improve a situation or offset crises were dubbed angels even if they were only human so to speak. Other Old Testament applications of the ambassador's activities include:

- Contracting alliances (Joshua 9:4)
- Solicitation of favor (Numbers 20:14)
- Remonstrating wrongdoing (Judges 11:12)
- Consoling the loss of a monarch (2 Samuel 10:2)
- Congratulating a king's enthronement (1 Kings 5:1)

Injuring an ambassador in a foreign land insulted the king or sovereign who sent the diplomat and there were grave consequences to pay for it that often escalated in Bible times into war (2 Samuel 10:5). Here is where the Old Testament and New Testament apostolism connection emerges. This premise

236

makes ambassadorship and embassies costly to all parties involved. Ambassadors assigned to foreign lands required protection and their host countries often incurred the expense of seeing that their foreign diplomats were protected and adequately supplied. Also, all efforts had to be made to avoid giving the impression of mistreating them because they were foreign citizens.

Consuls: Another Embassy Type

Another aspect or type of embassy is the consulate. It is maintained by agents called consuls. A consul is a member of an agency organized as a body of public officials on foreign soil similar to the embassy. Its center, a consulate, is kept by a government on foreign soil to serve as its international political, commercial, and economic center. Consular aims are to protect the persons and interests of its nationals outside its borders. *Consul* is the name for its staff official. They are recognized by foreign states through the issuance of a special authorization that may be revoked by the admitting state at any time.

Primary consul duties in foreign lands include promoting and protecting commercial interests. They verify citizenship and issue passports. The consul further assures the sanitary conditions of the cargo, crew, and passengers of vessels that sail to its homeports, while mediating with local officials in legal matters involving its dispatched or residents citizens. Consular service, typically combined with diplomatic service, appears to be mainly financial and commercial. Consulates, it seems, accentuate commerce and treasury matters where trade, port activities, cargo conditions, and their profitability upon leaving foreign shores are its chief concerns. Governments' commerce and treasury departments usually install attachés at consulate offices to see to these affairs.

Immunity, like that enjoyed by an embassy diplomat, is also granted to consuls. They benefit from the same extraterritoriality in all matters pertaining to their official functions as ambassadors, and their premises likewise are equally privileged. Such honors are granted either by courtesy or through special treaties.

Special Consul Privileges

Exterritoriality is privileged immunity from local law enforcement bestowed upon diplomatic aliens. It provides they be treated in foreign nations as if they were physically on their home soil. Thus by customary international law aliens are physically seen as under the legal jurisdiction of their native countries. A reciprocal arrangement between countries, exterritoriality is generally bestowed upon visiting heads of state, diplomatic agents and their families, and upon United Nations officials. Being exempt from civil and criminal action, such persons may be neither sued nor arrested. They, their property, and residences are untouchable. Exterritorialists are also usually exempt from personal and property taxes. Exterritorials, though not vulnerable to prosecution for illegality, are nonetheless expected to adhere to the laws of the land in which they serve. Serious misconduct or criminality may result in a formal complaint to their home government and possible expulsion from the assigned territory. The protection of extraterritoriality also extends to state-owned public vessels in foreign territorial waterways and ports.

Ambassadors, Consuls, & Embassies

Up to about five hundred years ago, informal international communications or negotiations were transacted strictly by ambassadors specially appointed by the heads of states. Distance coupled with the lack of electronic communications systems conferred upon them broad latitude while on

238

diplomatic missions. Once they were dispatched, it was accepted that communications and supervision of the ambassador would be difficult and therefore imposed upon the plenipotentiary authority. Any misconduct, disobedience, or abuse of power were sternly proved and admonished. Ambassadors had to be trusted to make the best decisions and take the most prudent courses of actions on their countries' behalf. They were empowered to act quickly when needed to take advantage of opportunities for its nation's initiative. Whatever communication attempted took ages because they were hand delivered by special couriers. As a result, the ambassador's decisions were frequently independent. Besides this, everything imaginable the ambassador would need in the foreign country was sent along with him or her. This included staff, supplies, materials, gifts, and even inventory. Ambassadors were dispatched well stocked. It should be understood that apostles are only be appointed and dispatched by their head of state to fit the ambassadorship classification that goes with the office. For apostles-ambassadors is always a head of state to head of state arrangement.

The Founding of Literal Embassies

In early times, physically sending ambassadors from nation to nation was the only way international relations could be built. The time and money it took to travel back and forth to especially distant lands after awhile became exorbitant, proving costly and risky as the embassy's exposure to peril and ambush increased each time they set out on a return voyage. Naturally, this practice was seen as ineffective over time, and so physical embassies were stationed on foreign soil to reduce the travel expense and risk of peril. Established embassies served the added purpose of situating ambassadorial sites in distant lands to expedite discussions, negotiations, and enactments that formerly took years to accomplish. Thus, the policy of countries permanently hosting foreign representatives and providing them limited access and influence on their soil became the rule. Toward the end of the 17th century, permanently stationed legates became widespread. The highest and most integrious of these groups though, remained the ambassadors, despite the time it took to perfect the arrangement to the mutual satisfaction of all involved. Nonetheless, agents of foreign countries enjoyed considerable status and influence.

Eventually, the early unwieldy system improved and diplomatic agents were ranked and classified. Out of the new system came the following ranks of embassy agents:

- Ambassador
- Papal Legate
- Papal Nuncio
- Minister Plenipotentiary
- Envoy Extraordinaire
- Minister
- Minister in Charge of Affairs

Ambassadorship Began in Religious Spheres

It is hard to overlook the strong ecclesiastical connotations in the preceding list. That is because of the immutable tie the ancient world had between the heavenly and earthly, the spiritual and the natural, and the human and divine. From the beginning of time, all diplomatic relations in early human affairs had their roots in forging and often merging divine and human sovereigns' relations where deities were thought to initiate and oversee their alliances through their human agents. Here is why the Lord of all creation promised His most impressive monarch's world dominance and imposing international acclaim. His fulfillment of His promises is most strikingly seen with David and Solomon and eternally Jesus.

The above list of titles settled the official status of the embassy representatives stationed in a land. Assigning them transformed the heretofore loosely formed agents into a professional organization handling diplomatic service. At this point, the embassy drew wide recognition and became valued as a credible branch of international public service. Upon becoming a regularized institution, diplomatic services and their associated functions grew. Quite apparently, order, structure, and titles stabilize and expand an organization.

Ambassadors still acted as **personal** representatives of their state heads, but their staffs expanded as attachés were assigned to their embassies forming what is presently know as an official diplomatic corps. A typical diplomatic corps encompasses secretaries, military, cultural, and commercial attachés, clerical workers, experts, and advisers. Then and now, diplomatic business is routinely conducted according to established custom, a large part of which, as a throwback to the pre-embassy era involves messaging. Communications are important to diplomacy and are generally relayed by memorandums, informal or formal, oral or written communiqués. As miscommunication and disagreement, lies at the heart of all diplomatic breakdowns, negotiations can be stalled because of it. That makes note taking and recording very important to the process.

In the United States, ambassadors are appointed by the President and approved by the Senate. Biblically, God's senate is the twenty-four elders of creation. Recall their part in the Lord's Jesus' post ascension activities in Revelation 4:4, specifically His opening the seven seals shows their involvement in heaven's earthly affairs.

A Legate

A legate is another type of sent one. From the Latin word *legare* that means *to send*, a legate,[29] is one sent as a state representative of a high authority. Devolving from Roman history, the senate sent legates to provinces as imperial envoys. Eventually the word came to designate a type of papal ambassador. Scriptures that refer to or exemplify ambassadors have been discussed. Another word that surfaced in some of them refers to this agent. It is the word *luwts*. Joining *malak, tsir, melits, and presbeia*, as well as the New Testament's *presbeuo*, it identifies a representative on what may be recognized as an ambassadorial assignment.

Recall the two New Testament passages of scripture that specifically support the apostle's ambassadorial nature. The first is 2 Corinthians 5:20: "*Now then we are ambassadors for Christ, as though God did beseech you by us: we pray you in Christ's stead, be ye reconciled to God.*" Ephesians 6:20 is the second rendering: "*For which I am an ambassador in bonds: that therein I may speak boldly, as I ought to speak.*" In both contexts, the word pertains to apostles and apostleship.

God's Calculated Use of the Word Apostle

A close study of the various particulars of the apostle's office shows how premeditated Jesus' appointment of the officer was as the Founder and Establisher of His church. Research shows the Lord's choice of the term *apostle* was calculated and meant to inject a staggering force of laborers into God's kingdom. The breadth of understanding to be gained from this chapter

---

[29] The word "legate" comes from the Latin legare ("to send"). It has several meanings, all related to representatives: A legate is a member of a diplomatic embassy. In ancient Rome, a *legatus* or legate was an official assistant to a general or governor of a province. A *legatus* (often anglicized as legate) was equivalent to a modern general officer in the Roman army. Being of senatorial rank, his immediate superior was the dux, and he outranked all military tribunes. Wikipedia.com

comes from a comparison study of the word *apostle*, and its related terms. Explaining how God arrived at His appropriation of the title and what it aimed to convey to the people of that day, and ours, paves the way for the wisdom of this material. It reinforces why apostleship is the first and highest officer of the New Testament church.

Christ's selection of the term *apostle* inferred in John 15:19 indicate apostles were a professional order in the empire's service of His day. They were not, for the most part foreign to people back then. The disciples who followed Jesus did not stumble at the idea of the Lord instituting His own order of apostles when He announced it to them. Peter, not unlike the Israelites with Moses years earlier, seemed quite comfortable with it. More than that, they relished it. They were apostles of the Lord Jesus Christ, the promised Messiah just like the others of their time. To the original twelve that meant something awesome. So clear were they on the matter that Peter was taken aback by Christ's revelation of His impending crucifixion later in Luke 22:31. Peter could not fathom it because of his understanding of them as apostles. His perception of apostleship was shattered by Jesus' revelation. In his and the others mind, Jesus had come to retake the Jewish kingdom from the hands of the Romans (look at Peter's confusion in Matthew 16:21-23). It took the Pentecost Baptism to show them otherwise. Until then, the idea of Jesus' death was beyond their imagination.

To familiarize them with their call to become His principalic officers sent to handle God's supernatural affairs as ambassadors of His eternal kingdom, Jesus connected years of societal apostolism to visualize it for them. By the time, Christ came to induct them into the office after His resurrection as ambassadorial agents to the New Creation Ecclesia. For the early church, the reality, necessity, of apostleship was a

243

foregone conclusion in their minds. A staff of workers known as apostles always helped founders of new faiths in the religious sphere and established the governments of kingdoms in the secular. Jesus' work was thus made easier by precedence, a principle typically employed by the Lord in the past to prepare the earth for some new spiritual practice He intends to interject and impose. The pattern continued up to the introduction of the era of apostleship.

The role of an apostle, as their culture understood it, was to take back what was stolen or illegally seized and restore it to its rightful owner. See their attitude in Acts 1:6. The apostles of their day established conquered territories in the ways and will of their new kings. That is how they came to realize that as Christ's post Pentecost messengers they were Redemption's Apostles. Though Jesus had died, He had returned to them. Surely now they would finish their mission and reclaim Israel's liberty by doing what apostles before them had done. They would usher in change, overturn God's enemy strongholds, free His captives, and take back the Almighty's nation for its true King. Certainly, now Israel would again be free. After all, that is what apostles did, didn't they?

Jesus, on the other hand, had greater plans global and cosmic plans in mind. He was not looking to restore Israel only, but to regain the whole of humanity for His Father. He was not looking to overturn the Roman Empire, but to overturn Satan's. He was not sent to apostle a nation, but the entire world. His mission was not just to save Israel from the Romans, but His entire world and its future generations from sin. Despite all the years, that Jesus explained to them His commission was to establish God's kingdom on earth, the message had not yet penetrated their fog. Yes, He was the apostle of a new move, but it was an unprecedented one. He was the apostle of the Creator's eternal kingdom sent to establish His body of "called out ones—the ecclesia as His Church." His mandate was the accomplishment of Daniel 7:13, 14, and the fulfillment of Genesis 3:15.

As the first apostle of the New Covenant, during His earthly ministry, Christ was to bring many sons and daughters to God. His success would set the stage for the final curtain of Satan's reign. He would take back the kingdoms of this world for the Lord God Almighty in much the same way earthly apostles were taking kingdoms for their kings. Although it was all so plain to Christ, the apostles believed otherwise. Luke 19:11 shows how the early apostles saw the Lord's and their own commissions. It was drastically different from what Christ was really sent to earth to do. Exploring the root of the word *apostle* shows it goes all the way back to before the Greek Empire, as its etymology found its way into their language.

The institution had become firmly entrenched in the Roman Empire's aggressive campaign of conquering nations to enlarge its territories. Their activities created the need for a word to define the commissions they were handing out to the ambassadorial military generals known as *strategi* in their empire, who helped them reach their goal. A single term was needed to classify those they sent out as ambassadors of the king's best interests and generals that conquered territories. The Romans drew on the Greek language for one. Research says they settled on *apostle* and used it in much the same way as the Greeks used it: To identify *an order of high ranking ambassadors with military might, powers of persuasion and diplomacy; and the ability to disciple captives and converts to the culture and laws and life of the Roman's kingdom.* It seems these diplomatic generals were accorded enormous powers and comprised an elite commission to propagate the aims of the empire and unify its citizenry. In addition, they were to, forcefully if need be, enlarge and settle the king's territory while at the same time stabilize its holdings.

This explanation coincides perfectly with Luke's parable of the Ten Mina illustrated above.

The core of these emissaries' authority it appears was created through overthrow, legislative license, judicial power, and governmental jurisdiction. They logically comprised the chief rulers of the region they apostled. Apostles were seen as influential leaders driven to induce converts to become settled and productive in their new kingdom.

The key terms used to define apostles and their customary usage further unfolds them as *generals*, *strategists*, and *territorial warriors*. They were purposeful, focused, and committed to the king's service with an unfailing allegiance. Winning such monarchical trust made defection or betrayal fatal. Their word, as fierce as their actions, promptly became law where they were stationed to demonstrate the powers and authority they were delegated. Lastly, for obvious reasons diplomacy being the mien of their responsibilities, these superior agents of the king's special service were highly educated and intelligent. The ability to communicate the mind of the king, his will, thoughts, and ways to those brought into the kingdom called for excellent communications. Therefore, the apostles were highly trained and extremely knowledgeable of their kingdom, its laws, philosophies, teachings, and sociology. Many of today's professing apostles would fail these simple measurements miserably.

Education, as is the case with any takeover or take-back campaign, is central to the orientation of a newly organized or restructured entity. Hence, catechism figures prominently in apostleship. Once a group has been conquered and inducted into the mainstream of their captor's society, the next most prudent step is to catechize them. The word *catechism*, which we have come to associate strictly with the Roman Catholic religion, has many meanings. It does have its roots in religion, but much of its object has to do with socialization. Catechism covers systemizing, indoctrinating, and teaching those that have been apostolized. Judicial features extend to interrogating possible resistors or criminals while education emphasizes the apostle's pedagogic tasks. Pedagogy identifies the apostles' duty to school thoroughly their new populace. This activity required illuminating, civilizing, thoroughly guiding, enlightening, and instructing those that once belong to and obeyed another kingdom. The word's use is expanded to include the formulation of beliefs, principles of doctrine and dogma, articles of faith, and philosophical creeds. These all aim to render every new member of the kingdom a productive, profitable, sociable law abiding member of the new society. For these very concrete reasons, apostleship also relies on citizenship instruction in the kingdom's culture and government. Such responsibilities are why the apostle's mandate demands extensive, sophisticated, and broad based education. The duty of properly orientating a soul to the Lord's kingdom of eternal life and its immortal protocols is weighty. Presenting everyone perfect in Christ Jesus as Paul understood in Colossians 1:28, is the apostle's ultimate measurement of success.

Whether in the Church or in another culture, the elementary principles of the knowledge and wisdom of the land they represent must be well learned by apostles. Without such, the possibly of making the new additions to the kingdom skilled, socially productive and functional citizens is slim.

In anticipation of the duty, the apostle's capacities are enhanced by strong articulation skills. Those appointed to the office need as their highest gift the ability to make the deep, mysterious, and obscure plain to their audiences. Effectively done, their vital truths become easy to apply. Institution building, development, and cultivation of other educators and leaders to continue developing and stabilizing new converts are innate to the apostolate. The ability to draft systematic means of positing orally relative, foundational teachings emerges as one of the mandates of its call by definition to explain the central need for commissioned ones to expertly communicate principle kingdom knowledge to those in their care.

Hence, apostles must be insightful and profound at once to expedite newcomers' adaptation to the culture of God's kingdom. It is the only way to nurture responsible converts to the government, culture, and commands of their new king. The last move's obsession with liberating Christians from God's law deviated from it in practice to the carnal trends of the era. They exemplify the sharp contrast between pastors and evangelists, and the apostles of the kingdom. Law, legitimacy, and legality are important to apostleship as the objective of displacing one government with another is at the heart of the mantle's purpose. Thus, apostles recognize, for instance, that the Ten Commandments and Moses' Law were never errant on God's part. What made them insufficient was that they were written on "tables of stone," rather than "tablets of the flesh," the human heart. Therefore, the apostle Paul said in Romans chapter seven that the law is holy, its commandments just and good. He understood the law to be spiritual but in conflict with the carnal soul sold under sin.

How Apostles See Law & Government

Apostles see the entirety of God's creation in heavenly and celestial terms. Primordial to the apostle means eternal, not ancient. That is contrary to how traditional religion sees it. Based on this, Christ's apostles comprehend what the Holy Spirit writes in the believer's heart upon redemption is not a new law but God's eternal government for immortal beings. Mortals need what Moses delivered to Israel in contrast. Because humans are born dead to God and confined to this

248

world, they are already judged as the race that failed God's creation law and government. Their being born to the doomed league of devils that revolted in creation with Lucifer settled the fact that no flesh could succeed in eternity's divine law. Although the sentiment of God's righteousness was never removed, God's legal objective for Moses' law was a codified means of accepting His chosen that allowed Him to bless them on earth. The Lord knew in advance that people could never live up to His immortal law on earth in the flesh; they needed everlasting life to do so. If they could, the need for Jesus would never be recognized.

God's law as the law of life is for immortals. It is how those of His spiritual realms live and prosper in all His created worlds. On earth, it kills the doomed but in eternity, it sustains creation. The Creator's spiritual law is for spirit beings; that is why people must be born again to pass from death to life, from carnality to spirituality. Once this happens, a person joins the ranks of those that prevent and harness sin, a view completely opposite of how the contemporary Christian sees God's government. To the redeemed today, God's law enslaves them and obstructs their freedom to sin. In no other government would such an attitude and its resultant behavior be tolerated. Such an attitude is what necessitates apostles. They are sent to overturn it by aligning their doctrine and its effects where they truly abide: with immortals, the true controllers of creation.

Mortality belongs to Satan who rebelled against the very law that God's people spurn today, but remember he did so as an immortal being. What Jesus accomplished did not eliminate God's spiritual law. It merely concluded its rituals, ceremonies, and observances, which only kept people's minds, stayed on their sin, distorting their relations with their covenant God (see Hebrews 10:1-5). Once the Messiah succeeded in His mission, these ceased to be needed because of what Jesus Christ

249

accomplished. What motivated their institution and their subsequent benefits from eternity were never erased. The Lord stills hates idolatry, fornication, adultery, and crime. He still wants His creation to behave as one big family treating everyone as a neighbor. Fear of loss and lack continue to inspire sin as do greed and desire.

God is the same and never changes, for Him to do so is to pattern (and subject) Himself after the author of sin and death. That is tantamount to dethroning Himself. In addition, to overlook in Christians what He condemned in angels and other immortal beings on the ground that the new birth, being born again as spirit beings is to set Himself up for a larger scale Luciferian revolt. No human in his or her right mind would do such a thing. The very faults and defects that caused Him to reject Lucifer still offend Him. Therefore, He sent the law of eternal beings to earth to offer His rescue and redemption to those that would keep it. Those that observe it, do so by becoming spirit beings. When they do, they qualify as heirs of eternal life to inherit it (read John 5).

Snapshot of Apostleship at Work

The chart below is an example of the apostle's prioritization. It depicts how the officer should organize his or her embassy and what should take precedence over what. Not meant to be a rigid, this chart aims to help new apostles structure their ministries to the King's best interests. It can serve as a guide to seasoned apostles trying to determine how on track they are in their apostolic commissions or to steer newcomers to the office in their God ordained direction.

Key Apostleship Actions

Apostles are action people. The very nature of their call is to action. Passivity is the apostle's furlough notice. Likewise, futility; it too signals the apostle's efforts are being thwarted and his or her skills and expertise either under utilized or misapplied. Review the following chart and compare its five categories of service (Kingdom, Church, Outreach, Enterprise, and Alliances) with how you presently see or execute your apostleship. Also, notice what should be important to apostles to ascertain if the service you are presently or contemplating rendering the Lord is comparable. By these, you will be able to judge yourself the extent and nature of harvest your ministry can expect based on the caliber of service your rendered. The following is merely a guide to provide a place of beginning: It suggests what percentage of apostolic concentrations should be stressed in every essential area of apostleship. They are cyclically applied. The list depicts major apostolic actions in relation to the other functions and duties assigned its role. The action columns list typical apostolic duties in contrast to their applied areas.

Quality Apostolic Concentrations

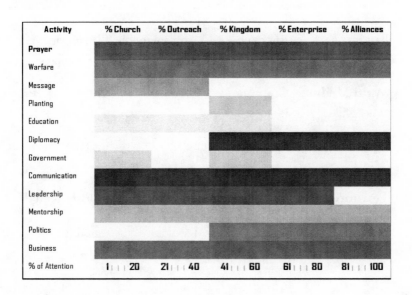

Activity	% Church	% Outreach	% Kingdom	% Enterprise	% Alliances
Prayer					
Warfare					
Message					
Planting					
Education					
Diplomacy					
Government					
Communication					
Leadership					
Mentorship					
Politics					
Business					
% of Attention	1 20	21 40	41 60	61 80	81 100

In addition to the above, apostles ought to be able to measure their effectiveness by identifying their routine activities. These should include, but not be limited to, the following:

Possible Apostolic Enterprises & Ventures

Stages & Accomplishments You May Want to Build

From Your Commission

Churches	Planting	Sustaining	Maturation	Multiply
Schools	Found Curriculum	Student Recruit	Educate & Train	
Community Development	Assistance	Improvements	Housing	Economy
Network	Relationships	Alliances	Exchange	Fortify
Business Ventures	Revenue	Employment	Prosperity	
Multi Media	Communicate	Illustrate	Inform	Propagate
Drama & Arts	Spread Message		Portray Doctrine	
Territorial	Establish Stronghold		Fortify Kingdom	
National	Create National Voice		Establish Nat Influence	

International	Globalization by Discipling Nations to Populate Kingdom
Publication/ Distribution	Produce Books, Tapes, Literature, Periodical, Courses

Ancient Terms Identify & Blend Apostleship with Militarism

As old as the ancient religious movements that preceded them, the shell Christ chose to sketch His Church's leadership and government comes from the Old Testament's *melakim*, the *eved* (or *evad*), and the *shaliach*. To conclude this chapter's discussion, the broadest military connotation relating to the apostle and apostolic ministry is proffered. It is another term that further isolates the nature and scope of the apostle's office. The Hebrew word *Tsava* clearly depicts the institutional pattern the Lord designed for the office. In particular, the word describes the officer and his or her work as it pertains to its stratospheric station and principalic function. This ancient term captures the call, its purposes, main activities, and range of authority most persuasively, integrating the apostle's military, gubernatorial and conversion responsibilities. Just look at some of *Tsava's* meanings below to picture the major initiating mandates of the apostle's commission. As the study advances, refer to them repeatedly to confirm the appropriateness of this application to the office of the apostle. The word *Tsava* essentially defines:

Meaning of the Word *Tsava* in Relation to Apostleship

1. A mass of persons or things, especially for war.

2. A campaign and its army or troops set in battle array.

3. A host; the host of heaven.

4. The angels or stars as assigned to the officer and those he or she musters for the warfare and/or the campaign that necessitated.

5. The call and dispatch of the officer in the first place.

6. The hosts of angels that surround God's throne.

7. A military service.

8. Warfare and the heavy service that result from it.

9. The miserable conditions that arise from war, such as hardship, injury, lack, and calamity.

10. Temple services, the priestly element of apostolic service.

11. Service done for a superior such as God and Christ, who are over the apostle.

12. A non-military host.

The military overtones connected with the word *Tsava* are similar to the Greek terms to define the apostle, its apostolate, and apostolos. Together the words complement each other even though their applications are centuries apart. Furthermore, *Tsava* leans more on the eternal and universal rule of God as implied in Job 25:2. It implies that portions of that rule are divided to Jesus Christ, and through Him to His servants (see Isaiah 53:12). As used in scripture, the word invokes God's Theo-militaristic roles in the life and defenses of His nation Israel.

Since Israel, like most countries of the day, was under theocratic rule, it was firmly Creator God's nation. Consequently, their clashes with their neighboring rulers and rivals came under the heading of religious battles, or holy wars. It was well understood at the time that whenever a nation went to war it was because the gods over those nations had engaged them. The territories up for grabs were spiritual and earthly, natural and heavenly. The presence of Jehovah's angels in every one of His nation's conflict supports this view, and the following passages of scripture exemplify it: Judges 5:23; 2 Kings 6:15-18; Isaiah 55:4; Joshua 5:14; and 2 Chronicles 32:21. What all of these passages share, is the reality of natural battles being supernatural in origin occurring at once on different planes of God's creation. Compare this statement with the words of the prophet Isaiah in Isaiah 43:12 where another word is used that can be a kin term to *Tsava: Tsawah.* It means to constitute, make firm and to establish. The word defines the acts, processes, and authority of appointing anyone over anything, such as the authority the apostle possesses to install, inaugurate, and ordain subordinate ministers to the various assignments that emerge from a commission. *Tsawah* expressly means to command, charge, ordain, and commission. Its inferences include a delegation (as embassy ambassadors) set or commissioned over something defined. Such ministers of the kingdom were initiated as messengers; officers furthermore charged with setting things in order. Lastly, the word refers to a superior giving a verbal communication to a subordinate.

What brings both words forward to the Greek renderings and definitions of the apostle is the last meaning for *Tsava.* It coincides with the final meaning of the word is *stratia,* one of the terms found in a long list of words that pertain to the apostle. Specifically, *stratia* pertains to the military aspects of the apostle's mantle. The word defines an encamped army (celestial or human) as numerous as the heavenly hosts. *Stratia* stresses the (spiritual) militaristic components of the apostolic mandate in the same way that tsava does.

Apostleship & Spiritual Warfare

As you can deduce, this teaching continues to unfold apostleship, showing how the two terms *apostle* and *warfare* are unavoidably inclusive. The office grew out of warfare and so cannot operate or exist apart from it. As a case in point, refer to Paul's words to Timothy in 2 Corinthians chapter 10. There he refers to weapons and warfare together in the fourth verse. The word used for warfare in those contexts is the one discussed above, *stratia*. It describes an *apostolic career* and its military campaigns. Its use links warfare in the heavenlies and the discharge of apostolic duties on earth. Furthermore, in 2 Timothy 2:4, Paul in his counsel to his young apostle uses a kin term to *stratia* to encourage the youthful minister in his apostolic campaign, another apostleship term. The word used for war in that passage is related to the apostolate as well. Not only is that the case, but the phrase refers to Timothy as a soldier, an enlisted one, and ties his service to the warfare of Christ that he has been inducted in the army of the Lord to lead and enlist others to fight.

Apostles as spearheads and catalysts of their commissarial movements gather persons and possessions to support and expedite their ministries. Theirs are ministries only in the sense that they are servants of Christ and through Him God. Also in this context, they serve His ecclesia as well. Generally, the people and possessions gathered are extracted from those discipled by the apostle's early ministry efforts. Usually launched by evangelism, early apostolism often begins by preaching God's move or present actions in the earth. Following this, the message turns to the salvation and conversion of lost souls. See Acts 4:32-37 and Matthew 10, along with Mark 3:13-19. Initially, the campaign (that includes warring with demons and resistant religious cultures and mindsets) makes up the apostolic mandate that first secures its army from the body of New Creation saints born into the kingdom of God. What adds to its supernatural and stratospheric nature is the role of the host of heaven, consisting of the entourage of angels dispatched to the earth to undergird the apostle's mantle. For the apostle this complement of spiritual assistance is critical to commission success because the apostle's main combat realm is in the heavenlies where both the angels, and the demons that oppose the mantle and its work on earth, dwell or confront. That is why Jesus gave Peter and later other apostles the keys to the kingdom of heaven, not the kingdom of God. Paul spoke along this vein often throughout his writings. According to his 1 Corinthians 9:7 counsel, Paul responds to people's refusal to support his ministry as part of his apostolic resistance. He comprehends the wisdom of Ecclesiastes 7:12 that say money is a defense and without it one's hedge of protection and performance are weakened.

Moreover, Paul informed Timothy that he was to wage war (spiritual warfare) in the heavenlies over his call to enable him to execute his apostolate. That warfare, he instructed the young man was to be fought with the prophetic word of the Lord that no doubt sent him into God's service, based on Acts 13:2. It was also based on the impartation Paul gave him by the laying on of hands to set him office. Timothy's warfare is pivotal to apostleship as explained by, for instance, Ephesians chapter 6. There, references to the spirits of darkness are frankly detailed by the apostle Paul. In Ephesians 3, he introduced the idea by revealing the invisible hierarchy of heaven. The passage makes it plain that the Lord God, Creator of all things, has ranked the authorities of His creation in a specific order. In addition, Ephesians reveals Christ as the Head of the Almighty's creation orders consisting of principalities, powers, dominion, thrones and so forth; all personified by angelic beings.

In the same statement, Paul shows his intimacy with the Creator's hierarchy by adding that the church is above them all as Christ's body and that, according to Ephesians 3:10, it is to demonstrate Creator God's manifold wisdom over creation's dark powers. In 2 Corinthians 10, the apostle spells it out far more specifically by detailing the scope, authority, spheres, and nature of apostleship as meant by God and Christ. Moreover, the angels constitute the supernatural agency force sent forth to minister to the heirs of salvation, serving the Father and Christ as spiritual messengers and guardians of the church. They comprise the network of principalic archons over creation that exercises the Savior's power and dominion in and through the church. This work identifies them as the seven principalic powers of creation with whom the apostle melds and interacts on God's behalf. See the book of Revelation for the list of them.

The term *angelic delegation* is the one coined for identifying every minister's entourage of heavenly support backing his or her work. This force is how the Lord dispenses His apostles' power. No apostle can really expect to be effective or established without them.

Angels & Apostleship

Angels, as a case in point, retrieved the apostles from jail, warned them of impending danger; and steered Paul through many perilous adventures during his missions. They supply God's spiritual military help to His human messengers on the earth. Military refers to the spiritual combat apostles are drawn into often in the course of ministry. It is not, as early church apostles succeeding the founding ones thought, the engagement of other countries or opposing faiths in physical combat. For the apostle learns early that the battles must be wrought and won in the realm of the spirit, in the heavenlies, the exercise of their right the to the keys of heaven's kingdom that Christ gave

Peter. Heaven is where the real command centers that govern the natural world are stationed. Therefore, inevitably astute apostles are well versed in the language and strategies of spiritual combat. Many of them over the years have been ridiculed for emphasizing spiritual foes over earthly ones and spiritual warfare above physical conflicts. Their wisdom has also been perverted by those assuming they know and understand what the apostle instinctually perceives about the forces of darkness. Hence, those who emulate what they see for selfish reasons strike an unhealthy balance between spiritual warfare and earthly pragmatism.

No bona fide apostle is ignorant of who and what his or her real foe is. They are well taught by God to identify the strategies and tactics of Satan poised to frustrate and overturn the work they are assigned. As a result, their apostolic language and actions accentuate spiritual combat and kingdom militarism above all. Strategy, planning, tactical maneuvers of a spiritual nature are integral to the well skilled and educated apostle's mantle regardless of its sphere of execution. Constant interactions with the Godhead see to it that the officer never forgets who the real target of their ministry is. Likewise, constant encounters with the Redeemer see to it that the apostle is never ill equipped to deal with the archrivals of Christianity and its truth. Those who meet them often find themselves flustered or perturbed at some of the remarks heard from apostle's mouths and they confront with the issues, stratagems, and manipulations of darkness. This is particularly so if they discern the presence or operations of Satan's spiritual guard using a person to unwittingly aid in their schemes. Here is where many people resent and oppose the apostle's mantle. Being well groomed generals and commanders, apostles can often receive at a moment's notice God's direction to tackle a pressing or irritating problem conjured by the demonic forces are now ready to be battled. Caught up in the Lord's assault on the problem, the apostle is likely to appear rude and unfeeling in the process. If the problem is connected with a person their rebuke or commands are not meant to be offensive since what is being spoken is aimed at the demonic forces attacking, deluding, or manipulating someone.

To biblically ground this truth, think back to the Lord Jesus' handling of Peter when the young apostle sought to correct the Messiah on the next stage of His mission. Refer to the account in Matthew 16:21-23. Onlookers that heard the Lord call Peter "Satan" could have easily misunderstood, and rejected the Christ after that incident. However, apparently their training helped them get through a naturally embarrassing moment meant to deliver Peter from the seductions of darkness that eventually led the man to betray a friend and Savior. A similar incident happened between Peter and Paul in Galatia, See Galatians 2:11.

After days of distressing divination from a girl possessed by a familiar spirit, Paul turned abruptly at the right time and rebuked the spirit. Those void of spiritual insight no doubt heard him speak harshly to the young damsel. However, the ones capitalizing off the young woman's *gift* knew full well what happened. Several more scripture passages make our point. The apostle's militaristic mandate is confrontational and frequently misunderstood as a result. For these reasons, it is constantly feared by darkness that pretends to be the light.

Chapter Summary

1. Apostleship began as a societal blend of the sacred and the secular.

2. Jesus' world strove to segregate one from another.

3. Ambassadorship is one of the several designated aspects of apostleship.

4. Ambassadorship is tied to apostleship in the Old and New Testaments.

5. Two words define apostleship in the New Testament: *Tsawah* and *stratia*.

6. Apostles are plenipotentiaries, diplomatic agents, consuls, and many other things that ground their territories to establish their embassies.

7. Diplomacy and tact are important to apostleship.

8. Four words designate an embassy and ambassadorship in the Old Testament: *Tsir, melits, luwts,* and *malak.*

9. Consul is an embassy type that focuses on citizenship, trade, and commerce.

10. God deliberately chose the word *apostle* to identify His principalic corps or plenipotentiaries.

11. Apostleship is a military call to arms to activate apostles as stratospheric warriors.

12. Military warfare is central to successful apostleship.

13. Angels partner with apostles in ministry and warfare.

14. Apostleship is an eternal public office in heaven and on earth.

Chapter Eleven

Apostolic Protocols, Etiquette & Interrelations

Chapter Discussions

This chapter seeks to present some tangible refinements to enhance apostles' ministry service and strengthen vital ministry relationships. The most fundamental relationship principles apostles today must embrace is that collaboration, alliances, and group ventures are essential to the institution's success. With the office of the apostle being initially ambassadorial, it is important that those occupying it comprehend what that means. While there may be apostles dedicated as apostolic ambassadors, others as ecclesiastical, and still others as political or entrepreneurial. All apostles are launched on some ambassadorial platform and that is the object of these discussions. From what has been seen to date, current apostles fall short in their expression of an ambassador as has been addressed so far. If world kingdoms relied on such disarray, discourtesy, poor professional etiquette, and protocol disregard there would be less peace accords on the planet than there are now.

A group that genuinely esteems itself and its station in society is usually motivated to unity, even if it is only for the protection of their order. Peer relationships, colleague regard and support, and professional courtesies are paramount to them. Realizing the damage disharmony and internal strife can do to any institution, the diplomatic officer makes keeping the peace within the ranks as important as establishing peace in their territories. That is not always the case with Christ's Apostles.

Remember, it was said elsewhere that apostles were installed into their offices *before* the church was born, making them immediate officials of the King. Apostleship is the single office of the King that is outside the bounds of the church. It is closest in proximity to the Lord and His rulership. If the church had not been birthed, as we know it, apostleship would have been the only office that the Lord Jesus instated in His kingdom upon returning home. No other office of the New Testament church would or could have existed. That truth on its own has sweeping implications, saying that all other New Testament sent ones are dispatched below the rank of ambassador if the word means what it says. Spiritually and organizationally speaking the remaining ministries in the church are thus sent out as part of the embassy head's attaché, Christ's apostles being that head.

It is an established fact that apostles are how the church was born. It was drawn into their office and mantle and not the other way around. Had they not preached Christ's message, the church as Jesus ordained it could never have been, for the Holy Spirit was dispatched to the earth for this very purpose. John 16:15-16 launched His earthly ministry through the apostles. Subsequently, it was their duty to receive and implement the Lord's ecclesiastical leadership plan for those born again on the first Pentecost. Their years of training and pre-ascension crash course inculcated them on how to install others into Christ's service under their pre-existing station. Had the apostles not done so, they would have been forced to return to Judaism from which they were all being called, and to their previous professions.

In addition, the ambassadorial function that grounds apostleship in and through the church annexed it to a bigger more complex vision that of occupying Christ's divine embassy on earth and seeing to His best interests in the planet as any foreign agent would do for his or her sender. Whether the first apostles understood this or not is debatable, but for sure their next generation apostle Paul did, which is why he could articulate their outreach, catechistic, government, institutional, and other establishment functions so clearly. Paul recognized that Jesus as creation's newest and final deity, once hidden in the Godhead, came to earth as its manifested eternal monarch. He understood that when Jesus established a nation by begetting His own offspring as scores of divine beings did before Him meant a kingdom was born. The Savior's task was comparable to any earthly ruler interested in enriching and enlarging His stronghold on earth. Paul no doubt had opportunity to draw on his vast political and religious knowledge to convey these ideas to the other apostles. As all consuming as it was, the ecclesia was not the apostles' sole responsibility. Acts chapter six says they knew this and determined to give themselves to God's word. Paul's ecclesiastical activities were as much aimed at the world and its government as they targeted the church. Collectively, these facts resolve the sphere and scope of the true apostle's service. Theirs is radically different from the pastoral mandate the church has grown up with for ages. Apostles could never be governed by the church as its foundational governors. The thought of doing so is just plain absurd.

Two other passages of scripture amplify these truths. Interestingly they come from Luke the physician, another professional whose standing in the community would have exposed him to this ancient office. Introduced earlier, they return us to Luke's gospel where he uses the term *ambassage* explained thoroughly in earlier chapters to show the embassy concept the Savior no doubt wanted him to grasp. Both times, using the word in parables allowed Jesus to veil His true objectives until much later. Surely, during their forty-day class with the Risen Lord after His resurrection made their applications more definite. The apostles would found His eternal embassy on the planet and set themselves up as heaven's celestial diplomatic corps. Back during that time, embassies were traveling caverns roving from place to place to whatever territories their rulers dispatched them to overtake, settle, or birth embassies. Official residences then were in tents.

As civilization grew up, fixed edifices were erected in places where another's diplomatic corps was welcome or authorized. Upon entering a land, the ambassador had to bring and distribute the proper gifts. These were selections of their finest objects, commodities, and treasures. Once this was done, usually ceremoniously in the highest and most prestigious places, the business for which the ambassador was sent commenced. Peace accords to avert war, joint ventures to strengthen both kingdoms' profitability or to form alliances that fortify each nation's territories to protect themselves from invasion constituted the usual business transacted. Another most frequent mission in early times linked apostleship to ambassadorship. It was when one deity determining to wage war against another for the sole purpose of seizing and annexing it to his or her own was the goal. The word *apostello* inserted in the above verse, by now self-explanatory alludes to this aim. It is the term used most often for sending apostles. *Pempo*, a word discussed elsewhere, adds the dimension of a hurried sending, normally stated as dispatch. For our purposes, the word *apostello* emphasizes ambassage, the topic of our discussion. Being an early word for embassy, it is best applied in a multi-national environment where people and nations spread out wish to interrelate. Embassies extend one government into the territory of another.

All this is to say much growth and maturity is needed by today's apostles stepping onto the world and church front. They are going to need greater refinement and grooming to be taken seriously. Apostles today shifting from another stream should surrender to mentors and coaches to help them successfully make the transition and acquire the skills needed to distinguish themselves as the world ambassadors they desire to be. Observing most of them in action is an almost frightful experience. Tact and courtesy are often wanting. Broken spirits and hearts have been calloused as defenses outweigh wisdom and knowledge. Professional and social ties rudely and abruptly severed, rather than use tense circumstances to hone apostolic skill for diplomatic tact and harmony. For the most part, this is routinely how Christian conflicts are resolved.

Many renowned apostles belie their grace by crudely snubbing peers and colleagues and crushing the spirits of those up and coming. The idea of uniting for a common cause is met with old errant rhetoric that failed its own generation. Schism is justified with "God called me to be different gave me something that cannot be blended with any other, sent me to work only with elites" and other uncooperative excuses that discredit the true call of the office. Communications are abhorrent as phone calls go unreturned, invitations rudely spurned, and contacts rejected for what is perceived as opportunities that are more lucrative.

Unsophisticated apostles trivialize social settings with conversations and brag fests where name-dropping, label comparing, and boasts about personal possessions accumulated in ministry dominate discussions. These tasteless practices are behaviors sophisticated ambassadors would abandon to avoid giving the impression of unchecked pride and arrogance. Such offensive behavior can offend relationships and risk vital business later. Besides this is the poor habit of using the religious guise of testifying to engage in these practices. Etiquette, ethics, and justice on all levels are lacking as the normal courtesies of hosting and welcoming peers; followers and colleagues are abandoned for a haughty superiority that would stall any international accord. The very simple regard for the office of apostleship itself and the exchange of mutual respect for those that walk in it, particularly in light of the severe trials and tests every apostle must face before promotion, is non-existent. Novices and young apostles envisioning a high spiritual climate and a flow of God's exceptional wisdom and grace to transpire in many closed apostolic gatherings are sadly disappointed and confused when they finally attend one. They often leave the encounter shocked to see the same carnality they suffered with secular leaders. Christ's vision is rarely touted at such 'after the service meetings', as alliances to support apostleship's corporate success are risked everyday on the altar of the fragile ego. All this is not to say that social chatter is inappropriate, it is the sometimes braggadocios spirit that creeps into them that is unprofessional.

Yet this generation of apostles claims a call to the world stage, its marketplace, and political arenas. To succeed in these territories much grooming and finesse has to happen. Conversations that saturate discussions with useless theological and worldly harangues must be abandoned. Encounters with all people should be governed by Hebrews 13:2; one simply does not know if one they snub is an angel unaware. A common affirmation of those among the ranks and all that are encountered should become a byword. Explaining snobbery and rudeness away with feeble excuses about personality shortfalls is no longer adequate. Ambassadors and public officials earn the right to their positions by conforming to whatever it takes to succeed. Far too long church leaders have avoided the necessary personal developments imposed upon our secular counterparts for their posts by claiming their antisocial conduct is spiritual or contemplative. A wiser and more sophisticated generation forced to take numerous interpersonal seminars will not accept that excuse anymore.

The byword for the entire church is to grow up. We must all bring and keep our emotions in check and avoid the appearance of selfish ambition by being kind and sociable to all, especially those that support us. Refusing to mature and overcome shyness and insecurity by cloistering does not serve an ambassador's purpose. A public office requires effectively mingling with the public. Those that would be mentors and coaches of apostles emerging today should include in their developmental programs, personal and interpersonal skills, communication and conflict resolution, diplomacy and tact as effective etiquette and socialization skills. Protégés should be taught positive ways to breach the uncomfortable barriers to getting to know, working with and bonding with people. They should be told the consequences to themselves and the Lord's kingdom for needlessly offending peers, colleagues, and superiors.

Protégés should be schooled on how to handle non-church public appearances from grooming and attire to dinner table and conversation etiquette. They should be forced into these environments until they are comfortable with breaking the ice with strangers and holding warm friendly social conversations. These skills are just as important as preaching, prophesying, teaching, and scolding the church. In some cases, they may be more important if the apostle wishes to access and enter a great ministry doors. This type of training should be included as part of every apostle's Public Ministry Refinement classes and students should be required to, more than barely pass them.

Apostolic Covering & Tithing

Of late, there is much debate and consternation over the matter of tithing. When it comes to spiritual coverings, the matter is intense. Those that have submitted to a covering are irritated by the demand to tithe to that covering for what are presumably spiritual services that have yet to be adequately explained. Elsewhere, we discuss spiritual covering from the perspective of a mentor, a tutor, an authority, and an influence. Just think for a moment of the demand all those different spiritual benefactions dependent upon the tithe. Does one tithe to the covering as a mentor, tutor, advisor, or promoter? Do they tithe to the influencer or the authority? Who makes the decision and what is it based upon?

Here, to wrap up the discussion, the matters of how to handle the tithe as a leader and to whom those in authority tithe are addressed. To do so, let us begin at the beginning by answering first what the tithe is, how it began, and its founding premise. Often when people can follow the line of thinking on a matter, they usually arrive at its soundest conclusions, policies, practices, and revelations on their own. First, we start with what is the tithe.

Literally, tens of thousands of dollars are given to spiritual coverings worldwide and precious few of the tithers can say what they got for their money, and the tithe is money. Since it is money, the question invariably arises, what does one get in return for the tithe to his or her spiritual covering? The number one premise of the tithe is that it is a war tax. That is how it came to God's people in the first place. The most basic return should be defense and protection from the customary onslaughts that are launched every time a newcomer enters Christ's service.

What is the Tithe?

Abraham, having won the war between himself and the five kings, as a thank offering to the Almighty who wrought his victory, rendered a tenth of his spoils to the Lord's lone priesthood on earth. That is how the war and tax piece applies to the tithe. Melchizedek met Abraham returning from his unbelievable slaughter and administered his first communion with his new God. Abraham's history as a Babylonian prophet no doubt educated him on divine protocol. For example, one always gives the first fruit of the war spoils to the god responsible for a victory.

Perhaps Abraham knew Melchizedek or he may have appeared in what were commonly accepted priestly garments for his day; either way, Israel's progenitor knew that the Almighty gave him his victory and was entitled to its war tax, also called back then a death tax.[30] The normal war tax for most kings, according to several sources, was half of the tithe. The other half went to the generals that won the battle. Abraham in effect gave the Lord a double portion, as it appears he gave his warrior's portion to the Lord as well. Melchizedek in turn blessed Abraham and ratified the Lord's covenant with the man that would found His only portion of the human race. The Most High's priest added Abraham's spoils to the Creator's temple treasury to continue to have meat in the Lord's storehouse for the priests under his care, the priestly village he founded and maintained for the Creator, which brings us to our next point.

Rightful Recipients of the Tithe

The tithe goes to the priest of the temple to maintain it, pay its workers, and provide for its replenishment. Back in Abraham's time, the temple precinct was the same as the village and most deities' temples were situated in the center of the village surrounded by the rest of its community. To be over the temple was to be over the region that housed it. That is how powerful priests were then. They represented the highest level of government and anointed every other official beneath them. What makes this important is the reason the Lord appointed

---

[30] Roget's International Thesaurus, St. Martins Press, 1965

the tithe in the first place and why it ends with the priest of the house.

Most people are familiar with the concept of a priest. They know that they are ministers ordained to officiate for their gods. The epistle to the Hebrews, chapters seven through nine, give an abbreviated explanation of priests, their minimal functions, and obligations to their gods and their people. Priests are ordinarily stationed at their temple sites in the temple or about its precincts. They receive offerings and sacrifices, slaughter and prepare them for presentation to the god of the land. The funds are used to train worshippers in divine service, how to correctly approach and appease the god of the land, and supply food and clothing for temple workers. The priests teach the god's laws and statutes, history, and testimony. They also prepare other priests to succeed them.

Other Priestly Duties Financed by the Tithe

In the book of Leviticus, the priests also diagnosed sicknesses and diseases, identified mold in the home, exposed adulterous wives, and overall mediated and governed in the name of the deity. The priests inquired of God, interpreted His divine responses, and supervised the temple workers and its possessions. They overall administrated its daily affairs. Furthermore, priests handled ceremonies, administered sacraments, and mediated controversies that arose among the people, aside from officiating at the sacrificial altar. Succinctly speaking, these are the gist of the priest's work for which he was compensated from the tithes and offerings collected. This is what Malachi 3:10 is addressing when it says the Lord's house must have meat in its storehouse. God is not overly concerned with stockpiling for its own sake. He needs His inventories to answer petitioners' prayers, avert or abate their crises, refurbish and replenish His household, and enrich those that have obtained or sustained His glory. Receipt of the tithe

272

forges a relationship closer than any other kind between a senior and a junior. Its payment solicits or retains a promise on the part of the recipient that the tither has reserved in advance the priest's attention, responsiveness, and intervention when the need arises.

The Melchizedek Tithe

One ongoing debate raging in the church is the validity of tithes under the New Testament. The argument is that the Lord did away with the reason for the tithe when He concluded the Old Testament and Moses' Law, which would be valid if the tithe bega n with Moses, but it did not.

The Bible introduces the tithe in Genesis 14:20 where Abraham gave Melchizedek, not Moses, a tithe of all he won in slaughtering the five kings. Peculiarly, the tithe like faith predates Moses and the Law. Both began as part of Abraham's covenant into which the children of Israel were born. That makes tithing an act of faith and not compliance with Moses' Law. Faith is what ascribed God's righteousness to Abraham, making the tithe a spiritual act of faith that ratified it.

The priest that administrated the first tithes to be paid on earth to the Most High is Melchizedek and not Aaron. Melchizedek is an eternal being. Hebrews chapter seven says that he is without father or mother, beginning of days or end of life. That makes him eternal (in our sense) and immortal. Hence, the first priest to receive the Lord's tithe was not human or earthly. He was sent from heaven by the Creator to lay the foundation for the birth of His first nation, Israel. Melchizedek is the priest of eternity and not earth. His prototypical order established the earthly priesthood that paved the way for the Lord Jesus' installation as High Priest according to the order of Melchizedek. Hebrews calls the Lord's first priesthood unending and unchanging. Jesus took over as High

Priest of an eternal priesthood that subsists on the power of an endless life.

What do all these facts about Melchizedek tell us but that tithing is an eternal and heavenly custom given as a gift to humanity? It assures God's vital transactions between heaven and earth remain unimpeded. Those who base the tithe and its cessation on Moses fail to trace its origins back far enough. If Jesus was the High Priest of eternity according to the order of Melchizedek, His priesthood on earth before Salem became Jerusalem and before the Jebusites took over the area, two things become evident. The tithe and faith are both eternal and that makes them both perpetual.

The New Testament church may not have to pay tithes according to the Moses' Levitical Priesthood as sinners kept for redemption, but it should pay tithes to the Lord Jesus Christ based on Melchizedek's priesthood to whom Abraham, the father of our faith, paid them. That is the gist of what Psalm 110:4 prophesies and Hebrews 7 says Christ accomplished. Study the chapter and pay close attention to verse eight: "*And here men that die receive tithes; but there he receiveth them, of whom it is witnessed that he liveth.*" The peculiar phrase "there he receives them" is replete with implications. There is an apparent reference to the heavens or eternity where Jesus and His Melchizedek Priesthood officiate. Spiritually, tithes are no longer going to Aaron's Priesthood because it eternally has no recipient. Now everything classifying as a tithe is rendered to the Lamb of God slain from the foundation of the world. The agency through which He receives them and dispenses them throughout the world, now His kingdom, is Melchizedek's Priesthood.

Of the nine times the word *tithes* is used in the New Testament, six of them are in the book of Hebrews and they are all about Melchizedek, the eternal priest. Each time the

Almighty declares Jesus' priesthood, He always decrees it is forever according to the order of Melchizedek. Therefore, if Melchizedek's priesthood came before Aaron and Jesus entered it as its High Priest, then Melchizedek and his priests were alive and well at the time of His resurrection and ascension. This eternal priesthood is apparently the one that received the spirit of all those animals Aaron's order offered up to the Almighty for centuries, confirming the principle that everything earthly has a spiritual prototype upon which the carnal subsists.

As a result, of this revelation, the argument about tithes in the New Testament church is unfounded. The Church is an eternal entity stationed on earth. When its natural founder paid the first tithes, it was to the eternal and heavenly priesthood that he paid them. Here is what Hebrews 7:9- 11 says: *"And as I may so say, Levi also, who receiveth tithes, payed tithes in Abraham. For he was yet in the loins of his father, when Melchisedec met him. If therefore perfection were by the Levitical priesthood, (for under it the people received the law,) what further need was there that another priest should rise after the order of Melchisedec, and not be called after the order of Aaron?"*

Understanding the Ancient Temple

Ancient temple precincts housed livestock, granaries, agriculture, beverages for the libations, war spoils, an arsenal, and a precious metals and gemstone vault, if it belonged to a famous and victorious deity. These storages were huge and maintaining them all employed extensive personnel beside the priests and ministers. From accounting to inventory, from collections to distribution, from security to supervision, the temple areas of the ancient world were busy industrial centers. They supplied the community, defended and horded the god's treasuries and wealth, and financed its people's individual and collective economies. What all this seemingly unrelated information shows is the importance of the tithe.

The accumulated tithe was intended to cover the living expenses of every member of the community. It provided the economy of the commonwealth, and the priest's sustenance for serving in the temple. Administrating it was part of their extensive duties and how they earned their living. When the church was born, the priests that received the hordes of the Lord were replaced by the apostles and that is the point of this discussion.

The apostles' early collections reminisced the extraordinary giving to the ancient temples. In addition, the apostles' purposes for receiving the bounty were the same as theirs: to distribute to the church at large, so that none among them lacked or had any need (read Acts 4:32, 37). Moreover, the ancient Levites were replaced by the seven deacons chosen to do for the church what the Levites did for ancient Israel (Acts 6:3, 4). Paul teaches us in 1 Corinthians 2:13 to compare spiritual things with spiritual. In relation to spiritual coverings and the tithes, coverers need to occupy the seat of the priest of the house and completely perform its functions to earn it.

As for tithing up, one wonders, where does scripture say the tithe of Israel made a national circuit? Where are we told that the northern temple precinct tithed to the south, the south to the north, the north to the west, and the west to the east? Would it not be redundant for them to do so if the tithe ended up where it began? While this was being done, how were the needs of the people handled and who administrated this circuit?

Today's ministers demanding the tithe because of being the seasoned or senior minister is questionable at best. What do they do with the tithe that even remotely resembles what the ancient Bible pattern portrays? How is the tithe of the coveree stored and for whose benefit? How is an accounting made and under what guidelines do today's recipients of the tithe perform 2 Corinthians 12:14? *"Behold, the third time I am ready to come to you; and I will not be burdensome to you: for I seek not yours, but you: for **the children ought not** to lay up for the parents, **but the parents for the children.**"*

Somehow, according to this wisdom, tithes received by coverers should be laid up for the coverees as a hedge against possible disaster in the future. The tithe is not only a war tax, but it is also a retainer that assures God's intervention when and if, a calamity strikes. If we are to use the Lord's handling of His tithes as a model then those requiring and receiving tithes from those they cover should be governed by the Creator's example. Tithes are a type of insurance payment that stores (lays up) claim money or resources in advance of crises. Lastly, the tithe is a guard that prevents encroaching terrorists from invading a saint's safety to wreak havoc at will. Coverers that demand and receive the tithe, especially from a church or individually ministers, should be as available to their coverees as the priests of the temples were under Moses' order. There should assigned personnel to assure access, communication, and intervention for those who tithe to the coverer.

Spiritual Covering & the Tithe

If all these requirements are true for those that receive today's tithes, then much more should be expected and given in return. Coverers are going to have to deliver more in exchange for the tithe they take in the name of a priest or its equivalent. Those that tithe to them should legitimately anticipate some hedge against disaster and hardship should it happen down the line. They should expect to be counseled, coached, mentored, advanced, and promoted because that is what secular counterparts to Christian ministry assure their supporters. Integrious leaders would never presume to take anyone's funds under false pretenses, coercion, or without giving them something of equal or greater value in return. Doing so on the ground of a purely ethereal return can appear to be a type of spiritual exploitation.

If your coverer requires the tithe, he or she will need to provide what the early church and ancient Israel provided for it. There should be discounts, rebates, savings, low interest loans, or something concrete in exchange, especially when the tither falls on hard times. The coverer should perform the same or equivalent priestly functions as those from whom they took their pattern. It is a risky practice to divert the tithe from the temple and its needs to one's personal interests. Hording that tithe for personal gain and not laying up some of it for the tither to fulfill the whole word of God is dangerous.

It may be better for coverers to assess a duty or fee for their services. Perhaps charging tuition for tutoring, counseling fees for mentorship and specific retainers for eventual services is more appropriate. A more sensible approach could be to assess a single monthly amount comparable to what the coverer includes in the arrangement.

A Model for Spiritual Covering

The term *spiritual covering* does not just mean heavenly or celestial, nor utterly out of the range of the definitive. The Church under the Holy Spirit is regulated by God's word as to what defines and qualifies as a spiritual covering. At face value, it simply means ecclesiastical, Spirit-filled and led, logos and rhema balanced. Spiritual coverers should avoid impressing ethereal motives upon their coverees that exempt them from attaching tangible values to their protection. Christian coverers' values should exceed prayers and extend to a concrete exchange of ministry services for funds received that at least somewhat mirrors what ancient tithe recipients provided.

Christ's apostles that received the membership's wealth laid at their feet provided the early church with tangible benefits of

278

their apostleship. They saw to it that there was no lack among any of them from what was laid at their feet. It should not be that a network with faithful tithers has no means of helping its supporters in times of crises. It may be that aid is only a referral databank of proven community agencies that can help; however, a dollar-for-dollar or equivalent exchange should figure somewhere in the arrangement. Leviticus 27:30 makes it plain that the tithe is the Lord's. It is His because whatever one acquires from his or her labors was made by Him. Whatever qualifies as a tithe is composed of, and come from God, making it inherently His. While there is no question that a laborer is worthy of his or her wages, as the Lord says, the Church needs to be sure that wages are what is owed one's spiritual covering rather than the tithe if that is the goal. If the tithe is due one's covering, they should provide, even if only minimally at first, the full range of services typically performed by priests.

A Biblical Pattern for Spiritual Covering

A responsible model for spiritual coverings' to earn their tithe is no different from what the church was built upon. The Bible is explicit about how to receive and process, store, accumulate, and distribute the tithe. Coverers themselves need to have stationed headquarters with reliable communications systems to receive and respond to calls and correspondence from those they cover. There should be a personnel staff to meet, greet, and serve those committed to the ministry. Tithers should insist on it. The inexcusable attitude of today's great ministers that they have no obligation to their supporters and tither because they are too busy getting more to ignore is unfortunate and borderline abusive. It confirms the sinner's negative opinion of the Church because its leaders do not grant the same latitude to subscribe to such professional protocols. A number of legal guards hold them accountable for the funds they receive and see they are responsible to those that patronize their secular businesses. After all, as we like to say in ministry circles, the church is a business; and if this is true, it should act like one, especially in the area of the tithe.

Quality Spiritual Covering Protocols

A good spiritual covering protocol resembles this: A contact begets at contact; colleagues and peers personally return calls to colleagues whenever possible; assistants respond to other assistants; and contacts to all others are made by lower staff. Everyone that reaches out to a ministry they have supported in any way should receive a return communication in some format that shows interest in them and the intent to address their concern. Promises should be kept in a timely matter with delays adequately communicated. Gratitude should be expressed for loyalty. Orders and requests should be processed promptly and shipped expediently. Errors should be frankly admitted and reversed speedily. Promised compensation for losses and missed dates should be quickly remediated.

Criticism, problems, and complaints should generally receive even cursory investigation and be followed up with explanatory responses as a matter of courtesy. Christian leaders must become as bold and adept at handling the unpleasant tasks and events associated with their vocations as they are about the pleasant ones, or the souls, opportunities, and contacts they court. Staff members should be well trained in customer service, courteous and diligent. Supervisors should regularly review operational and administrative procedures and correct deficiencies promptly when possible. When people deal with ministers, they should feel they are being served by the Lord and every effort should be made to avoid misrepresenting Him and disillusioning them. These are some minimal integrity protocols that all those entrusted in public service, ministry or not, should implement and observe.

Staffing Protocols

In addition, coverers should be full time, like the ancients' priests before them. Sufficient staff or technology should be employed to take calls, make callbacks, and schedule meetings. Tithers should receive discounts on products, though they should not be necessarily free, and honored for keeping the coverer's ministry thriving. The most successful coverers should have prayer teams on hand to take prayer requests and counselors to handle the problems their tithers encounter in the course of ministry life, or just as part of the warfare assigned to the apostle's ministry. These could be assigned to subordinate ministers the coverer has engaged with part of the tithe money received from those covered. Coverers should accumulate developmental resource tools to offer their tithers and supporters on a variety of topics, themes, and issues and have a means for them to access or acquire them for ministry. There should be designated recognition, reward, and award protocols in place to distinguish those that tithe as supporters from the others the coverer relates to in ministry. Tithers should get something for their money, starting with special attention and preferential treatment.

All these benefits the Lord gives His Church for their tithes. Besides them, He gives them preferential treatment and elevated status among His other spiritual hosts, and releases upon them exceptional favor in the realms of men. God opens doors, rescues, enhances productivity, enriches, and blesses His tithers' hands and lands. He teaches, guides, counsels, heals, intercedes, and intervenes for them, replenishing and unifying His people from His abundance. Continually, the Lord fellowships and communes with His family remaining intimate with them as a Provider and Father, fully earning the awe and offerings He expects to receive in return. He tends to their sorrows, averts or reverses their crises, and overturns their calamities. The Lord uses His reputation to influence their lives, prosper their endeavors, and return what was stolen or lost to them, sending help and provisions in times of need as well. He does not respond to His tithers crises with indifference or censures about their lack of faith, poor coverer support, or treatment; He shows compassion. These He does because He has vowed to do so because He is faithful and He earns His tithe.

Tithing Protocols

It is incumbent upon God to earn the advances paid Him for His ongoing and unexpected services. His people secure these by the tithe. God's is an institution, an organization that, like the ancient temple precincts, provides a multitude of essential and intermittent services to His creation. These are compounded when they are delivered to His ecclesia. As due remuneration for His services and a hedge against disaster, deprivation, or disease, He ordained the tithe. God's kingdom is tantamount to a nation with the duties and responsibilities of a government that the tithes support.

In addition to the tithe being a war tax also constitutes a citizen's tribute. Consequently, one would hardly think of giving one's taxes to anyone other than the government officials appointed to receive and distribute them. Once remitted, citizens of a government's communities expect that in return it will render the services promised its citizenry. Moreover, citizens would hardly continue paying taxes to a government that gave them nothing for it in return; they would only revolt after awhile. This is just basic monetary reasoning. A regularly assessed fee is meant to pay for services, not just concepts and abstract ideas.

It should never be that anyone who tithed faithfully to a ministry or minister for years who undergoes crises receives nothing from that ministry in times of trouble. They should not be told to tithe and not get the same spiritual advantage and economic leverage the Lord gives immaterially and materially to His tithers. Those who take the tithe should use their influence and authority to intervene on tithers' behalf and pull from the accumulated resources that years of tithes help to build or aid those that have been supporting them. If the aid cannot be material, then it should be contacts, referral and referral services, counselors, guides, the wisdom and word of the Lord. That calls for a staff, an agency of services, and an inventory or goods and products accumulated from what is taken. Tithers to spiritual coverings should never receive for their faithfulness a wall of silence. That is not why the Lord entrusts His tithe into any leader's hands. He expects them to respond with His response systems and be there for His people in His stead as He would be if He were physically present. Here is the reason the Lord determined to prosper certain skillful and administratively talented people more than others.

Deciding on the Right Covering

In the wake of prolific teaching on spiritual authority and the need for everyone in the Body of Christ to submit to it, ministers of all kinds are feverishly looking for their spiritual covering. They spend money on meetings, conferences, and classes trying to determine who should be their spiritual covering. Most of them are looking for what they have been taught is the ideal covering: someone they can trust, look up to, and most importantly, obey. Obedience and service seem to feature most prominently in the requirements of today's spiritual covering that tend to often emphasize the *coverer* more than the *covered*. Frequently, covering seekers are told only what they must do, how they must comply, and all they need to bring to the relationship. Often there is little talk about what they, the *coveree*, will get from the arrangement, even after they have jumped through hoops to meet all its requirements. Many times, their benefits are usually quite vague so that what they get from the spiritual covering and the role the covering is to fill in their life and ministry are assumed. Questions that arise regarding spiritual covering concern the type of coverings one should choose. Where should one look for his or her spiritual covering? What commitments should be made to one's spiritual covering, and should they fill the role of teacher, trainer, intercessor, coach, collaborator, influence, or authority? The last two questions are quite pivotal.

It is essential to determine whether a spiritual covering is to become an influence or authority in your ministry and life in general. The answer to this question determines the extent of involvement and submission to be covenanted. People generally feel a call to more than one person as their covering. Some are drawn to one person's mantle, another's anointing, someone else's wisdom and counsel, another's teaching, training or mentorship; and still another's strength and leadership. If you look at the list you will see that one protocol principle surfaces. Only one person in the group can be the authority figure in the spiritual covering spectrum; all the others are influencers in some capacity or other. Classifying all the others as *influencers* means what they provide does not require any more obedience and submission than is needed to benefit from short term or incidental service.

A mantle attraction or affinity may be intermittent, active only when the services of apostleship in general are being rendered. The same is true for the anointing; its settings are situational. Wisdom is based on the need for counsel and likewise training and mentorship; when the class is over or the coaching complete the need for that type of ministry subsides so the influence wanes. These interactions or encounters may sway decisions, affect actions, and even give some direction, but what they lack is the governing aspect of authority in the spiritual covering context. For any number of reasons, that person's mantle fails to inspire a consistent obedience from you, though what they say is heard and respected. Therefore, ministers, especially apostles, should be careful about how they invite someone to cover them. There should be extensive discussion and thorough investigation to confirm that all parties to the agreement benefit. Perhaps a stipulated probationary period should be suggested to allow both sides to dissolve the union without hard feelings and undue costs should it not work out.

What to Consider in a Covering Relationship

Personality, viewpoints, and beliefs should be frankly discussed. Limits of authority and commitment should be established with some type of loose scheduling agreed upon to reduce overwhelming demands that can overtax either member with consuming tasks and assignments. A designated review period should be set to determine the success of the arrangement and identify ineffective areas and activities. At this honest session, what is working well should be recognized and applauded and what needs help or elimination should be voiced without tension or offense. The boundaries of authority and influence should be set so that the accountability and responsibility of the covering and the one covered are clearly defined.

Those who take on a spiritual covering should benefit from the arrangement commensurate with the one providing it. It should not be a one-sided arrangement and compatibility issues should be strongly considered. Spiritual covering arrangements where the one covered is incompatible with the one chosen to cover, or where there is imbalance between the two that causes friction should be averted. Smoldering resentment or unavoidable antipathy can ruin the relationship, allowing hurt feelings to impede its potential effectiveness. Envy, jealousy, rivalry and competition can color discussions, motivate unfair treatment, and expose every one concerned to unintentional hurt. If such emotions exist on the part of their authority figure, much damage can be done to the submitted minister. If it is the other way around, the subordinate minister the coverer hoped to benefit can defame their authority figure.

Choosing Influence Rather than Control

Often ministers in their eagerness to comply with the Lord's governmental system and means of regulating and protecting His ministries jump headlong into covering relationships without giving them enough forethought. Simply because they want to be accepted and provided an outlet for their ministries, too many people find themselves bound to spiritual coverings that conflict with their callings or clash with their mantles. When the covered minister is an apostle, he or she can end up being suppressed, rashly promoted, dreadfully used or abused, or constantly at odds with the spiritual authority. The cause of the situation is not taking time to determine what was intended by the spiritual covering and what he or she is to expect from or contribute to it.

Mostly, when people say they want a spiritual covering, what they really mean is they desire a devoted counselor, advisor, door opener, or ministerial backer. Not wrong in themselves, these desires can misrepresent the goal of a potentially good spiritual covering or frustrate it altogether. On the other hand, there are those that see the need for authority figures over their ministries, and sometimes over their lives. Such people are drawn to extremely charismatic leaders, especially if they are prominent or strong dominating ministers who tend to take control of their charges' lives. In these cases, an indolent minister can risk being told what to do, how to do it, when to minister, and when not to minister, or even what to minister. Submitting to a strong apostolic authority figure can be positive if the one submitting is of a strong character in his, or her, own right; otherwise, such an arrangement can be crippling.

Negatively, the control figure becomes the lone commander and chief over weaker ministers because that is the sole reason the pact was made. There is little thought of training, development, skills building or inner personal enrichment. The commander speaks and rules, and the subordinate listens and obeys. Again, if one feels the need to cast all his or her care onto an elder minister to feel validated for ministerial service, it is no crime. Once more, such an arrangement is not inherently wrong in and of itself. However, over time, an overbearing covering will ultimately spoil the relationship and the future ministry of the subordinate, crippling dependency that stagnates the novice's growth, ability and confidence.

What needs to be explored by the one seeking spiritual covering is the reason they see a spiritual covering as necessary in the first place. Why should they be covered by anyone at all, and what type of covering is best for them? Some people, for instance, have pastoral covering because a strong pastor is sufficient. However, apostles tend to outpace their shepherds once they are awakened to the office, and that can be unsettling as the apostle's insight and range of spirituality can overshadow the pastors after awhile. Tensions under these circumstances easily build between the faithful shepherd and the emerging apostle so that they have to separate. Tragically, the separation caused by sharp contention often divides the sheep and shepherd for an extended period of time simply because the pastor as a parent did not connect the young apostle with a senior one for development.

Stronger apostles need stronger ones covering them, but even under these conditions, the terms of the accord should be thoroughly assessed. Many factors go into forming the best covering arrangement, most of which are ignored until a crises forces their handling. While such reactionary methods of problem resolution or troubleshooting may eventually work out, they tend to take more effort and cause much anxiety in the process and over time take a brutal toll on the relationship.

Wise spiritual covering arrangements are better served by anticipating the likely disruptions or conflicts that invariably crop up in any kind of alliance, collaboration, or spiritual union. Below are some issues or questions that could be addressed. One can use some of these guidelines to draft and answers their own questionnaire on this subject.

Thoughts to Consider for Spiritual Coverings

- Why should the covering arrangement be established in the first place?

- Is the lesser in the agreement really to be blessed by the better and is it clear who is the lesser and the better?

- If the subordinate has more to offer, will the tables turn and the *coverer* become the subordinate?

- Is the ideal arrangement to be based upon influence or authority? Is it to be a professional alliance or a parental connection?

- What are the limits of authority and control and who decides them?

- Are decisions to be joint ventures or does the *coverer* retain all control?

- What happens as the subordinate grows? If he or she increases in stature, how does that affect the initial arrangement? Should it continue as is, or be modified or dissolved. Is so, how?

- Who evaluates the subordinate's growth and by what standards and criteria is it done?

- If the relationship is to be based on authority, what in action does that look and sound like? If it is based on influence, then what is the ground of the influence?

- Is the best covering arrangement to be one of mutual control, unilateral authority, or hierarchy? If it is to be mutual, how are conflicts and disagreements to be resolved?

- Is a third party needed to arbitrate, or are the two parties involved agreed on some strategic points of resolution?

- What arbitration and advocacy guidelines will the relationship draw from in its journey toward the ideal arrangement?

- If it is a mutual arrangements with both sides watching each other and enjoying equal privileges (or rights), what are the checks that balance the relationship to keep one or the other on point according to what guidelines?

- Are questions of control and authority versus protection and provision adequately answered by both groups? If they are, how are they to be treated in the future?

- Does the subordinate understand what spiritual authority means as opposed to spiritual influence?

- Does the authority figure intend to balance authority and control with suitable protection and provision?

- What about economics, finances, and profitability? If everything else goes well, the one thing that can destroy any sort of an alliance is monetary. Are all parties to the arrangement willing to discuss frankly any money aspects of the covering arrangement so expected rewards are balanced by prudent responsibilities and outcomes of the alliance?

- Are character and integrity, morality and ethics frankly compared? Do those entering the arrangement agree on what makes for godly character, biblical morality, and overall minister integrity?

- Have preliminary discussions assured due regard for each party's views on critical reputation building or destroying issues?

- What happens to one if the other parties to the covering fail or falter in critical areas?

As you can see, the questions and matters concerning spiritual covering are vast. It is rare that those embarking upon such alliances thoroughly investigate any serious aspects and potentials that lie ahead of them. Far too often, the covering arrangement is based upon spiritual enthusiasm, flattery, or emotional fervor, which cannot withstand the inevitable onslaughts all relationships face. Misunderstandings, feelings of inadequacy or unfairness can so deteriorate the union that hostility and anger fester because key questions and answers were not resolved in advance. Review the previous list and carefully consider if you hold the proper views and expectations on any proposed spiritual coverings, you may be contemplating.

Settling Lesser Better, Stronger Weaker Questions

Previously, the phrase "lesser and better" was used to call into question the viability of certain covering arrangements and those considering them. It is common for newcomers and unknowns to seek covering from forerunners and renowned ministers for a myriad of prudent and self-serving reasons. Initially, the arrangement works but only for a while until its inherent weaknesses outweigh its strengths.

If the newcomer is not a novice but merely an unknown or even more threatening an up and coming catalyst for what the Lord will do next, the outcome of such a covering relationship can be disturbing and activate the Saul-David Syndrome. Here is where the incumbent authority figure recognizes the Lord's intentions in their subordinate and fears the inevitable effects of having brought the newcomer into their sphere of ministry. Once the awareness becomes public and the incumbent begins, like Saul, to hear the undercurrent of those beneath them who also recognize God's intentions, things turn sour. Spite, competition brew, and hatefulness can take over. The once valued subordinate is pursued and discredited mercilessly for being chosen.

This crushingly painful scenario is all too frequent and hardly anyone rising from the ranks of the unknown escapes it. Although it is impossible to avoid completely since our Savior endured such hostility, it is possible to foresee and avert its constant repetition. Here are a few clues to the possible pitfalls of an unhealthy or imbalanced spiritual covering relationship.

Evaluating the Health of a Spiritual Covering Relationship

To examine the nature, present and future effectiveness of a spiritual covering, everyone involved should ask the following:

1. Is a proposed mentor, parent in the Lord, or spiritual covering on par with you experientially, intellectually, or emotionally? This hard to consider question should probably be resolved in the prayer closet and then discussed among trusted friends first because most Christians confuse genuine prudence with pride. Nonetheless, it should be explored in light of the historical record of the proposed covering. If he or she lag behind in critical biblical, spiritual, and professional areas because of having been assigned to the preceding move, it may be that they are not ready to appreciate a rising minister's fresh wisdom and valid spiritual contributions for long. These could clash with an old mindset that is not willing to risk reputation and rewards on it.

2. Has the *coveree* achieved more spiritually, practically, or ministerially in their short time in the Lord than the one considered for covering? Has the novice or unknown done more with less and remained faithful despite hardships and opposition? Does the proposed coverer realize it and offhandedly comment on the difference a little too often or sarcastically? If so, new gifts can be either suffocated or wrongly harvested. Not everyone makes a good surrogate parent, and not all adopted children are prized. A strong parent embraces and encourages a strong child. Those that are not as strong tend to punish or ignore the child of special talent or strength. Worse yet, they may overindulge the youngster and fail to perfect what God needs for their calling. It is

the same with strong or weak leaders. They make wonderful friends, occasional counselors, but that Ahab insecurity cannot help but creep in from time to time. Genuine parents know the importance of encouraging their bright stars and not every parent or mentor can do so.

3. Does newcomer brilliance, enthusiasm, or keenness bother the spiritual covering? Do they seem to always say tone it down, and warn you not to rock the boat, or to keep your words and revelations silent? This **could** be a good sign of linking up with one who appreciates but cannot respect a subordinate's anointing or its place in their world. That could be costly over time.

4. How about wisdom, knowledge, and understanding of the scriptures? Typically, if the proposed covering downplays God's word in favor of more external or sensual approaches to ministry and spiritual contact, it may suggest a resolve to do just what it takes in ministry and no more, to play it safe. A novice's or unknown's overwhelming embrace of God's whole counsel as is usually the case with apostles who takes the full gospel as written, may be unnerving to such a covering. It may also agitate those whose spiritual lives are not quite as active. This situation is more like Eli and Samuel.

To discover where a prospective covering stands on these matters, listen to what is said, when it is said and how. What is declared or inferred about God's truth, Spirit and the needs and state of His church can be insightful. If a senior minister sees ministry shifts or improvements as miles away from what the Lord declares is His works, His will, and plans for His church, it may mean a God conflict in the future.

293

5. Be alert to unfounded criticism, abrupt dismissals, or refusals to allow contributions to covering minister's world. How ministers share their heart, handle what newcomers or enamored subordinate's submit can frustrate an intimate and long-term relationship. Routine requests or admonitions not to be so spiritual or too religious, or legalistic upon bringing up obedience, holiness, or God's righteousness should be openly discussed. Criticisms about being too preachy when Bible references are made should raise a flag. It may be that the covering under consideration is not where they appear to be publicly in the things of God. When you are told you are two narrow in your thinking or that you see things too black and white, further investigation should be made into the motives behind such remarks.

Grooming for successful and effective ministry requiring seeking God less and regarding or listening to the people more, or suggestions to gather messages from extra biblical sources rather than the Holy Spirit, from a mentor covering could veer genuine ministers away from their first love and Christ's foundation in ministry.

6. How people criticize others in the body of Christ is important. What they judge as God or not is worth studying. How prospective coverers view the present state of the church in comparison to scripture and what they propose God feels or should do about it are all good thoughts to hear regarding those to effectively cover a ministry.

A Guide for Those Spiritually Covering Others

No fruitful relationship can endure one-sidedness. Just as the person seeking a covering must examine his or her motives so too must those who feel the call to cover others. It is not enough to care about an up and coming or dynamic minister. Questions concerning the need to commit to another in ministry and take responsibility for their success should be honestly answered.

Assessing Integrity of Spiritual Covering Commitment

In addition to the previous recommendations, here are a few introspections for coverers to assess the integrity of a proposed or present covering relationship to start with:

1. Why should you bother assuming responsibility for another?

2. What do you get, or expect to get out of it?

3. What would I give to such a relationship and what do I expect to receive in return?

4. What type of people do I work best with and what type of people do I least effect?

5. How do I determine those to benefit most from my tutelage and covering?

6. Do I have a successful enough record of accomplishment with empowering people for ministry to undertake this assignment?

7. Am I a better influencer that an authority or vice versa? How do I discover the answer to this question?

8. Am I good at confrontation, evaluations, and objectivity?

9. Am I to cover as a parent, a coach, a mentor, or a trainer?

10. Am I expected to provide ministry outlets, to open doors otherwise closed to those I cover, and somehow

reciprocate their service to me? How do I feel about this, and how much am I willing to meet such expectations?

11. Honestly speaking, am I looking to develop people or to be served?

12. How are my interpersonal and people building skills? Are my social skills up to par and am I emotionally giving or honest?

13. What developmental resources do I have on hand or at my disposal to develop an apostle?

14. What am I prepared to impart to others as a spiritual covering?

15. How much authority should I require from the relationship? Am I willing to take on the duty of spiritual parent?

16. Is the person approaching me as a covering willing to submit to me? Do they know me enough to conform to my style or successfully integrate it with their own? What will they do with my handprint on them?

17. How long do I want the relationship to last and how will I measure its success and effectiveness?

18. How many people should I mentor and cover at once? What is the prudent limit of my ability to meet their needs, support their works, and empower their service?

19. What standards and obligation should I set for the arrangement?

20. Are my ministry resources, training and development materials, sufficient for this person's apostolic needs?

21. Do I have a good sense of their calling and the breadth of knowledge and information they require to be equipped for God's service?

22. How am I to evaluate my potential to develop this person as an apostle?

23. What tools do I need to confirm this person's apostolic call and ability to glean from me? Where may I get any essential materials I do not have that may be needed?

Of course, there is more but you do get the point. Furthermore, it is understood that matters of integrity, criminality, addictions, abuses, and reputation are to be uncovered before the covenant is sealed. Anyone convinced they need a spiritual covering or should be one, ought to take steps to understand why and how anyone can benefit from, protect, and guide either ministry.

Apostles should not rely on non-apostolic ministers and leaders to cover them who have no real apprehension of God's apostolism and their spheres. Do not fall into the trap of just getting a covering to comply with popular trends. The arrangement has to bless and empower as much as it exalts and encourages. By all means—and it cannot be said enough—make sure one's covering is leagues ahead in ministry, mantle, Bible knowledge and wisdom, spiritual understanding. Evaluate the range and depth of their spiritual and apostolic insight and make sure their overall maturity will enrich your calling.

Gifts and anointing in themselves do not guarantee maturity or stability, and generosity is no substitute for integrity or godly opportunities. For instance, some seemingly successful ministers have brilliant staff people that help them get to and remain where they are. Their initial promotion may have been the result of means other than those you need or deem necessary for proficient ministers of the gospel. Your choice of

297

such people for a covering may prove disappointing if this is the case, as they may not possess the superior gifts and abilities you think they have to pass onto you.

The type of covering settled upon should be clearly defined and established as envisioned by both parties to not unduly stress either party. If it is to be one of influence then a network not interested in telling ministers what to do or assuming control of their ministries may be enough. Should authority figures be sought to entrust one's leadership and government to, then more than an association network will be insufficient. A spiritual parent, direct leader, or outright superior is a better choice. The decision to enter all alliances and the relationships that affect ability to hear and obey the Lord must be made with eyes wide open.

The Apostle & Covering

No comprehensive treatment of this subject would be complete without a discussion on mentoring. Mentorship is an official function where a seasoned, well-connected veteran of the field takes a novice or junior under his or her wing. Spiritually speaking, mentorship is a joint agreement where one who is called to a specific sphere of God's service seeks and surrenders to a like-minded senior in their calling to learn the ins and outs of the office.

Mentorship may or may not include tutoring but it always involves coaching, counseling, guidance, and practice. What is scarcely known is that mentorship is supposed to provide skill outlets and professional opportunities at some point in its season. Otherwise, why would a junior or novice submit his or her life and liberty to another's care or will? Here is where the conflict begins because both parties to the arrangement must agree on its purposes, goals, and objectives. They must together identify and employ proven methods, requirements, and the standards by which their mentorship is measured.

Mentorship must be distinguished from personal attendance where a servant attaches himself or herself to a seasoned professional for the specific purposes of attending to their private affairs and personal needs. In this instance, the primary goal is to see to the senior's comfort. That is, unfortunately, how many Christian mentorships are conducted as overworked and overwhelmed ministers entrust their menial tasks and personal need to an eager soul yearning to be used of God. Frequently in these types of arrangement, the server may or may not understand that the developmental and opportunity aspects of their services they secretly hope for will not happen. Frequently, this is because they may have only existed in the mind of the attendant and may never been directly voiced to the one thought to be a mentor.

To avoid such confusion frustration and anguish such situations can breed a candid understanding of the nature of a servanthood relationship and its outcomes or benefits should be spelled out in advance. Those attending to prestigious ministers should be honest about their motives and the limits of their service. They should frankly disclose what they expect from their services, whether it is prayer, personal gratification, finances, opportunities, etc. Senior ministers should likewise be open and honest about what they need from an attendant and what they are willing to supply in return. If the minister is willing to be a mentor, not only should he or she say so, but also the terms and conditions under which the veteran is willing to lend his or her expertise to the junior's development should be specified.

Traditional Mentorship Formation

Ordinarily, mentors choose their mentees and not the other way around. The child rarely chooses the parent, and if so, it does not nullify the parent's obligation to the majority of the provision and training involved. The idea of a newcomer or unknown minister approaching a well-known one to and declare him or her to be their mentor though commonly done is spiritually and naturally unwarranted. It is not only awkward; it is inconsistent with the natural order of life. Juniors may easily latch on to their elders but they do not dictate the elder's response or agreement. A negative outcome of this practice is that the junior that forged the mentorship on their personal grounds tends to sever it at their will, when things do not go their way. Once the mentor takes the union seriously, the junior minister or novice can balk at its demands and structure and feel free to abandon the mentorship because it was their idea in the first place. Many times, this is how Christian mentorships are born. The elder minister is approached, often at a very vulnerable time, and told by some eager young minister that God told them, "You are my mentor." Expecting joy and confirmation, they can meet with a very different response. A mentor that has been there before may flat out discourage the novice. Wounded at the unexpected response, many of them walk away from the encounter confused. While there are numerous reasons for this reaction, sometime it is simply because experienced ministers respond with caution and do not jump at the chance to obey another's word to them from the Lord. Another equally imprudent response is when the tenderhearted elder minister just acquiesces to the declaration, unsure of how to, tactfully get out of it. Generally, these two models are how Christian mentorships form and depending upon which of two birthed the arrangement, a healthy or extremely dysfunctional relationship begins.

A third scenario is where a weighed down minister realizes that he or she has grown to the point that personal assistance beyond clerical and administrative is needed. This is the most difficult and vulnerable position a harried minister can be found in because it exposes their intimate concerns to another that they must rely on handle their personal needs. Aside from the fact that many people filling this role in a minister's life have no idea of the inner struggle most of them experience before entrusting their private selves to another's care, this can be reckless. Such exposure can be helpful or detrimental and choosing the right person to handle the task is crucial.

Often the overwhelmed minister waits, usually for the above reasons, until the situation becomes dire and is forced to appoint someone to their personal or sensitive matters hastily out of sheer necessity. Unwise in itself, should this be done with someone with high ministry aspirations who feels personal service is the fast track to success the outcome can be disastrous. Numerous negative developments can unsettle the arrangement. For anyone seeking mentorship, it will certainly end in disappointment. For the minister, an even sadder situation can occur.

If the most available person has not been purged, groomed, and pruned by the Lord for the assignment, the results can be ruinous as a critical spirit mercilessly uncovers the elder minister spreading private matters abroad. The converse of the situation is when the elder seeks to offload quickly personal matters and implies to a willing candidate that more will come out of the relationship than actually will. Here is where a dutiful servant diligently attends to the elder minister with the hopes that he or she will be rewarded with promising ministry opportunities later. Such an arrangement can go on for years until the servant wakes up and realizes the implied promise is never going to happen. Feeling hurt and betrayed, the naive attendant severs ties seriously wounded. Such an attendant can turn vengeful and bitterly retaliate against the unsuspecting minister.

Again, the outcome is tragic as a once or potentially wonderful attendant is jaded and embittered at having been abused. This is called the "Ahab-Jacob Syndrome." We all know the story; Ahab promised Jacob something for his services for a specified period time with no intention of honoring his word (though that may not be the case with your mentor at all). He deceived Jacob until the young man by God's providence forced Ahab to perform his word. Many young attendants have been burned by the Ahab Game and are quite cynical as a result, which is a prudent reason to explore prospective mentorships carefully.

What all these examples share is wisdom for determining the success of failure of a mentorship. To avoid difficulties, everyone involved should be clear about the aims of the mentorship they want to form. Here are a few things to consider when deciding the outcomes of your mentorship.

Indicators of a Promising Mentorship

A promising and fruitful mentorship should offer:

1. A unique wisdom and practicality for what you are called to do.

2. Protection from failure, faults, the unscrupulous, and naiveté.

3. Specific preparation for God's eventual use or promotion.

4. Instillation of knowledge, astuteness, vocational insight, and protocols.

5. Perspective shaping that alters previous views and unrealistic expectations to the realities of the call.

6. Impartation of the spirit and sentiments of the calling.

7. Practical skills building that reflect the demands and duties of the calling.

8. Agency support as the mentor reaches out to his or her constituency to pave for the mentee's eventual entrance into the field.

What Mentees Must Do

In order to succeed, the mentee must be available, submissive, diligent, and teachable. Instructions must be followed, details completed, assignments and tasks carried out as instructed. Excuses and task evasion should be avoided, and open and honest behavior and conduct expectations defined and followed. If you are prescribing to the Bible's model, the mentor has the right to set schedules, make unusual demands, and do all possible to simulate the world of the calling the mentee is aspiring to enter. Realism is the greatest tool of an effective mentorship as the mentor includes true reenactments of what the mentee will face in the field as a regular part of the development. Here is where novice mentors fail in the mentorship. A mentor on the rise cannot lift a mentee above where he or she has not gone. Following are some other significant factors to take under advisement as you consider the best mentor for you.

Suitable Mentor's Essential Service Requirements

1. Most importantly, encounters with your mentor should reflect he or she has prayed for you or at the least heard from the Lord about you (where you are and what you face).

2. The mentor must admire and appreciate you as a person and a future peer and colleague.

3. The mentor must be able to relate to your readiness journey, the experiences, and processes you encountered along the way to them.

4. The mentor must appreciate and understand the wisdom and value of the life experiences that made you who you are.

5. The mentor must not envy you, who you are, and what you bring to the relationship. Here, Hebrews seven's lesser is blessed by the better principle especially applies.

6. The mentor must not need what you have more than you need what they can deliver to get you where you are going.

7. The mentor must not view you as a rival and a contender for their fame and success.

8. The mentor must have an honest insight into the struggles and warfare you face being uniquely you pursuing your particular call.

9. The mentor must exceed you in knowledge, competence, wisdom, and exposure to the field.

10. The mentor must enjoy observing your present capabilities and delight in developing them further to ready you for God's service

11. The mentor must enjoy hearing the details of your development process as you review what you have learned, and where and how you have improved under their hand.

12. The mentor should not see your faults and shortfalls as confirmations of a major "overhaul" project.

In addition, it is helpful to recognize the signs of an unsuitable mentor. Unsuitable, in this case, means unsuitable for you, not necessarily unsuited to the call of mentorship. Human nature being what it is relational chemistry is largely emotions driven. Sometimes for any number of reasons personalities and temperaments clash and that makes for a bad mentorship mix.

Below are some points that can prove insightful to the mentor and the mentee as they probe the feasibility of forming a mentorship together. A mentorship arrangement should be avoided if too many of the following indicators are present.

Indicators of an Unstable Mentorship Mix

1. The mentor starts out with a list of "fix you's" before identifying your strengths, learning your world and your life.

2. When the mentor builds the mentorship primarily around them and ignores your development needs.

3. The mentor limits access to his or her expertise and assistance by being routinely unavailable.

4. The mentor makes definite demands but gives vague commitments.

5. Your servanthood is more important than your development.

6. Your labors are praised while your growth, skills, and development are ignored or minimized.

7. The mentor does not value your professional contribution to the relationship.

8. The mentor disdains your wisdom and advice when it is right. You observe this by the same words being accepted from others that were rejected from you.

9. Most sessions and encounters with the mentor center on disapproval and correction.

10. Your strengths and weaknesses are inequitably recognized and treated.

11. The mentor relentlessly crucifies your natural ability, temperament, and personality, preferring to alter who you are and how you are made rather than cultivate your gifts and talents for the purpose for which you were made.

12. The mentoring atmosphere seems to be constantly one of threat and censure.

13. The mentor readily receives your ideas and creations and uses them personally and professionally without giving you due credit as their author or creator.

14. The mentor regularly harvests your gifts and talents for personal gain never giving you a platform to practice them or an audience to field test your skills.

15. The mentor refuses to acknowledge you in public.

16. The mentor refuses to give you the time and attention you request to grow, improve, and become competent in your calling, dismissing your requests for special instruction, attention, or opportunities.

17. The mentor consistently compares you with others and demeans you publicly under the guise of humbling you so you don't fall in the future.

18. The mentor does not seem to value your time, obligations, and need for his or her attention as demonstrated by ignoring calls, overlooking your presence in special sessions, and not ever choosing you to be part of significant events or to perform a significant role with them, even after years.

19. You often leave your mentor's presence depressed, devalued, and frustrated rather than motivated.

20. The mentor responds to your experiments and best efforts with callousness and your achievements with disinterest.

21. Your mentor is oblivious to your challenges and responds to them with accusations or judgment.

22. The mentor shows little interest in you as a person outside of your service, gifts, and contributions to him or her personally.

23. Your mentor finds it difficult to be in your presence for long.

24. Your mentor frequently forgets promises made to you.

25. You mentor ignores your suffering and appears out of touch with your life experience.

These are but a few of the behaviors that you should consider and note as you give your mentorship the trial run and probationary period it deserves to prove itself valuable to you and the mentor. Mentors ought to review them to detect nagging thoughts or resistance to mentees that they cannot quite identify. It may be the mentor is not the one for the person in determined to force a veteran to take them under their wing. That constant irritation you vaguely wrestle with concerning them just may be God's way of saying this one is not for you to groom.

Coming Under Your Mentor's Wing

Taken from the book *Church Prophets*, by this author the following suggestions are made concerning yielding to a mentorship. At the least, be ready to comply with the following:

1. Be honest about your actions, reactions, motives, offenses, and defenses as you enter and interrelate in your mentorship.

2. Honestly confront yourself and question your motives; truthfully appraise your real self through another's eyes.

3. Analyze yourself in view of your required mentorship duties and your attitude toward them.

4. Face and explore your relational and service history, fears, doubts, anger, and resistance; in particular as they pertain to authority figures.

5. Ask yourself how selfishly motivated you may have been in establishing your mentorship and if you have a real problem committing to its development in any area connected that should be promptly handled.

6. Are you really interested in being successful in God, and what will you sacrifice for that success?

7. Will your pride, your ego, and your independence get in the way of you receiving from, serving, and benefiting from your mentor's expertise?

8. What did you expect to get from and give to and for your present and future ministry success?

9. Are your expectations fantasies or not? How realistic are they?

10. Now that you have given your word to be mentored by this person, are you going to back out of it or will you see through to the end what you know the Lord called you to do?

Chapter Summary

1. Modern apostles require professional refinements.

2. Professional, ministerial, and peer relationship skills are essential to successful apostleship.

3. Apostles stepping onto the world front must grow and reflect the maturity routinely exhibited by their secular counterparts.

4. The tithe must be earned by priestly actions.

5. New Testament tithes are based on faith, eternity, and Melchizedek.

6. The tithe goes to the temple priest for household maintenance and treatment of its members.

7. The tithe was never meant to enrich its recipients only.

8. The tithe is to finance a priest's duties and sustain God's kingdom temple.

9. God meant the tithe to be a hedge against disaster, lack, and shortfall.

10. Spiritual covering must earn and allocate portions of their tithes for those that surrender them.

11. Spiritual coverings are not merely heavenly and ethereal.

12. The term *spiritual, covering* is meant to identify the Holy Spirit leading the New Creation nature of the arrangement and its participants.

13. Effective apostleship requires observance of standardized ministry protocols.

14. Careful thoughts and discussions should precede and determine the formation and maintenance of every spiritual covering.

The above suggestions when implemented will produce a well thought out mentorship with minimum surprises.

The call to apostleship is great. Its demands and requirements are immense as the call spans eternity and time, heaven to earth, the human to the divine. Despite apostles today not having much of a model or platform for readiness training, it is incumbent upon those surfacing today to take the reins of this movement and correct the errors and deficiencies prevalent in people's mind about the office. This book is but a step in the process. The remaining cogs in the wheel are vast and intricate. They will take the whole being of apostles and their cabinets to prepare to occupy a seat that has undergone centuries of perversion, abuse and neglect.

Glossary
Key Terms & Phrases

Adam The name of the first man created. Means red man, earth man or man of the clay.

Agencies Plural for the organizations, offices and their activities authorized to represent the interests of another.

Agency Singular for agencies above.

Almighty All encompassing name of God as Creator and all powerful over creation.

Ambassador One sent to transact business in a foreign land for another called a sent one, delegated, or diplomat.

Ambassadorial What pertains to an ambassador or what comes from a representative sent to foreign land

Ambassage Bible name for ambassador or embassy.

Ancient From a very old period in history. Archaic, primeval, before counting eras.

Annex The state of being added to and cared for thereby.

Anointing The word for the spiritual appointment for installation into an official position. Signifies ancient practice of pouring specially made oil of an authority figure.

Apocalypse A natural event brought on by spiritual, heavenly, or celestial sources that occurs because it was foretold.

Apocryphal That which related to or the source of the mythical, forged, or imaginary.

Apostello Greek word for sent one, often found in scripture for apostolize.

Apostle The first ranking officer in Christ's kingdom beneath Him and over the church.

Apostleship The duties and activities of an apostle.

Apostolate The ambassadorial institution of

the apostle as exercised through the ecclesia.

Apostolic Pertaining to apostleship.

Apostolic Age A period in Christian history where apostleship dominated its ministerial spheres and positions.

Apostolic Annexation Defines the Lord's extension of His kingdom into this world under the ambassadorsial leadership of His apostle. The act establishes the apostolate as an embassy. Politically, speaking, embassies are designated government franchises.

Archaic Old, ancient, belonging to antiquity.

Assignment A delegated task of duty short or long term in duration.

Authority The lawful right to enforce obedience, control, or restrain behavior, compel performance to a power or position.

Authorization The license or permission to do perform some task, action, or event given by one in a position of authority.

Bible General word for book. Traditionally applied to a sacred book, specifically that containing the inspired word of Creator God.

Biblical Order Ecclesiastical structure, hierarchy, policy and government based upon the Bible, see above.

Bishop A church leader usually responsible for a network or region of churches. Often believed to be an apostle, although there is no scripture basis for this belief.

Cabinet, Apostles The body of officials, ministers, and staff that comprise the apostlle's support team. Generally these are apostolic people that share many of the traits and character of apostleship lacking only the characteristics that emphatically exemplifly the apostle.

Cain Adam's firstborn son that killed his brother. The apostle John calls Cain the son of the wicked one.

Canon The word for society's religious spheres. In scripture it is the sphere of the new creation as established by apostleship.

Canon Law Law and government founded upon the word of God as ecclesiastically translated by the leaders of the New Testament church. Canon comes from the Greek, Kanon, referring to the New Creation in Jesus Christ and all that pertains to or emanates from it.

Catechism Word for the instruction and orientation of a convert to a religious order.

Commandments Order, edicts, or mandates issued by an authority over a subordinate.

Commission An official position or charge given to another assigned to handle a principal's affairs. The delegated tasks assigned to one dispatched away from the sender to accomplish. Commissions are usually accompanied by special signs and authority to prohibit the commission from being opposed.

Constitution The codified collection of rules, regulations and laws that establish a country, company, religious order or other organization. The formal document drafted by entity founders that legitimizes its right to exist and forms the basis of its order, structure, government and authority.

Corinthians The name of two epistles written by the Apostle Paul in the New Testament.

Cosmogony Word for the origins of the world.

Counsel Guidance, advice, direction.

David Israel's second king after whose lineage Jesus Christ was born.

Deity Another word for a celestial or divine being.

Delegated Assignment of a task, commission, or project by one in authority that is initially responsible for them, to another to handle on his or her behalf.

Delegation A deputation, commission, authority and charge.

Demonics The antics and effects of demons.

Diplomacy The art and practice of negotiating treaties and agreements in a foreign land on behalf of one's home country.

Diplomat One who engages in diplomacy.

Directives Another word for command; a direct order or decree to carry out some instruction or edict.

Disintegrate To break down, fall apart or to pieces.

Dismantle To disassemble, take apart, defrock or deauthorize.

Dispatch To send forth on a mission, journey, task, or commission to accomplish express duties or to execute determined orders.

Dispensation A form of the word dispense, refers to God's outpouring and its economic and managerial requirement at an appointed time or under partiular circumstances.

Divine Celestial, spiritual, heavenly and eternal. What empowers and governs our world.

Doctrine Teaching, curriculum, thoughts and ideas communicated in an instructional manner. Biblically, didactics; theologically the Didache.

Duties Responsibilities, tasks, and assignments associated with an office or official position and its labors.

Ecclesia The New Testament name for the church of the Lord Jesus Christ. The Greek word meaning, "called out ones."

Ecclesiastical What pertains to the ecclesia, the church or a body of worshippers.

Education An encompassing term for the arts, acts, and process of teaching, training, and instructing another.

Elijah One of ancient Israel's most notable prophets, known for great exploits and repeated challenges to Israel to repent of baalism and return to its covenant God, Yahweh.

Embassy Ambassadorship

Ensis Ancient term for primitive villages priest king rulers. Melchizedek fits the description of an ensi.

314

Entrepreneurialism The sphere of business and enterprise.

Epistle A letter , biblically the word for an official correspondence. In relation to the New Testament church in Bible times, epistles served as official documents that governed the church. It was understood during the years of the Church's formation that epistles that commanded the church were exclusively written by the apostles. Any other author attempting to influence the church with no apostolic authority was considered spurious.

Ephesians One of Paul's epistles written to a capital city where goddess worship prevailed because its deity Diana was believed to have fallen into their land from the sky. Ephesians is one epistle that sets forth apostleship's eternality.

Eternal That which is without beginning or ending.

Evangelist Third ranking member of the five-fold, following apostles and prophets. This office is not mentioned in Paul's 1 Corinthians 12:28 list of officers. Evangelists concentrate on replenishing the body by converting believers with the message of the gospel.

Extra-Biblical Religious material written apart from the canonized scriptures of the Living God, referred to as the Holy Bible.

Franchise

Franchise Annexation A phrase that names the direct collaboration of the apostle with the Lord in the matters of that pertain to the earth, humanity, and their governmental administrative.

Functions The roles and tasks connected with or that explain an operation, occupation, or purpose.

Generation The origination, era, age, and zeitgeist of a given group of people or series of events, either alive or dominant throughout one time period.

Genesis Means the origin or birth of; name of the first book of the Bible. Moses' the Lord's fifth generation prophet is its accepted author.

Godhead The biblical term for the collective rule of the Almighty as Creator. Its members include Creator God, His first begotten Jesus Christ, and the Holy Spirit dispatched into the world to adminstrate redemption through the church. The word *trinity* is not found in scripture.

Govern To administrate the laws, regulations, and policies a founder or superior impose on the entity over which he or she is assigned; often delegated.

Government The system of laws and its administration that rule and protect a country, company, or group.

Great Apostle Hebrews 3:1 title of the Lord Jesus Christ as the Head and Founder of the office of apostleship because He came to earth as eternity's Sent One, another name for the apostle.

Guards Those that by occupation, officially protect others, property, and activities.

Heaven God's abode at its highest level. The area, expanse, above the earth, the sky.

Holy Spirit The third member of creation's Godhead, comprised of God the Father, His Son Jesus, and His Eternal Spirit.

Humanism What pertains to humanity as devised by people. Scripture calls it carnality.

Humanist That which pertains to or promotes humanity, its cultures and societies above or in place of its Creator.

Immortal Unable to be put to death or cease to be.

Influence Power to sway opinions of action, exert pressure, or persuade without necessarily exercising the authority of an office.

Institution The formal organization of a body, class, or group as held together by its prescribed order, constitution, and government all designed for its prosperous perpetuity.

International Activities or business conducted in two or more nations.

Isaiah One of the Old Testament's major prophets. A 66-page prophecy is named after him that is called the "little Bible" since its chapters coincide with the exact number of books in the Bible.

James The name of the apostle John's twin brother. Also the name of the Lord Jesus' brother who is believed to replace Peter as head of the Jerusalem counsel. Wrote one epistle in which he identifies himself as the Lord's brother.

Jeremiah One of Israel's major prophets that prophesied the nation's downfall and deportation of Babylon by Nebuchadnezzar.

Jesus The Savior of the world, second member of the Godhead, Creator God's first begotten Son.

Judaism The system of religious worship, rituals and observances commanded by Israel's God, Yahweh, for His progenitorship and redemption of the nation.

Jude The Lord's brother, his epistle identifies him as the brother of James who says he is the Lord's brother. Jude's epistle is the next to the last epistle of the New Testament coming just before John's Revelation.

Jurisdiction A region or territory where an official's word is accepted as law.

Kanon Greek word for the New Creation born of God's Spirit, its sphere of existence, and the eternal law that governs it, as well as the sphere of the apostle's ministry and authority. **See Canon.**

Kingdom The physical territory or realm of a monarch.

Koinonia The Greek word for fellowship and communion used to expressed a unique intimacy.

Language The words and speech that comprise a talk or other communication as understood by a particular group.

Law A single term that describes a body or collection of rules, commands, decrees and bylaws that govern a particular group or oganization; includes the theories, formula, and principles that inspired them.

Legal That which conforms to the established laws of a

group, organization or government.

Legate A subordinate sent one, usually in the ecclesiastical sphere.

Legislate To enact laws and government.

Lucifer Satan's pre-damnation name when he served the Most High as a covering cherub.

Mandate An order or command issued by an authority to be performed.

Mantle The biblical name for the spiritual garment that serves as the uniform of service for a particular office.

Marketplace Apostle An apostle not called to the local church or specifically the ecclesiastical sphere of God's kingdom. One that is assigned to the field of the world wher e business and enterprise is their primary objective.

Measure of Rule The sphere of authority and rewarded accom-plishment of an apostle.

Melchizedek Founder and holder of the office of Creator God's eternal priesthood into which all New Creation members of Christ's body belong, and over which He was installed as High Priest. Occupied pre-Jebusite and Davidic Jerusalem until Abraham's covenant was ratified.

Mentor A skilled professional or veteran in a certain field that guides, aids, and equips another for success who is rising in his or her field.

Mentee One who is mentored.

Mentorship The arrangement between a mentor and mentee.

Message Communication of one's thoughts, feelings, ideas, and will to another for information or activity purposes.

Messenger One sent on an errand or assignment to voice the will, thoughts, and actions or intents of another. Official messengers were thusly authorized to perform the assignment or otherwise act out the message in the sender's stead.

Messiah Greek term for Christ. Comes from the Hebrew *mashiach*.

Ministers Official servants that hold the public offices of a country, temple, court or palace.

Ministry Occupying the office and executing the duties of a minister.

Mission A journey from one land to another to handle the affairs or transact business in the name or on behalf of another.

Moses Yahweh's first institutional prophet. Returned to Egypt after fleeing it in order to deliver God's people from Egyptian captivity.

New Testament The 27 last books of the Bible. Pertains to the ecclesia the spiritual Israel purchased by the blood of Jesus Christ.

Office A position of public trust one is appointed to by a ruler, leaders, deity, or other entity.

Officer One who occupies an office.

Offspring Another name for children, seed, or descendents.

Old Guard Those that formerly performed the duties of a guard who are now outdated because of having completed their assignment and about to be replaced.

Old Testament The first 39 boods of the Bible consisting of the Psalms, the Prophets and Moses' Law and the Wisdom Books. It chronicles the kings of Israel and the Lord's dealings with His nation until its deportation to Babylon.

Ordained Appointed and installed by law or edict to an official capacity to carry out ministerial, legislative, or judicial details.

Pagan That which is birthed, venerated or observed instead of the Creator. Usually, refers to nature worship and its various demonic forms.

Pastor Fourth member of the Ephesians 4:11 staff. A stationary office, the pastor's sole duty is to attract, receive, maintain and nurture sheep.

Paul The apostle to the Gentiles that wrote the major portion of the New Testament. Responsible for writing at least 14 books of the New Testament.

Pantheism From pantheon, a council of gods.

Pentecost Meaning fiftieth, Pentecost refers to the day the new creation church was born and how it changed the world and its era forever.

Peter One of the original twelve apostles. The first to occupy the seat of Chief Apostle on the Jerusalem counsel. Contributed two epistles to the New Testament.

Plenipotentiary A synonymic name for the apostle's ambassadorial status. It means to be dispatched with full delegated power and authority to act in the Sender's stead.

Polytheism Many gods.

Powers People and agencies that exert force or exercise strength and authority in various affairs or upon others.

Praxis Practical application or exercise of a branch of learning; Habitual or established practice or custom; translating an idea into action.

Priest A little stronger than the word minister, a priest is the specific servant representative of a deity appointed to mediate between the god and his or her people.

Priesthood An order of priests. The Bible's are first Melchizedek, second Levitical under Aaron, also called the Aaronic Priesthood, and third the New Creation priesthood according to Melchizedek's order under Jesus Christ.

Principal Chief or head. Applied apostolically to those that send apostles forth on their commissions.

Principalities The ruling territory of a king. The regions or spheres ruled by the offspring of royalty.

Prophet Second member of the Ephesians 4:11 staff who operates as the mouthpiece of God to creation.

Protocol Actions and initiatives, rules, practices, etiquette, and behaviors that regulate the conduct, policies and procedures of a particular group. The response codes or reaction guidelines peculiar to a particular body. They regulate its conduct, manage its operations, and order its procedures.

Revelation Unveiling of present truth. Also called apocalypse.

Revival Events, words, or actions that restore life to a thing.

Royal Ruling that which pertains to a monarch.

Rule Leadership, government, authority, and power over others.

Satan Lucifer's adversarial name inherited after revolting against the Most High's rule and seducing other spirits to do the same.

Scripture Another name for the Holy Bible. Also called God's Holy Word.

Secular Worldly, carnal, cosmo-politan. Also defines what is sensual and demonic.

Specially Commissioned A term used to identify the apostle's call to service and dispatch to preach the message given to establish his or her portion of the Lord's kingdom.

Sphere Orb, world, an invisible circle of beliefs, trends, or attitudes that influence a culture within a society. Also explained by the word zeitgeist.

Spirit What is celestial, ethereal, non corporeal and heavenly. What pertains to the higher world as opposed to the physicality of the earth.

Spiritual Covering An abstract term to identify the loosely arranged relationship a senior minister has with a junior or novice whereby the senior implies prayer, counsel, guidance, and intangible support of the junior's ministry.

Staff A force of workers employed or engaged by an entity to man its facilities, operate its business, and overall promote, prosper, and protect its affairs.

Strategy The plans, policies, and tactics devised to guide an approach or attack.

Strategize The act or process of developing a strategy.

Strongholds A fortress or fortification that defends and maintains its grip on something. Stated in scripture as a castle or citadel.

Supernatural That which is otherworldly but more supra

than preternatural. What is spiritual, celestial, and normally beyond human concept or capability.

System The orderly method of ranking, arranging, structuring or classifying anything, including the logic and techniques used to do so. What is or become routine because of common practice or usage.

Teacher The fifth office of Ephesians 4:11. Also mentioned with apostles and prophets in 1 Corinthians 12:28.

Tithe Bible word for a tenth. Also called the firstfruits, increase, the tithe is returned to the Lord as Creator as His earned portion for supplying the earth's provisions and acquisitions.

Title The name of an official position into which authority those appointed to public office enter.

Traditional What is or has become culturally or religiously accepted as the normal standard or orthodoxy for a group or belief.

Truth What conforms or evidences to creation and its design, laws, and government as upheld by the Creator's invisible agents and agencies.

Vision The inner ability to see with the mind's eye or the heart's view what should manifest as reality in this world. Seeing the unseen in this world.

Wisdom Combined knowledge, facts, information and details that provide functional understanding to be acted on, obeyed or performed for success.

World The cosmos, the earth, its spheres and realms, contents and inhabitants.

Yahweh Jehovah, Israel's covenant God's name.

Index

Bibliography

Dictionary of Christian Lore & Legend, JCJ Medford

Thames & Hudson, LTD, London 1983

The Original Roget's Thesaurus of English Words & Phrases, New Edition

Revised by Robert A Dutch, O.B.E.,

St. Martins Press, New York, 1879, 1936, 1962, USA 1965

Zondervan Compact Bible Dictionary

Zondervan, Grand Rapids, 1993

Random House Webster Collegiate Dictionary

Random House, Inc. 1995, 1992, 1991

The Barnhart Concise Dictionary of Etymology; The Origins of American English Words

Robert Barnhart, B. H Wilson Company, 1995

The World Before and After Jesus: Desire of the Everlasting Hills &

Civilization and the Gift of the Jews

Thomas Cahill, Nan S. Talese, Anchor Books, New York, 1994, 2001

A Reader's Guide to the Great Religions

Edited by Charles J Adams, the Free Press, A Division of the Macmillan Company 1965

The Harvard Business Essentials: Coaching & Mentoring

Harvard Business School, Publishing Corp. 2004

People Skills

Robert Bolton, Ph.D., Simon & Schuster, Inc. 1979

A Latin Dictionary, Freunds Latin Dictionary

Charlton T Lewis, Ph. D. & Charles Short, LL. D., Oxford at the Clarendon Press, 1966

International Standard Bible Encyclopedia

Electronic Database copyright 1996, Biblesoft

The New Ungers Bible Dictionary

Moody Press of Chicago, Illinois, 1988

Merriam Webster's Collegiate Dictionary 10th Edition, 1994

Merriam Webster's, Incorporated, Springfield, Massachusetts USA

The Dictionary of Classical Mythology, Religion, Literature, and Art

Oskar Seyffert 1841-1906

Revised and Edited by Henry Nettleship and J. E. Sandys, Gramercy Books, Distributed by Random House Value Publishing, Inc., New Jersey 1995

The Leadership Bible

General Editor Dr Sid Buzzell, Ed. Dr. Kenneth Boa & Bill Perkins, Zondervan Publishing

Shades of Meaning

Samuel R Levin, Westview Press, 1998

World Religions

Simon Schuster, 1998

The Hebrew Goddess, Jewish Folklore & Anthropology

Raphael Patai, Wayne State University press, Detroit, MI 1967, 1978.

The Christ of the Mount

E. Stanley Jones, Abingdon Press, 1931

The Witness of the Stars

E. W. Bullinger, Kregel Publishing, 1893, 1967

The Release of the Spirit

Watchman Nee, Sure Foundation, Grand Rapids, MI, 1965

Life is in the Blood,

Larry Ollison, Larry Ollison Ministries,

What The Bible Is All About

Hennrietta C Mears, Gospel Light Publication, 1952, 54, 1960, 66, 1983

The Story of the Christian Church

Jesse Lyman Hurlbut, D.D., Zondervan Publishing House, Grand Rapids, MI, 1918, 1933, 1954; Holt, Rinehart & Winston Inc., 1970, Zondervan Publishing

The 1599 Geneva Bible,

LL Brown Publishing, Ozark, MO, 1990-2000

The Scepter & the Star

Anchor Bi le Reference Library, John T. Collins, Doubleday 1995

Serving Humanity

From the writings of Alice Bailey, Lucis Publishing, 1972, 78, 99

America

Hendrick Van Loon, Boni & Liveright, Inc. 1927

Dictionary of Biblical Imagery

Gen. Ed. Leland Ryken, Kames C. Wilhoit, Tremper Longman III, Intervarsity Press, 1998

Who Were the Amorites?

Alfred Haldar, ©E. J. Brill, Leiden Holland 1971, Lonsdale & Bartholomew, LTD, England

Military Correspondence Reports & Orders,

Lucius Hudson Holt, Ph.D., Frederick A. Stokes Company, NY

Brotherhood of Darkness

Dr. Stanley Monteith, Hearthstone Publishers, OKC, OK 2000

Dictionary of Judaism

Dagbert D. Runes

Citadel Press, Carol Publishing, NJ 1959, 1987

The Book of Jasher

Artisan Publishing, Muskogee, OK 2002

God the Master Mathematician

Dr. Noah Hutchings, Hearthstone Publishers, OKC, OK 2002

The Book of Enoch, From the Ethiopic

Richard Lawrence, LLD, Artisan Publishing, Muskogee, OK 1980

How to Think Like a CEO

D. A. Benton, Warner Books, 1996

The 12th Planet

Zechariah Sitchin, Avon Books, 1994

Soothsayers of the Second Advent

William M. Alnor, Power Books, Fleming H. Revell, NJ, 1989

Signs in the Heavens

Marilyn Hickey, Marilyn Hickey Ministries, Denver, CO, 1984

The New English Bible, New Testament

Oxford University Press, Cambridge University Press, 1961

The Future War of the Church

Chuck D. Pierce & Rebecca Wagner Systema, Renew Books, from Gospel Light Publishing, CO, 2001

Now is the Dawning of the New Age New World Order

Dennis Cuddy, Ph. D., Hearthstone Publishing, OKC, OK 1991, 2000

The Tabernacle of David 1976, The Temple of Solomon 1988, The Tabernacle of Moses 1976, The Book of Acts 1992, `Interpreting the Book of Revelation, 1995,

Kevin J. Conner, City Bible Publishing (Formerly Bible Temple Publishing), Portland, OR

How to Become a CEO

Jeffrey J. Fox, Hyperion NY 1998

The Catholic Encyclopedia

Kevin Knight, 2003

The Diplomat's Dictionary

Chas. W. Freeman, Jr., United States Institute of Peace Press, Washington, D.C. 1999

The Arts of Power, Statecraft and Diplomacy

Chas. W. Freeman, Jr., United States Institute of Peace Press, Washington, D.C. ©1997

About the Author

Paula A. Price is vastly becoming the international voice on the subject of apostolic and prophetic ministry. She is widely recognized as a modern-day apostle with a potent prophetic anointing. Having been in active full-time ministry since 1985, she has founded and established three churches, an apostolic and prophetic Bible institute, a publication company, consulting firm, and global collaborative network linking apostles and prophets together for the purpose of kingdom vision and ventures. With an international itinerant ministry, she has transformed the lives of many through her wisdom and revelation of God's kingdom.

As a former sales and marketing executive, Paula blends ministerial and entrepreneurial applications in her ministry to enrich and empower a diverse audience with the skills and abilities to take kingdoms for the Lord Jesus Christ. A lecturer, teacher, curriculum developer, and business trainer, she globally consults Christian businesses, churches, schools, and assemblies. She has, over a 20-year period developed a superior curriculum to effectively train Christian ministers and professionals, particularly the apostle and the prophet. Her programs often are used in both secular and non-secular environments worldwide. Although she has written over 25 books, manuals, and other course material on the apostolic and prophetic, she is most recognized for her unique 1,600-term *Prophets' Dictionary* and a concise prophetic training manual entitled *Church Prophets*.

Beyond the pulpit, Paula is the provocative talk show host of her own program, *Let's Just Talk: Where God Makes Sense*. She brings the pulpit to the pew, weekly applying God's wisdom, and divine pragmatism to today's world solutions. Her ministry goal is to make Christ's teachings and churches relevant for today. "Eternity in the Now" is the credo through which she accomplishes it.

In addition to her vast experience, Paula has a D.Min. and a Ph.D. in Religious Education from Word of Truth Seminary in Alabama. She is also a wife, mother of three daughters, and the grandmother of two. She and her husband Tom presently pastor New Creation Worship Assembly in Tulsa, OK.

Other Books by This Author

♦ *The Prophets' Dictionary: The Ultimate Guide to Supernatural Wisdom*

♦ *The Prophet's Handbook: A Guide to Prophecy and its Operations*

♦ *Prophecy: God's Divine Communications Media*

♦ *Divine Order for Spiritual Dominance*

For additional copies of this book or other works by this author, call 918-446-5542 or visit our website at www.drpaulaprice.com.

LaVergne, TN USA
14 April 2010
179246LV00002B/112/P